Too Darn Hot

THE BROADWAY LEGACIES SERIES

"South Pacific": Paradise Rewritten
Jim Lovensheimer

Pick Yourself Up: Dorothy Fields and the American Musical
Charlotte Greenspan

To Broadway, to Life! The Musical Theater of Bock and Harnick
Philip Lambert

Irving Berlin's American Musical Theater
Jeffrey Magee

Loverly: The Life and Times of "My Fair Lady"
Dominic McHugh

"Show Boat": Performing Race in an American Musical
Todd Decker

Bernstein Meets Broadway: Collaborative Art in a Time of War
Carol J. Oja

"We'll Have Manhattan": The Early Work of Rodgers and Hart
Dominic Symonds

Agnes de Mille: Telling Stories in Broadway Dance
Kara Gardner

The Shuberts and their Passing Shows: The Untold Tale of Ziegfeld's Rivals
Jonas Westover

Big Deal: Bob Fosse and Dance in the American Musical
Kevin Winkler

Pal Joey: The History of a Heel
Julianne Lindberg

Oklahoma! The Making of an American Musical, Revised Edition
Tim Carter

Sweet Mystery: The Musical Works of Rida Johnson Young
Ellen M. Peck

The Big Parade: Meredith Willson's Musicals from The Music Man to 1491
Dominic McHugh

Everything is Choreography: The Musical Theater of Tommy Tune
Kevin Winkler

Yankee Doodle Dandy: George M. Cohan's Broadway and the Making of American Identity
Elizabeth T. Craft

Too Darn Hot: Kiss Me, Kate & the Making and Remaking of a Broadway Musical
Hannah Robbins

Too Darn Hot

Kiss Me, Kate & the Making and Remaking of a Broadway Musical

HANNAH ROBBINS

OXFORD
UNIVERSITY PRESS

OXFORD
UNIVERSITY PRESS

Oxford University Press is a department of the University of Oxford. It furthers the University's objective of excellence in research, scholarship, and education by publishing worldwide. Oxford is a registered trade mark of Oxford University Press in the UK and in certain other countries.

Published in the United States of America by Oxford University Press
198 Madison Avenue, New York, NY 10016, United States of America.

CIP data is on file at the Library of Congress

ISBN 9780190082406

DOI: 10.1093/9780190082437.001.0001

Printed by Integrated Books International, United States of America

The manufacturer's authorized representative in the EU for product safety is Oxford University Press España S.A. of Parque Empresarial San Fernando de Henares, Avenida de Castilla, 2 – 28830 Madrid (www.oup.es/en or product.safety@oup.com). OUP España S.A. also acts as importer into Spain of products made by the manufacturer.

MIX
Paper
FSC FSC® C183721

For William Peter Robbins and all the women with spirit to resist

Contents

Foreword

Kiss Me, Kate is a familiar show to musical theater scholars and fans alike. Often touted as Cole Porter's "late masterpiece," the 1948 musical enjoys a prominent place in American musical theater history. *Kiss Me, Kate* famously won the inaugural Best Musical award at the Tonys and has been a staple in musical theater scholarship for decades. Geoffrey Block, Joseph P. Swain, Raymond Knapp, and more have discussed the show in books on the Broadway musical. Yet *Too Darn Hot: Kiss Me, Kate & the Making and Remaking of a Broadway Musical* marks the first full-length monograph on the show.

Founding series editor Geoffrey Block commissioned and worked with Hannah Robbins's project through the proposal and early drafting stages. Unsurprisingly, he was drawn to a project on the most acclaimed show of Cole Porter's career. In a communication with me, Block noted that a volume on Cole Porter had been a long-held hope for the series. Furthermore, Block warmly supported Robbins's work not only for its strengths in archival research, but also for its critical approaches to *Kiss Me, Kate*. These aspects, which Block clearly identified as strong points within the proposal, continue to loom large in the final book. As the first book in my tenure as series editor, Robbins's nuanced exploration of a beloved yet complicated musical has been a real treat.

One central aspect that I found particularly impressive is the book's extensive archival research. Robbins provides evidence from the Bella and Sam Spewack Papers at Columbia University, the Cole Porter Papers at the Library of Congress, and various selections from the New York Public Library, to name a few. By making this material accessible, readers have a fuller understanding of *Kiss Me, Kate* and the creative process of the collaborators. The first chapter of *Too Darn Hot* sets the stage by breaking down the most common ways that *Kiss Me, Kate* has been framed in the existing literature: as a "Shakespeare Musical" and as a "Cole Porter Musical." At the same time, they highlight screwball comedy's influence as a genre in the show.

Even for readers familiar with the musical, the book will show you findings from deep within the archives to construct a thorough narrative of the complex genesis of *Kiss Me, Kate.* Using strong evidence, the opening chapters offer new insights into the show's development and illustrate the highly collaborative nature of making a Broadway musical. As such, Robbins details how Bella Spewack, Cole Porter, and John C. Wilson became involved in the project. They also delve into the earliest drafts of the show (first called *Backstage*) and consider the adaptation process, looking at how the creators treat *The Taming of the Shrew.* The process of adaptation was deeply collaborative, and Robbins contends that it was "clear that the team found creative sympathies while addressing the Shakespearean aspects of the show." Bella Spewack, Sam Spewack, and Cole Porter all interpret elements of the Shakespeare source material in their own way while experiencing a close creative relationship. At the same time, I found the examination of Cole Porter's interpretive contribution to be a strong addition to the existing musicological scholarship. Robbins analyzes sketches, along with various accounts from the collaborators, to piece together a picture of Porter's process. They consider Porter's musical impact on the show, splitting the song analysis by love songs and "manifesto music." Moreover, considering the direct lead-up to the Broadway production further demonstrates the collaborative realities of preparing a Broadway production. Casting, final edits, design, and the role of choreographer Hanya Holm all play a role in the discussion of *Kiss Me, Kate*'s formation. Additionally, the difficulties Bella Spewack experienced with the producers are addressed in the final chapter related to the genesis of the show. Throughout the first half of the book, the deep engagement with multiple archives ground this thorough exploration of the "making and remaking" of this well-regarded Broadway musical.

Another captivating aspect of this book is the close look at the "after Broadway" life of *Kiss Me, Kate,* which highlights the show's continued legacy. The book's focus on three stage productions reveals both tensions and successes between the Spewacks in particular, and producers as the show transferred to the UK and Austria. And the discussion of the musical's move to Hollywood examines the process and impact of adapting *Kiss Me, Kate* for film. Most fascinatingly, Robbins outlines similarities between drafts of the film scripts and Bella Spewack's early drafts of the stage version. They also consider changes to Porter's songs, including the role Hollywood censorship played in softening the lyrics.

Too Darn Hot concludes with a discussion of how contemporary productions and audiences have dealt with the problematic gender politics that stem from *The Taming of the Shrew*. Throughout the book, Robbins illustrates Bella Spewack's use of her authorial voice at various stages of creation to disrupt or comment on the original Shakespeare. Through their nuanced, evidence-based discussion of gender in *Kiss Me, Kate*, Robbins presents a show that has always been more complicated than it seems on the surface. This basis regarding the gender politics in *Kiss Me, Kate* then informs modern understandings of the show.

Too Darn Hot: Kiss Me, Kate & the Making and Remaking of a Broadway Musical offers as comprehensive a picture of this popular, well-respected show as any scholar could hope for while simultaneously using an engaging and provocative style for all readers. What emerges throughout the book is a clear sense of the intensely collaborative nature of the Broadway musical, encouraging us all to "brush up our Shakespeare" and revisit this show with new eyes.

Megan Woller
Series Editor, Broadway Legacies

Acknowledgments

For a few whirlwind minutes of October 2013, I sat anxiously staring at a borrowed mobile phone in the laundry room of a student dorm in New Haven. On the other end of the line was ninety-eight-year-old Patricia Morison, the first woman to star as Lilli/Katherine in *Kiss Me, Kate*. She chatted and giggled, remarking that it was thrilling that young people still cared about the show. At the end of our brief, and totally impromptu call, she told me I was funny, and that she was glad she'd stopped watching her shows to talk. I couldn't be more thrilled that my journey of researching *Kiss Me, Kate* began with her and with her memories of the fun and doubts that shaped the development and early days of the original Broadway production, which opened just over fifty years before I was born.

I have been with *Kiss Me, Kate* for more than ten years now. I don't think I could have imagined how much I would think about the tap solo in "Bianca," gush about Sammy Davis Jr.'s recording of "Too Darn Hot," lament the failed ambitions to film the original Broadway production, or mourn the fact that I never got to reach out to Bella Spewack while she was alive. This book has been a labor of love for a work that has an unparalleled place in my life. It is a complicated musical, riddled with limitations and challenges, but also full of personality, charisma, and a deliberate intention to entertain us. When I talk about the musical now, I think of it as testament to collaboration and shared creative vision, so it feels more than right to begin here with thanks to all those who have walked alongside me for some, or all, of this project.

Above all, this book would not be possible without the support of numerous colleagues at the various archives that I have consulted. To Mark Eden Horowitz, who met me in the opening days of my PhD, only days before the call to Patricia Morison, and following a government shutdown that threatened my entire trip to the United States, you have been so warm in helping me navigate different topics and collections across the years. I can't wait to meet with you again. My gratitude also to Roberta Staats at the Cole Porter Trust, Richard Boursy at Yale University, and Jennifer Lee at Columbia University for their assistance in accessing those materials. To Joshua Goodman and Andy Buchman, who visited collections in California that I could not reach, thank you for reading lots of scripts and sending me excited emails about what you found. To the late Ned Comstock at University of South California, I'm sorry I didn't ever get to express my appreciation in person. Lots of people touch a project briefly and I'm also thankful to James Hepokoski, Robert Kimball, Jeffrey Magee, Tim Carter, Robert Gordon, Olaf Jubin, and David Charles Abell for their different encouragement and assistance early in my research journey.

Thank you to all the people that have listened to papers on *Kiss Me, Kate* or read my work on this topic. To Geoffrey Block, Norm Hirschy, and Megan Woller, who have offered me kindness and generosity, I am grateful for your care in supporting a new author through this process. I'm especially grateful to Geoffrey for his warm and persistent encouragement of my research and professional development since we first met in 2014. To my academic family—Furaha Asani, Leighan Renaud, Kirsty Sedgman, Katy Jayasuriya, Royona Mitra, Emma Nagouse, Harriet Boyd-Bennett, and Henry Parkes—thank you for your encouragement, the space to moan, and for cheerleading me on to the bitter end.

I could not have reached this stage without all those people who have offered me practical and personal support over the years. To my family, Rachel, Simon, Ian and Anne, Alison and Jay, Tracy, Ruth, thanks for believing I could do it and encouraging me to try. To my long-suffering friends Alex Rose Cocker, Miranda Debenham, Doug Dunn, Danielle Fairbrass, Naz Gayle, Phoebe Savidge, and Katie Woodward, who have come to know and have opinions about this musical and writing an academic book, it's helped more than you know to be randomly asked "how *Kiss Me, Kate* is." To Larry (we miss you), Gilly, and Lawrence, thank you for welcoming me into your family and caring about me and my work. Finally, I would like to extend my deepest love and gratitude to my mentor and dear friend, Dominic Broomfield-McHugh. I would not have begun my PhD project or submitted this research for publication without your support and guidance. It changed my life.

I dedicate this book to my grandfather Peter, who loved to play, read about, and listen to music. An accomplished amateur violinist and pianist, he championed me in my different musical exploits across the years. Even when he started to lose a sense of us, and of himself, certain songs and symphonic movements would resurface his younger personality for a moment. Gramps, I wish you could see this book and hold it in your hands. I would have loved to share a chocolate bar and listened to the original cast album while chatting about the show. I'm sorry it's not your favorite *West Side Story*, but we both know you loved a Porter tune or two.

Kiss Me, Kate: A Commercial Force

The most commercially and critically successful work by beloved American songwriter Cole Porter, *Kiss Me, Kate* remains one of the most popular musical comedies of all time. The libretto was coauthored by Sam and Bella Spewack, with direction by John C. Wilson, costumes and set design by Lemuel Ayers, and choreography by Hanya Holm. Nurtured by this team, *Kiss Me, Kate* opened on December 30, 1948, at New York's New Century Theatre, running for 1,077 performances, with a reported $350,000 in advance ticket sales.[1] Its plot combines an opening preview performance of Shakespeare's *The Taming of Shrew*, newly musicalized, with the backstage shenanigans of its leading actors. Its unusual but memorable plot is amplified by an outstanding score of songs with broad appeal and a bold visual and choreographic aesthetic that has persisted in over seventy-five years of performance and translation into over twenty languages.

The original Broadway production garnered numerous accolades including the inaugural Tony Awards for Best Musical and Best Book of a Musical as well as Best Original Score, Best Costume Design, and the now defunct Best Producer of a Musical. In addition to many Broadway revivals and American tours, *Kiss Me, Kate* has enjoyed productions around the world, including in Australia, Britain, Sweden, Turkey, and Japan. It was the first American musical to be performed in Vienna following Austria's return to full independence in 1955 and later the first to play in communist-allied Poland, opening at the Teatr Komedia in Warsaw on September 14, 1957.[2]

In 1999, British theater director Michael Blakemore mounted a revised version of the show at the Martin Beck Theatre (now the Al Hirschfield Theatre) in New York that became the most nominated musical revival in Tony Award history to date. The changes Blakemore oversaw led to the licensing of a new, updated version of *Kiss Me, Kate* for modern productions. More recently, *Kiss Me, Kate* has been further monumentalized in a critical edition by David Charles Abell and Seann Alderking, which offers a third licensable version.[3] Then, in 2019, Kelli O'Hara, Will Chase, and Corbin Bleu starred in a seventieth-anniversary revisal that made additional changes to the script, stage directions, and, for the first time, Porter's lyrics. This ignited

Too Darn Hot. Hannah Robbins, Oxford University Press. © Oxford University Press 2026.
DOI: 10.1093/9780190082437.001.0001

conversations about ways to keep *Kiss Me, Kate* (and other classic musicals) in the contemporary repertoire.

In addition to a prolific stage performance history, *Kiss Me, Kate* has also had significant screen treatment. The 1953 MGM film adaptation *Kiss Me Kate* (no comma), directed by George Sidney, has given the musical a wider audience. Filmed in both 2D *and* 3D, MGM's *Kiss Me Kate* has a key position in the history of film technology as one of the earliest, and highest-budget, screen musicals to be made in 3D. Meanwhile Sidney's adaptation also provides a lasting case study of fidelity to source material in a screen version of a stage work. Alongside the film adaptation and recordings of the 2001 and 2024 London stage productions, there are also several television versions of *Kiss Me, Kate*, such as the 1958 Hallmark Hall of Fame television special, a one-off recording for the launch of British television channel BBC 2 (1964), a 1968 television film starring Robert Goulet, Carol Lawrence, and Jessica Walter, a live television presentation in Japan, and at least two Italian and German television versions that appear to have been lost.

In this book, I argue that *Kiss Me, Kate* reveals the profoundly collaborative nature of making a Broadway musical. I show how the Spewacks wrestled with adapting *The Taming of the Shrew* and characterizing modern marriage while Porter became increasingly invested in honing the score to both celebrate the premise and exemplify his personal writing style. Importantly, I demonstrate that these creatives understood their task and the challenges of adapting already sensitive Shakespearean material, but that this has not always been recognized or reflected in the choices made by later interpreters of the musical. I also highlight how other members of the creative team made significant interventions that helped refine *Kiss Me, Kate* into a commercially adaptable property. This frames the second half of this book, which offers a partial reception history of *Kiss Me, Kate* beyond Broadway, on screen, and in public and academic dialogues.

The Plot

The original Broadway production of *Kiss Me, Kate* begins onstage at the Ford's Theatre in Baltimore. It is the afternoon before the first preview of a musical adaptation of *The Taming of the Shrew*, which is produced by, directed by, and stars Frederick Graham (Fred), an established stage actor trying to secure his status as a theatrical impresario. As the overture ends,

Fred gives notes to the company and prepares to rehearse the bows ahead of the evening's performance. After speaking to Harry Trevor, who plays the Shakespearean patriarch Baptista, Fred calls forward Lois Lane—the nightclub singer cast as Baptista's younger daughter Bianca. Lois is still learning how to play to a large theater, and she flirts and coos with Fred as he gives her instruction that she does not quite understand. Fred then moves onto the bows for the principals. They are: Baptista, Bianca, Bianca's three suitors—Gremio, Hortensio, and Lucentio—Petruchio, and Katherine. However, it becomes clear that one performer—Bill Calhoun (Lucentio), Lois's boyfriend that she has secured a prime part for—is not in the theater. Lois steps into make an excuse for him and Fred seems to move on to stage the final bow, featuring him and his ex-wife, the film star Lilli Vanessi, who is playing Katherine.

Lilli has been onstage for the duration of the scene and is clearly seething over his attentions to Lois. As Fred calls her forward, he delays the moment, turning to Lois and asking her not to leave the theater and she departs the stage with a "whatever thou say, Fred."[4] He then fusses with the remaining bows, further irritating Lilli, finally asking: "Now, how about a smile, Miss Vanessi?"[5] She obliges, following his new blocking, but as he turns to her, she calls him a bastard and storms off the stage. Embarrassed and surprised at the outburst, Fred thanks the rest of the cast for their hard work and leaves the remaining company of actors and stagehands to anticipate the coming preview ("Another Op'nin', Another Show").

Backstage, Lois goes to the telephone to try and locate Bill when Fred's dresser, Paul, interrupts her. Paul asks Lois for $2 to pay Bill's taxi fare and he enters the theater. Lois is frustrated—"Bill, you've been gambling again"—and Bill reveals that he's lost $10,000 and spitefully signed the debt with Fred's name. Lois is horrified and warns Bill that she'll never forgive him if he ruins her chance at making a name for herself. Softening at Bill's obvious jealousy of Fred, she soothes him, claiming that there's "nothing wrong" between her and Fred—"he's culturing me"[6]—before asking why Bill he must be so unreliable when they could settle happily together ("Why Can't You Behave?").

In Lilli's dressing room, Fred is shouting at her for calling him a bastard in public when she receives a call from her fiancé—the Washington aide Harrison Howell—and she gets to speak, interrupted by Fred, to the President. After hanging up, Lilli flaunts her enormous engagement ring and Fred reflects bitterly on her wealth, suggesting she has sold out while he has been trying to make ambitious theater. Lilli mocks his lack of critical and commercial success, but the bickering is interrupted when Fred spots a photograph of himself as a young child on her dressing table. Lilli presents the photo to him and offers him the champagne cork from their wedding night, as a marker of the first anniversary of their divorce. They fall into increasingly happy reminiscence about their married life and the roles they played in their early careers, leading to a reconstruction of a scene from a badly conceived operetta that they had both been in ("Wunderbar"). At the end of the song, the couple embrace, becoming sober as they remember how the marriage failed. Fred pulls away and returns to his dressing room, saying they must prepare for the performance.

In Fred's dressing room, two men are waiting. Sharply dressed, they are clearly gangsters (known as the gunmen), and they begin to size Fred up. He asks them to leave but they warn him that they have his signature on a gambling debt and have come to collect the due. Fred calls Bill's fraudulent signature a fake and the gunmen reflect that everyone who owes money suddenly forgets their debts. However, they relent for the time being, exiting the room, and promising to return when Fred has had time to recall his mistakes.

In Lilli's room, Paul greets Hattie, Lilli's maid, and gives her a box of flowers from Fred for her mistress. Hattie shows them to Lilli, who is taken aback to see the flowers of her wedding bouquet and moved that Fred has remembered them, and the date. In that moment, she recognizes that she is still emotionally connected to him regardless of whether they reunite ("So in Love"). Unaware of what has passed, Fred chastises Paul for letting the gunmen in and then asks about the bouquet and if Paul gave it directly to Lois. Paul is horrified, tells him what he has done, and Fred trepidatiously goes to smooth things over with Lilli. But she is delighted to see him and overcome with nerves about giving a good performance. As they are called to starting places, Hattie unearths the card accompanying the flowers and hands it to Lilli, who starts to open it. Fred stops her, describing the romantic message it contains, as he tries to extricate the card from her. Impressed by his words, Lilli tucks the card into her costume next to her heart, and promises never to call him a bastard again as she exits for the stage. He says to empty room, "You will, my sweet, you will!"[7]

Onstage, the *Taming of the Shrew* begins in front of the curtain with a quartet that introduces the four main actors—Fred, Lilli, Lois, and Bill—as a "troupe of strolling players" touring productions around the country ("We Open in Venice"). This prefaces the first Shakespearean scene in which

Baptista, a wealthy merchant, refuses to marry his younger daughter, Bianca, off to one of her many suitors until he has found a husband for his first, intemperate daughter, Katherine. Bianca sighs at his decision and performs a modern, up-tempo number with her three suitors about the anticipation of dating whoever presents himself for her attention ("Tom, Dick, or Harry"). Lucentio (played by Bill) remains after the song ends, having caught a rose Bianca has thrown to him, and dances a romantic duet with it as though the flower were Bianca ("The Rose Dance"). We understand then that their courtship will be the successful one.

When Lucentio has finished, Gremio and Hortensio enter ready to start trouble, but the brawl is curtailed by Petruchio who enters the scene, extricates his friend (Lucentio), and defuses the moment. Surprised to see him, Lucentio asks why Petruchio has come to the city, and he explains (and sings) to the surrounding crowd: "I've Come to Wive It Wealthily in Padua." Petruchio explains that he will tolerate any personal flaw if he can find a woman rich enough to marry. The suitors see their opportunity, and despite their description of her, offer enough indication of Katherine's wealth that Petruchio agrees he will marry her should Baptista guarantee the dowery. The suitors hurry to strike the bargain with Baptista and Petruchio follows behind them.

On arrival at Baptista's home, Katherine is suspicious of the men's excitement and threatens Lucentio as Baptista quickly draws the suitors away to discuss the possible marriage. She is left alone and explains to the audience that she does not trust the ways men have agency over the women they romance and marry ("I Hate Men"). Ironically, her father then reappears announcing Petruchio's hope to marry her, which she rejects, leaving the stage as Petruchio arrives. The men negotiate the terms of Katherine's dowry and Baptista leaves to find a notary. Aware that Katherine is on the balcony and has overheard some or all of their conversation, Petruchio begins his campaign to win her over ("Were Thine That Special Face"). Baptista returns concerned that Katherine is unmoved by the song, when Lilli flies angrily onto stage, wielding the wedding bouquet from her dressing room. She has entered early and speaks off script, leaving Fred scrambling for a way back to the Shakespeare. Lilli hurls the bouquet at him before removing the card from her costume.

As she rips the card up, Harry (Baptista) flees and Lill continues to ad lib—"Speak, Petruchio . . . though thy message is not meant for me,"[8] throwing the pieces in his face and beginning to call him a bastard once more. Fred interrupts her, speaking loudly to the audience and then to her, "We're on stage, now, Lilli . . .,"[9] and they proceed with the scene. As a prelude to a proposal, Petruchio attempts to lavish Katherine with disingenuous praise, and she mocks his attempt. However, Lilli continues increasingly disruptively, using the opportunity of mocking Petruchio to bite, slap, and kick Fred, and he begins to lose his temper, finally warning: "You keep on acting just the way you've been doing, Miss Vanessi, and I will give you the paddling of your life and right on stage."[10]

In the *Taming of the Shrew*, Petruchio asks Katherine for her hands to begin the proposal, but Lilli resists the gesture. They struggle and Fred seizes the moment to temporarily restrain Lilli. As some time has passed, Baptista and the suitors return to see if everything is settled and, although they can clearly see that it is not, Baptista gives his blessing when Petruchio says they are agreed on the match. In this time, Lilli has been working free of Fred's hold and kicks him as she escapes. He continues in character, inviting the company to the wedding, but she slaps him and Fred snaps: "All right, Miss Vanessi—you asked for this, and you are going to get it."[11] He puts her across his knee and begins to spank her behind as the scene dissolves into chaos.

Backstage, the argument continues as Lilli screams for Hattie and Fred rails that "the name of this piece is *The Taming of the Shrew* and not *He Who Gets Slapped*."[12] He accuses her of being jealous of Lois and she mocks him for chasing a young girl to appease his lack of professional success. He threatens to teach her manners, and she threatens to walk out of the production, exiting after landing another slap to his face.

In her dressing room, Lilli phones Harrison and says she is giving up acting and leaving the show. Fred overhears and calls her bluff, saying she'd never go through with it, but Lilli throws him out. Waiting for him are the gunmen, ready to collect the outstanding funds, and Fred spots an opportunity to leverage his need for the money from the show's box office and encourage the gunmen to compel Lilli back onstage. Taking the hint, they visit Lilli with Fred and "suggest" that she should continue with the show. Initially, she stands up to them but gives up, appealing to Fred, who feigns outrage.

In front of the curtain, Lucentio, Bianca, and members of the ensemble perform "I Sing of Love," extolling the (somewhat ironic) romance of the moment while the sets change in preparation for Katherine and Petruchio's wedding. When the curtain rises, we begin "on book" with Baptista, Lucentio, and Bianca emerging from the church, horrified by Petruchio's bizarre dress and behavior. He enters in a bold, mismatching outfit, carrying a whip, and summons Katherine, eventually cracking the whip to hasten her. Lilli/Katherine arrives flanked by the two gunmen in *Taming of the Shrew* costumes. They disrupt the blocking of the scene and Fred attempts to move them, finally cracking his whip at the gunman who has just noticed the audience over the headlights. Startled, the man pulls out a gun, at which point Lilli attempts to get away and Fred catches her, returning to the Shakespeare to announce that Petruchio and Katherine will leave Padua immediately.

Initiating the end of Act 1, Petruchio asks Katherine to kiss him ("Finale Act One"), and she refuses, eventually interrupting the ensemble with an elaborate cadenza on the word "never." She duets with a puppet bird (musicalized by flute in the orchestra) until one of the gunmen eventually shoots the prop and the company hurry through the remaining song, while Lilli/Katherine tries to make good an escape. Fred/Petruchio finally catches her, in the closing bars, throws her over his shoulder as she hits and kicks him, and the curtain comes down.

Act 2 begins during the interval of *The Taming of the Shrew*, in the alley by the stage door where Paul joins two friends who are playing cards, and they lament the heat ("Too Darn Hot"). This eventually turns into a full ensemble dance extravaganza featuring Bill and Paul before everyone is called back to stage. While they are returning, Fred appears before the curtain to announce that the next scene, which should feature Katherine riding on a donkey, has been cut due to injury and that they will continue the performance after the characters have arrived in Petruchio's home.

Petruchio welcomes Katherine to his estate by abusing the servants, throwing away their dinner, and refusing her a handsome cap that he has had made until she behaves better. Initially, she is accompanied by the gunmen, but Fred eventually encourages them to leave the stage and Katherine retreats to bed in preparation for a return journey to her father's house the next day. Now alone, Petruchio extols his method of taming Katherine, but she has locked him out of the bedroom, foiling his plan to disrupt her sleep. Frustrated at her antics, he begins to feel nostalgic for his single days when he could flit nonchalantly from woman to woman ("Where Is the Life That Late I Led?").

Backstage, there is a major disturbance as Harrison Howell arrives with an ambulance in tow, demanding to see Lilli. Fred appears briefly to quiet the noise, accompanied by the gunmen, and on meeting Howell, begins to sow doubt about the voracity of Lilli's tale that she has been injured and cannot escape the theater. As Fred returns to stage, Lois appears and spots Harrison, whom she recognizes as one of the many wealthy men she has previously entertained in exchange for luxurious gifts. Perturbed, Harrison asks her to keep quiet given his position and his engagement to Lilli before fleeing to the dressing rooms. During this, Bill arrives, witnessing the conversation. Lois reproves him for being jealous and tells him that she will always be devoted to him, but also like nice things and knows how to get them ("Always True to You (In My Fashion)").

When Lilli discovers Harrison has come for her, she is initially happy but becomes increasingly frustrated that he does not believe her account of what has happened. She challenges the gunmen, but Fred calls them apprentice actors and Howell, already under the impression that Lilli has been overly dramatic, accepts his more mundane suggestion. As this happens, Fred takes the opportunity to take stock of his rival for Lilli. With the gunmen and Lilli looking on, Fred lulls Harrison to sleep while he explores how boring their married life might be. Lilli sends Fred away, but it is too late. Harrison begins to snore.

In the corridor, a procession of parcels arrives for Lois while members of the backstage crew and ensemble look on and laugh. Bill sees their reaction but tells the assembled crowd that he is so in love with Lois that it just doesn't affect him ("Bianca"). As Bill draws the audience away, the gunmen appear, still in their *Taming of the Shrew* outfits, to telephone their boss but learn he has been assassinated, writing Bill's debt off. They tell Fred he is released, say goodbye to Lilli who has come out of her dressing room with Hattie and a suitcase, and leave. Fred asks if Lilli is taking Harrison with her, but she has left him to sleep. Fred begs her not to leave, asking if he'd imagined their reconnection, but is interrupted by the doorman who announces Lilli's cab. She leaves and Fred realizes, now alone, how much he wants and needs her ("So in Love: Reprise").

Instead of leaving the theater, the gunmen turn up in front of the curtain, seemingly lost, and the orchestra starts to play so they sing "Brush Up Your Shakespeare" before bowing out of the performance. The curtain raises on Baptista's house, decorated for a wedding, and the guests dance a pavane before Baptista introduces Bianca and her new husband, Lucentio. Fred enters as Petruchio, and they greet him expecting Katherine with him. After briefly stalling, Harry/Baptista sends a dancer to get Katherine, covering the absence and the gap in dialogue. A moment later, Lilli enters as though simply late for her cue and Fred briefly breaks character but recovers and they play the end of the scene in which Petruchio asks Katherine to tell other women "what duty they do owe their lords and husbands"[13] ("I Am Ashamed That Women Are So Simple"). As Katherine finishes her song, he proclaims the final line of the piece "Why! There's a Wench! Come on and kiss me, Kate" before the closing number ("Finale: So, Kiss Me, Kate!") with Fred/Petruchio and Lilli/Katherine reunited at the helm of their show.

Unpacking the Story

Within this plot are many important strands that I unravel across my narrative of the musical. The bipartite structure—of a play within a play—and the adaptation of *The Taming of the Shrew* are perhaps the most appreciated qualities of *Kiss Me, Kate*. Alongside this, many scholars have highlighted Porter's construction of the score to elaborate on the plot and characters, unlike many earlier musical comedies where the songs served more as embellishment than progressing the drama. More broadly, *Kiss Me, Kate* addresses the act of creating a stage work, of being an actor, of being in and out of love, of being married, and the experience of gender inequality. Long-standing criticisms of Shakespeare's *Taming of the Shrew* emphasize the ways the play can make light of and even glorify misogyny and domestic violence. *Kiss Me, Kate* introduces a new, more contemporary vantage on this through the backstage plot in which Lilli is rich, successful, and has already been married to Fred. Their life experience, and understanding of one another, is essential to the narrative truth of this musical and the explorations of power at a time when female writers and actresses were making waves as interpreters of works and creative projects historically dominated by men.

In *Too Darn Hot*, I explore how intricately the creative team envisaged *Kiss Me, Kate* for stage while recognizing all the themes I have outlined. This was a second collaboration between the Spewacks and Cole Porter which moved from an intensely topical subject—international diplomacy in the prelude to World War II in *Leave It to Me!* (1938)—to more universal themes of entertainment, love, and relationships. While more commercially accessible than *Leave It to Me!*, which had some characteristics in common with a musical revue, *Kiss Me, Kate* includes similar high spirits, wit, sharpness, and broad appeal through laughing at big topics to their first project. However, *Kiss Me, Kate* also harnesses the skills of Bella Spewack in representing modern women, exemplified in her previous work with Sam, and Cole

Porter's appetite for mischief and romance. This harmonized through the provocative and bawdy elements of Shakespeare's play and the new backstage plotline.

Above all, they worked together, agreeing a skeleton for the musical only weeks after beginning work, revealing considerable joined-up thinking that allowed *Kiss Me, Kate* to stun and surprise audiences around the world. Arguably their collective masterwork, *Kiss Me, Kate* survives where much of their previously successful work has dwindled, because of their deep understanding of the topics of the show, their ambition to entertain, and the risks that Bella Spewack and Cole Porter took to maintain their creative authority, even when that presented challenges beyond their individual ambitions for this musical.

In this book, I explore the creative collaboration and interests of various figures involved in the construction of *Kiss Me, Kate*. I show how the Spewacks wrestled with adapting *The Taming of the Shrew* and characterizing a modern remarriage while Porter entered the project tentatively but became increasingly invested in honing the score to exemplify his personal compositional style. I also highlight how other members of the creative team made significant interventions that helped define *Kiss Me, Kate*. For example, I show how choreographer Hanya Holm and director/producer John C. Wilson introduced editorial and staging insights that streamlined a script initially more suited to screen than to live performance. In the second half of this study, I reckon with *Kiss Me, Kate*'s life beyond Broadway, on stage, screen, and in various areas of its reception. Throughout, I argue that *Kiss Me, Kate* reveals the profoundly collaborative nature of making a Broadway musical where practical and dramaturgical questions are raised from multiple vantage points. I also demonstrate that these creatives understood their task and the challenges of adapting already sensitive Shakespearean material, but that this has not always been recognized or reflected in the choices made by other interpreters of the musical.

The portrait of marriage and of female emancipation in *Kiss Me, Kate* is limited by the conditions that Bella Spewack experienced and knew to be real. Although contrived for comedy, the challenge of this musical is that it refuses to give us the ending many feel that Lilli, *and Katherine*, deserve. Our heroine does not overcome the patriarchal environment she is situated in, and, in the end, she chooses partnership with Fred over the "independence" that is fleetingly shown in the penultimate scenes of the show. *Kiss Me, Kate* is frequently tasked with redeeming the messages in *The Taming of the Shrew* and can be criticized for extending the comedy related to misogyny, female subjugation, and patriarchal violence. In this volume, I propose that Bella Spewack and Cole Porter not only were conscious of these challenges and worked to find solutions that suited their agendas (regardless of whether we think this translates in performance or not), but they also remind us that, for most women, it is impossible to fully resist a patriarchal society. Instead, I demonstrate how the layers of *Kiss Me, Kate* explore societal limits on female agency within and without the Shakespeare. As will be shown in the genesis chapters, Bella Spewack spent more time constructing Lilli/Katherine than any other character, ultimately working with Porter to produce a romantic, feisty, glamorous, spiteful, and frequently comic leading role that does not mask the realities of the material, their industry, or the society it is set in.

1

Critical Approaches to a Broadway Hit

Kiss Me, Kate opened in a rich creative climate across the American cultural landscape. On the musical theater stage, 1948 saw Broadway productions of *Allegro*, *Angel in the Wings*, *The Cradle Will Rock*, *High Button Shoes*, *Inside USA*, *Lend an Ear*, *Love Life*, *My Romance*, *Small Wonder*, and *Where's Charley?* while longer-running musicals like *Annie Get Your Gun*, *Brigadoon*, *Finian's Rainbow*, and *Oklahoma!* continued to perform to busy houses. Beloved film musical *Easter Parade* (1948) had become an immediate hit in cinemas alongside recently released classics *The Red Shoes* and Lawrence Olivier's *Hamlet*.[1] T. S. Eliot was awarded the Nobel Prize for Literature while James Michener, Tennessee Williams, W. H. Auden, and Walter Piston each received Pulitzer Prizes. The 1948 Oscars were dominated by *Black Narcissus* (1947) with other nominations for the Christmas classics *The Bishop's Wife* and *Miracle on 34th Street* as well as the David Lean adaptation of *Great Expectations*. Meanwhile, controversial spiritual-inspired "Zip-A-Dee-Doo-Dah" won Best Song for Disney's *Song of the South* (1946)[2] and actor James Baskett was given a Special Award for his "able and heartwarming characterization of Uncle Remus, friend and storyteller to children of the world."[3]

The New York classical music scene was also thriving, with Bruno Walter conducting Kathleen Ferrier at Carnegie Hall and productions including *Un ballo in maschera*, *Louise*, *Rigoletto*, *Aida*, and *Lucia di Lammermoor* playing at the Metropolitan Opera. Even the less well-remembered film musical *Words and Music*, which celebrated the partnership of Richard Rodgers and Lorenz Hart, achieved good box office receipts, with *Time* magazine describing it as "just the right proportions of garlicky bad taste and more than Oriental splendor which (plus Technicolor) add up to a Hollywood dream of heaven."[4] Simultaneously, Dale Carnegie, author of the infamous *How to Win Friends and Influence People* (1936), achieved his second *New York Times* bestseller with *How to Stop Worrying and Start Living* (1948), while Norman Mailer's debut novel *The Naked and the Dead* otherwise dominated the charts.

Too Darn Hot. Hannah Robbins, Oxford University Press. © Oxford University Press 2026.
DOI: 10.1093/9780190082437.003.0001

Kiss Me, Kate opened at a time when audiences (and critics) were receptive to a considerable range of dramatic and artistic content. Therefore, its balance of musical genres, a familiar Shakespeare play, and screwball comedy was well conceived to appeal. As this chapter will explore, *Kiss Me, Kate* has been contextualized against a backdrop of commercial failure for Cole Porter and personal turmoil between Sam and Bella Spewack. As a result, its success feels even more miraculous, despite its having many of the same qualities as other successes in both their portfolios and being staged at a receptive time. In fact, the Spewacks, Porter, Lemuel Ayers, Arnold Saint Subber, John C. Wilson, Hanya Holm, Pembroke Davenport (the musical director), and the orchestration team led by Robert Russell Bennett and Don Walker co-created a hit show during a period in which stylistic variety was still popular, a Shakespeare film was dominating cinemas, and Christmas and Disney movies, romanticizing even the sharpest themes, were garnering Oscar nominations.

The complex mixture of content in *Kiss Me, Kate* is part of its appeal but has also challenged biographers, scholars, and critics as we all seek designations to communicate the nature of works to a readership who may not have immediate access to the material. Therefore, I begin *Too Darn Hot* with a survey of existing approaches to the musical and how they help us to examine it. This serves as a preface to the deep analysis of how *Kiss Me, Kate* was developed for Broadway in 1948. It is also important to acknowledge that while *Kiss Me, Kate* is often viewed as a "Porter musical," it was produced during a peak period of writing by women for the American stage and screen. *Playbill* reported that the 1949/50 season, of which *Kiss Me, Kate* was part, celebrated the joint highest representation of new musicals with female writers.[5] It took seventy-three years, until 2023/24, for equivalent representation to recur. Among the works playing alongside *Kiss Me, Kate*, Jule Styne and Leo Robin's *Gentlemen Prefer Blondes* (1950) with book adapted by Anita Loos also engaged directly with gender, sex, marriage, and power, prefacing the iconic film adaptation starring Marilyn Monroe and Jane Russell a few years later.[6] Dorothy Fields, writing with brother Herbert, had coauthored books for three successful, though lesser-known, Cole Porter shows—*Let's Face It* (1941),[7] *Something for the Boys* (1943), and *Mexican Hayride* (1944)—and shared responsibility for the script for *Annie Get Your Gun*, which stands with *Kiss Me, Kate* as one of two relics of musical comedy on "post-*Oklahoma!*" Broadway. *Kiss Me, Kate* and *Annie Get Your Gun* would be compared together for some years because they revealed each new ambition in Porter and Irving Berlin's respective songwriting, and yet neither has so far received book-length treatment, despite their obvious appeals. This volume aims to fill one gap while emphasizing the role *Kiss Me, Kate* plays in musical theater repertory more generally. While undeniably a product of its time, the material of *Kiss Me, Kate* also reveals forward thinking and complex handling of topics that we do not frequently recognize in its reception today.

The Shakespeare Musical

The categorization of *Kiss Me, Kate* as a "type" of musical makes up a significant proportion of the scholarship on this show. For musicologists and theater historians, this musical provides a fascinating challenge among Cole Porter's catalogue of work and the evolution of musical theater writing that took place in the 1940s. Contemporary songwriters and lyricists undeniably responded to the commercial trailblazer *Oklahoma!* (1943) and began to transition away from using songs decoratively to focus on connecting their content, mood, and vocal writing to each dramatic moment. In this space, *Kiss Me, Kate* is placed as simultaneously sophisticated and old-fashioned.

Unlike many of Porter's previous musicals, *Kiss Me, Kate*'s songs clearly belong to this show. Many are settings or bastardizations of *The Taming of the Shrew* text, and Porter employs several musical jokes that evoke the mock-Tudor across the score. Simultaneously, there are wider comments and explorations of theatricality, sex, love, and marriage that are easily tied to *Kiss Me, Kate*'s plot points but are also sufficiently generic to appeal to listeners not intimately familiar with the show. It is striking that, although popular, many of the songs in *Kiss Me, Kate* have *not* been uncoupled from the musical in the way that material from previous Porter shows (e.g., "It's De-Lovely" and "Ridin' High" from the comparatively obscure *Red, Hot and Blue* [1936]) has survived away from their original commercial vehicles.

In addition to rich discussion of the genre of Porter's score by musicologists including Joseph P. Swain, Geoffrey Block, and Lynn Laitman Siebert,[8] commentators and scholars all place *Kiss Me, Kate* as an important example of "the Shakespeare musical"[9]—a shorthand that has been used to contain all musicals adapted, derived, or in conversation with the life and work of the English playwright. With similar priorities to the score analyses I have previously mentioned, Shakespearean approaches to *Kiss Me, Kate* consider how it crosses boundaries of adaptation and blurs aesthetic delineations by situating "Shakespeare" (high art) in a musical comedy (middlebrow entertainment). A melting pot of references, *Kiss Me, Kate* acknowledges a broad range of American and European cultural touchstones including previous productions of Shakespeare, other musicals, opera, film, and vaudeville. Broadly speaking, this makeup has placed *Kiss Me, Kate* among popular reimaginings of Shakespeare like Rodgers and Hart's earlier adaptation of *The Comedy of Errors* retitled *The Boys from Syracuse* (1938) and Gil Junger's cult teen movie *10 Things I Hate about You* (1999), also adapted from *The Taming of the Shrew.*

While being grouped with other light and commercial proliferations of Shakespeare's works, *Kiss Me, Kate* has also been distanced from "serious" adaptations of Shakespeare's plays, such as the infamous Zeffirelli-directed *Taming of the Shrew* film made in 1968 starring Richard Burton and Elizabeth Taylor. This differentiation is important for my account of the musical, where I suggest that Cole Porter and the Spewacks have not been given adequate credit for their engagement with *The Shrew* or its capacity to comment on modern times. In this context, there are some ironic parallels between *Kiss Me, Kate* and the Burton/Taylor *Shrew* even though Shakespeare's text has been shredded into its barest constituent parts for the musical. Both versions demonstrate the value of a production conceived to show the range and dynamism of its leading cast and that deliberately "stagey"—over-the-top and mannered—acting and use of sets can offer important comment on the text. It is striking that George Sidney, the director of the MGM film adaptation of *Kiss Me, Kate*, also came to the musical having just made a particularly theatrical movie *Scaramouche* (1952), which used the architecture of the stage and gimmicky special effects to amplify the performance culture in its plot.

With different applications of adaptation and appropriation within its repertory, the Shakespeare musical emerges as its own tricky yet influential phenomenon in which *Kiss Me, Kate* and Arthur Laurents, Leonard Bernstein, and Stephen Sondheim's musical *West Side Story* (1957) remain landmark successes. More recent shows including *Play On!* (1996), *Something Rotten* (2015), and *& Juliet* (2019) are also included alongside *The Boys from Syracuse* (1938) as a body of material adapted from the works of Shakespeare or set in the contemporary period. Less successful examples, including *Swingin' the Dream* (1939) and the Renaissance (though not Shakespearean) *The Firebrand of Florence* (1947), are also associated with this grouping, along with other small productions like British musical *Da Boyz* (2003).[10] Important to the story of this genre is the concept that musicals tackling

Shakespeare and the Shakespearean era face particularly adaptation challenged that pose greater financial risks than other types of show. This is used to metricize *Kiss Me, Kate*'s unprecedented success, still running after seventy-five years with comparatively little change.

Separate to this possible subcategorization, *Kiss Me, Kate* offers multiple points of interest for Shakespeare scholars. It uses *The Taming of the Shrew* as part of a metatheatrical puzzle, where Bella Spewack's contemporary 1940s plot echoes, revises, extends, and innovates the narratives and characterization in Shakespeare's play. For example, the song "Tom, Dick, or Harry" compresses an entire subplot from *The Taming of the Shrew* into a few minutes of music while also mapping Shakespeare's characters onto different gendered stereotypes. *Kiss Me, Kate* also includes what Julie Sanders calls a "quasi-Shakespearean"[11] musical-within-a-musical familiar from the original structure of *The Taming of the Shrew*, which begins in the "real world" and moves to a performance of its cautionary tale. To achieve a similar effect, Porter and the Spewacks developed several metatheatrical gestures, including writing *Kiss Me, Kate* two opening numbers: one that begins *Kiss Me, Kate* generally ("Another Op'nin', Another Show") and the other ("We Open in Venice") launching the performance of the *Taming of the Shrew*. There is also an "onstage" intermission immediately after the break between Acts One and Two, various asides about the backstage plot during the *Taming of the Shrew* performance, and blurred boundaries about what is and is not a "known performance space." For example, several musical numbers happen in Fred and Lilli's dressing rooms, but they are set "backstage." Meanwhile, the two gunmen appear on the wrong side of the safety curtain for "Brush Up Your Shakespeare" recognize that they are "onstage" and are encountering a real audience in the amphitheater.

In her monograph *Adaptation and Appropriation*, Sanders frames *Kiss Me, Kate* as "both adaptation and appropriation at the same time":

> Audiences register two levels of adaptation and appropriation. The embedded "The Shrew" musical is a more straightforward adaptation, . . . reworking the characters and events in a song and dance format. As a result, many of the central songs, including "I Hate Men," derive from the musical-within-the-musical. . . . If the pure adaptation rests in the embedded musical, then the appropriative aspect is found in the wider framework story of the US theatre performers and in the related subplot of the Mafia henchmen seeking debt repayment.[12]

Here, Sanders characterizes all of *Kiss Me, Kate* as in debt to *The Taming of the Shrew*, taking the material and subthemes and reconfiguring them in this new format. Irene G. Dash echoes Sanders, noting that the Spewacks created *Kiss Me, Kate* to evoke the structure of *The Taming of the Shrew*, "borrowing . . . from Shakespeare's play but transforming it."[13] However, while Sanders suggests that Porter's song "I Hate Men" derives from the process of "musicalizing" *The Taming of the Shrew*, this flattens Porter's unexpected advocacy for the character Katherine who does not have a comparable speech in Shakespeare's play. *Kiss Me, Kate*'s appropriation of *The Shrew* is perhaps most interesting in its attempts (successful or otherwise) to modernize and emancipate Shakespeare's Katherine from the restrictions that define the role in the play.

Sanders's important exploration of the relationship between play and musical also downplays the extent to which the creative team decimated the Shakespearean text, abridging, paraphrasing, and discarding anything from the odd line to entire scenes to satisfy their creative vision. According to James Shapiro in *Shakespeare in a Divided America*, Bella Spewack "understood that the proportions had to be right; by her rough calculation, Shakespeare was responsible for twenty-two pages of the script, Porter for sixty, and she herself for the remaining seventy-two."[14] Bella and Sam were ruthless in their cutting down of Shakespeare's play, removing the framing Induction and cutting thousands of lines from the scenes about Katherine, Petruchio, Bianca, and the other characters. In fact, *Kiss Me, Kate* abandons most of the "taming" scenes from Shakespeare's *Shrew*, using the conflict from Fred and Lilli's contemporary (1940s) relationship to present the power struggles and enduring patriarchal oppressions experienced by women who do not appease the men around them.

A Cole Porter Musical

The other key point of focus for approaching *Kiss Me, Kate* is its place as the commercial peak, and most enduring stage work, of Cole Porter's career. Porter came to true prominence comparatively late, at around thirty-six, when his musical *Paris* (1928) opened on Broadway, featuring the enduring song "Let's Do It, Let's Fall in Love." Like most Broadway composers, Porter experienced varied success across the four decades he wrote for stage and screen and, as noted previously, many of his most well-loved songs including

"Night and Day," "Love for Sale," and "Ev'ry Time We Say Goodbye" have transcended the popularity of the musicals that they originated in.[15] Really, only the revised *Anything Goes* (1934) and *Kiss Me, Kate* remain at the heart of stage musical theater repertory. There have also been larger revivals of *Can-Can* and *Silk Stockings*, but these are undeniably obscure works to a general contemporary audience.

Because of the second life of many of his songs in commercial recordings by artists from Bing Crosby to Debbie Harry and Iggy Pop, Porter is often placed alongside contemporaries including Irving Berlin, George and Ira Gershwin, and Harold Arlen as a defining voice in American popular music as much as a key figure in the development of the classic Broadway musical. In addition to his quintessential musical style of short and catchy songs layered with "tricky rhymes"[16] and memorable repetitions, Porter's personal and social life have also caught public attention. Associated with America and Europe's wealthy elite through his marriage to the socialite Linda Lee Thomas in 1919 and immortalized in photographs with major figures of his era including Noël Coward, Lord Carnarvon, and Marilyn Monroe, Porter excites romantic and salacious interest as a figure beyond his musical career. In this context, *Kiss Me, Kate*, as his most commercially successful and enduring stage musical, is rich with interest.

Following the old Broadway adage that "you are only as good as your last show," Porter was in precarious professional straits when he joined the *Kiss Me, Kate* creative team in early 1948. His preceding stage projects—contributing to Billy Rose's revue *Seven Lively Arts* (1944) and a collaboration with Orson Welles, *Around the World* (1946)—had been critical and box office failures. Porter was also unsettled by the ongoing conversations about the style and role of songs in musicals on Broadway, following the success of *Oklahoma!* Like Rodgers and Hart, Porter had been a major force in the musical comedies of the 1930s, which showcased his contrasting repertoire of tender ballads and playful comedy numbers, often layered with double-entendres and gags for a quick laugh. This style of songwriting was increasingly framed as out of step with the new trajectory of musicals.

When interviewed late in his career, Porter reflected on the changing aesthetic qualities of musicals describing newer musical comedies, including *Kiss Me, Kate* and Berlin's *Annie Get Your Gun* (1947) as more "musicianly" than in earlier years thanks to the collaborative work of Rodgers and Hammerstein after *Oklahoma!*[17] He also characterized his later songs as "easier than they used they used to be, musically and lyrically."[18] Porter's descriptions of his compositional sound and ambitions position him reactively to innovations in musical theater songwriting, and this has become a defining quality of how *Kiss Me, Kate* is placed among other classic musicals including its immediate competitor *South Pacific* (1949) and later rival *Guys and Dolls* (1950). *Kiss Me, Kate* is frequently presented as Porter's most deliberate attempt at writing a Rodgers-and-Hammerstein-like piece, where he responded to the dramatic needs of Sam and Bella Spewack's libretto and the broader subject matter of the musical. However, it bears saying that the similarities between *Kiss Me, Kate* and *Annie Get Your Gun*, written by two forces of 1930s musical comedy and commercial music, both including performances within performances that allowed a variety of musical styles, are more striking than those found in comparison to the more narratively driven *Oklahoma!*, *Carousel* (1945), or *South Pacific*.

As noted previously, chapters in survey volumes by Geoffrey Block and Joseph P. Swain situate *Kiss Me, Kate* most clearly in the evolution of the American musical.[19] Although different in focus, both authors suggest that Cole Porter was simultaneously responding to his own professional decline and to the unprecedented popularity of Rodgers and Hammerstein's collaborations together. Lynn Laitman Siebert also develops this argument, summarizing her doctoral thesis on the (musical) themes of *Kiss Me, Kate* in a chapter for *A Cole Porter Companion*.[20] Siebert connects Porter's musicality with his extensive music education, including at Yale and Harvard universities, and uses this context to celebrate *Kiss Me, Kate* as the most successful manifestation of Porter's musical abilities. Michael Buchler also provides a structural reading of the songs,[21] expanding Raymond Knapp's theory that we can deconstruct *Kiss Me, Kate* into pairs of complementary musical numbers.[22] Universal to each of these approaches is the conviction that *Kiss Me, Kate* is made significant to scholarship through the quality of Porter's songs. In *Enchanted Evenings*, Geoffrey Block also amplifies the score's significance to *Kiss Me, Kate*'s enduring commercial impact.[23] The unexpected sophistication of the songs in *Kiss Me, Kate* showcase Porter's capacity to write range of styles, moods, and pastiche while also speaking to the musical's core themes. As a result, they now represent some of the most celebrated works in Porter's prolific career.

This book builds on existing musicological overviews of *Kiss Me, Kate* while reframing Porter as one of several collaborative forces that led to the success of the musical. Sam and Bella Spewack identified a system of working successfully with him, following their previous collaboration on *Leave It To*

Me! (1938) a decade earlier. This allowed Porter to flourish, and, in turn, he supported Bella Spewack in disagreements with producers Subber and Ayers. He also introduced his own creative and dramaturgical interventions while the musical was in development. Despite the emphasis on Porter and his impact on the show, the later chapters will highlight that he largely retreated from *Kiss Me, Kate* to work on new projects after the Broadway opening and that, in many ways, the Spewacks became the custodians of the property until Sam's death in 1971. Above all, I reveal a juxtaposition between narrative songwriting that Porter undertook in the early stages of writing *Kiss Me, Kate* and the musical comedy numbers that supplanted this material around the show's rehearsal period. While *Kiss Me, Kate* reveals Porter's capacity to respond to text and drama in newly sophisticated ways, it also spotlights his ability to repackage legitimate drama into modern, witty, and commercially appealing comment that speaks profoundly to his work in the 1930s and less to the emerging musical dramas like *Oklahoma!* and *South Pacific.*

Screwball and the Comedy of Remarriage

In *American Cinderellas on the Broadway Stage*, Maya Cantu characterizes *Kiss Me, Kate* as part of a wider trend of "battle of the sexes" musicals in the post–World War II era.[24] She particularly aligns the narratives in *Kiss Me, Kate* with the theme of remarriage, which was regularly used in screwball comedy films including *The Awful Truth* (1937), *His Girl Friday* (1939), *The Philadelphia Story* (1940), and the Spewacks' screenplay for *My Favorite Wife* (1940).[25] Intended as light relief for a Depression era audience, this format reconfigures potentially serious dramatic narratives (e.g., investigating the murder of police officer in *His Girl Friday*) into improbably chaotic and farcical plots featuring miscommunication, competition, and escalating physical comedy.

Screwball films employ sharp and rapid dialogue between two (or more) charismatic stars, often additionally coupled with partners-in-crime and/or insipid rival lovers. Importantly, these films featured rich, fashionable, and attractive people overcoming spiteful manners and resentment to fall in love. Duane Byrge and Robert Milton Miller especially highlight how screwball comedies depict characters behaving in irrational and disreputable ways:

> combining slapstick with sophistication, characters who supposedly had ample reason to follow strict social convention took leave of at least some

> measure of their comfortable sanity and reverted to childish pranks while in evening dress, unabashedly wearing their egos on their sleeves.[26]

Hinting at the impropriety and adolescent behavior that typify these films, they capture the glamour and comedy that made them widely appealing. For *Kiss Me, Kate*, the subgenre of "remarriage" films includes an extra reference point as the drama is driven by protagonists who already know each other. Therefore the romantic thrust of the film, or, in this case, musical, is about solving the problem of separation that has happened before the start of the entertainment.

The Spewacks' screenplay for *My Favorite Wife* provides a useful example of this infrastructure. It follows the exploits of the main protagonist Nick Arden (Cary Grant) who marries his new lover Bianca (Gail Patrick) immediately after his first wife Ellen (Irene Dunne) is declared dead, having gone missing after a boat accident seven years earlier. As Nick and Bianca arrive at their honeymoon destination, he discovers Ellen in the lobby of the hotel as she and another passenger have just been rescued from a rural island. Nick is overjoyed but gets caught in a string of lies to Bianca while spying on Ellen and the handsome man that she was stranded with, investigating why he failed to locate them himself. The plot ends with a chaotic court scene where Ellen is declared "not dead," the new marriage is annulled, and the old one is rekindled.

A deeper examination of this screenplay also sheds light on the internal culture of *Kiss Me, Kate*. Both feature an attractive and talented man who has interest in two desirable and self-composed women, one of whom he has been previously married to. He immediately causes conflict by favoring his new love and dismissing the other. The drama is then extended by the interruption of a plausible, if unlikely, rival in love whom he seeks to undermine, while his former wife exploits the jealousy that this competition elicits. We see the same action play out in both of these Spewack scripts, reminding us that, while *The Taming of the Shrew* is vital to the fabric of *Kiss Me, Kate*, other formulas and stimuli were also significant to its creation.

The popularity of screwball comedy was partially pioneered by female screenwriters like Bella Spewack and Viña Delmarin, writing at a time when "no fault" divorce had not been legalized in the United States. In their work, these authors were often looking for routes to explore contemporary female agency and the ways men reacted to it. In a similar vein, Anita Loos's *Gentlemen Prefer Blondes* and her work with Jane Murfin adapting Clare

Boothe Luce's *The Women* (1939) are also relevant context. *The Women* follows a predominantly, and often solely, female cast as the protagonist Mary Haines discovers her husband is having an affair. Toni Anita Hull highlights that Loos particularly toughened the characters from the original play, showing them to be strong and independent, and balancing Mary's triumph over her usurper, Crystal, by making the rival a well-rounded character who is neither innocent nor victimized in the film's outcome.[27]

The Women is not a perfect film, but it interacts powerfully with *Kiss Me, Kate* as Loos's "unique fascination of [*sic*] men, women, sex, and relationships"[28] is undeniably similar to what we see in Porter and the Spewacks' respective works. The screwball comedy also provides heroines prepared to fight gendered expectations of mild-mannered meekness. They are romantically available but self-empowered and meet their lovers/antagonists with equal fire. Where Shakespeare's Katherine is wholly reactive to patriarchy, Lilli is the instigator of the commotions in *Kiss Me, Kate.* She also presents a viable threat as she wields the power to decimate and undermine the production regardless of the intervention of the gunmen. The drama is constructed through, and propelled by, her resourcefulness regardless of how we perceive the conditions that she faces.

Bella Spewack's history as a screenwriter is essential to understanding why *Kiss Me, Kate* treats Lilli/Katherine as it does. Like a musical comedy, the screwball remarriage trope assumes that the characters love one another and want to be together but are going to do ludicrous (and sometimes terrible) things while they figure it out. Therefore *Kiss Me, Kate* partially remakes Katherine through the intertextual connection to Lilli and her capacity to ruin Fred's life. This does not close arguments about the content of *The Taming of the Shrew*, but it contextualizes how Bella Spewack might have viewed her authorial voice and writing havoc for Lilli from her own professional expertise. She (and Sam) modernize Katherine by matching her to a screwball heroine who can, and will, fight her own battles against a challenging opponent.

If we dispense with the inference that the creative team were unaware of the harms in *The Taming of the Shrew*, we can also situate the construction of Fred and Lilli's relationship within the Spewacks' wider body of work. There are undeniable parallels between *My Favorite Wife*, their hit play *Boy Meets Girl*, and their Oscar-nominated script for *Weekend at the Waldorf.* In all these works, the Spewacks place their romantic protagonists in open conflict, which is resolved in differently ludicrous ways. If we acknowledge screwball comedy as an ingredient in the making of *Kiss Me Kate,* we offered a format that celebrates the performance of violence between consenting actors, using it as a means to an end.[29] This is not comparable to the harm sustained against Katherine in *The Taming of the Shrew.*

Reviving Classic Musicals

In recent years, musicals like *Kiss Me, Kate* and *Carousel* have been subjected to new attention as audiences, creatives, and critics have begun to challenge limited representations of women, queerness, and people of color in American musicals. Much scrutiny of *Kiss Me, Kate,* especially in Shakespeare Studies and in the press connected to #MeToo and Broadway, focuses on whether the values of this musical are suitable for modern audiences. This debate was made prominent in 2018 by a popular *New York Times* article, titled "The Problem with Broadway Revivals: They Revive Gender Stereotypes, Too," by Michael Paulson.[30]

Because of the interplay between the backstage narrative and *Taming of the Shrew* scenes in *Kiss Me, Kate,* a lot of critical reception has focused on the Shakespeare and the extent to which it has substantially shaped the representations of gender and power in this musical. The criticisms center the significance of *The Taming of the Shrew* to *Kiss Me, Kate* and the value system it provides for the violence enacted against Lilli on- and offstage. Paulson describes this relationship as "often vexing to contemporary audiences," presenting *Kiss Me, Kate* as a show in which "a fierce woman is persuaded to humbled herself to please her husband."[31]

Symbiotically, these interpretations foreground the legacy of *The Taming of the Shrew* in the musical as one of the undeniable flaws of the work. From this, most arguments about *Kiss Me, Kate,* feminism, and gender emphasize three aspects of the musical, which are, in some way themselves, grounded in *Kiss Me, Kate*'s relationship with Shakespeare's play text. They are "the slapping scene" at the end of Act 1, Scene 5, the spirit behind "Brush Up Your Shakespeare," and the use of Katherine's final soliloquy as a preface to Fred and Lilli's romantic reconciliation.

These "problematic three" represent several bigger themes in *Kiss Me, Kate* and force us to consider the motivations of physical and threatened violence against Lilli by Fred and the gunmen, which has been extensively covered by the academic reception to *Kiss Me, Kate.* For example, Barbara

Hodgdon highlights a "dominant-submissive undertext" of Shakespeare's play,[32] while Carol E. Silverberg argues that considerable sections of *Kiss Me, Kate* validate, and make light of, domestic violence.[33] In her doctoral research, Silverberg suggests that this stems from Bella Spewack's lived experience and poor treatment by Sam: "Without the emotional slapping around that Bella received from her unfaithful husband, she would have lacked material for her somewhat subversive libretto."[34]

Scholars have particularly grappled with *Kiss Me, Kate*'s "happy ending" because it seems a betrayal of Lilli's personality and a capitulation to the most limiting aspects of *The Taming of the Shrew*. There is also considerable debate about whether Katherine's spirit is broken by the treatment she experiences or if she decides to play along. Productions and film adaptations of *The Taming of the Shrew* present the conditions of the marriage in widely varying terms. For many feminist scholars, *The Taming of the Shrew* presents a bigger concern because the patriarchal culture of the play repeatedly denies Katherine's agency (before and after her marriage) and almost all the characters find enjoyment in, or relish in, her mistreatment regardless of how she responds to it.

Howard Bloom controversially defends the politics of Shakespeare's play, describing it as "as much a romantic comedy as it is farce."[35] He suggests there is legitimate romance among the ridiculousness of the play. Ann Blake also suggests that it is important to defend *The Taming of the Shrew*, in which modern readers have located darkness rather than exaggeration for the sake of comedy.[36] Blake reasons that the verbal comedy, the "nonsense game"[37] where Petruchio and Katherine size each other up, and the acts of violence against several characters of different classes and genders speak to constructed comedy, rather than a drama about domestic violence. In Blake's view, it is also dangerous to conflate historical records with creative works because it is easy to undermine subversive comedy that challenges rather than agrees with social norms.

Frances Teague concludes that any liberal gestures in *Kiss Me, Kate* "finally collapse into cynical conservatism" as the writing ultimately "backs down for safe conventionality."[38] It feels impossible to untangle the romantic resolution of the musical from Katherine's declaration that women should capitulate to their husbands. The flippancy and showiness of other songs, including the variously misogynistic numbers performed by Petruchio and the gunmen, is contrasted by the sparse and tender arrangement of "I Am Ashamed That Women Are So Simple," indicating that we should pay deep attention to Lilli/Katherine in this moment.

Although these issues have been referenced in press for many productions, much of the promotional tour surrounding the 2019 Broadway revival directly engaged with staging *Kiss Me, Kate* in the post-#MeToo era, and making changes to ensure a balance of power between Lilli/Katherine and Fred/Petruchio. In one interview for *Variety*, star Kelli O'Hara explained that they reformed their Lilli/Katherine:

> As opposed to crying or putting her head on her pillow or begging him back or running away . . . she beats the shit out of him. . . . It's a different response, but I think most women have been at the place where if they could, they would.[39]

Other coverage of the production describes how it navigates the "antique attitudes" of the Shakespeare so that "we view the vicious scrapping of these ex-spouses as hilarious, not creepy or lopsided."[40] Bailey Sincox suggests that the changes made in the 2019 *Kiss Me, Kate* "changes the problem of the unruly woman to that of partisan dissension,"[41] and I propose that this is exactly what the original creative team intended.

While it is clear that Lilli's agency in *Kiss Me, Kate* is inextricably bound up with Katherine's, it is an oversimplification to say that Fred draws only misogynist power and status from Petruchio as well. Instead, Porter and the Spewacks inject fragility and toxic masculinity into his character. His need to win is contrasted by his lack of success in controlling Lilli, in maintaining Lois's interest, and in mounting a smooth-running production. Unlike in *The Taming of the Shrew*, where Petruchio's ambition to be wealthily married underpins the priorities of the play, Lilli/Katherine's disruptive force is more prominent and equally central to *The Taming of the Shrew* in *Kiss Me, Kate*.

Supporting this, Kristen N. Gragg argues that Shakespeare's Katherine does not embody a typical shrew in English literary history. In the play, she is relatively quiet and speaks defensively in response to criticism rather than being abrasively gregarious and goading.[42] Gragg notes that Katherine has only 82 speeches throughout *The Taming of the Shrew*, in comparison to Petruchio who has almost double (158). In the original Broadway script of *Kiss Me, Kate*, Katherine has only 33 speeches. However, there is a proportionally larger amount of her Shakespearean text (37.5% of her dialogue), whereas Petruchio's speeches are more significantly truncated. The general retention of Shakespeare in *Kiss Me, Kate* is around 12% of the total play so

Katherine is remarkably well served in a superficial model of representation from the original text.

The scholarship on *Kiss Me, Kate* offers a complicated mix of readings because interpretations like Irene G. Dash's chapter in *Shakespeare and the American Musical* argue that almost all of the creative content of the musical is traceable to *The Taming of the Shrew*.[43] Assuming that *The Taming of the Shrew* overwhelms the creative input of the Spewacks, Porter, Hanya Holm, and others, readings of *Kiss Me, Kate* argue that *The Taming of the Shrew* imposes an element of horror—misogynistic violence—onto the backstage plot because of the constructed parallels between the characters and their situations. Therefore, Fred hitting Lilli and the gunmen's threats to her freedom and safety are escalations of the worst behavior in *The Taming of the Shrew*. From this perspective, Barbara Hodgdon argues that *Kiss Me, Kate* "not only rigorously polices excessive desires but also tolerates no ruptures in male dominance."[44] In different ways, Barbara Hodgdon, Irene G. Dash, Frances Teague, and Robert Lawson-Peebles (*Approaches to the American Musical*) each address *Kiss Me, Kate* as an extension of *The Taming of the Shrew*'s misogynistic legacy, encouraging the audience to enjoy violence at the expense of Lilli/Katherine.[45]

In my source analysis, I agree with Dash's appraisal that *Kiss Me, Kate* "doesn't try to solve but rather illuminates [the problems of *The Taming of the Shrew*] in twentieth-century terms."[46] I evidence how the creative team explored different ways of commenting upon and reframing *The Taming of the Shrew*, contrasting Porter and the Spewacks' experimentation with Shakespeare's play with Blakemore's 1999 revised script and the "tweaked"[47] 2019 Broadway production. Here I examine what priorities are foregrounded in different versions of *Kiss Me, Kate*, reflecting Ann Blake's warning that it is easy to impose unilateral assumptions about the social values of people because of when they lived rather than through what they said and did.[48] While far from utopic, *Kiss Me, Kate* also provides a vital glimpse of the lived experiences of women in theater as experienced by Bella and imagined by Porter.

Kiss Me, Kate in the Archive

My account of *Kiss Me, Kate* is largely constructed from the published and preserved accounts of people who were there, a patchwork of archival sources, public records, press reports, and textual analysis of the musical through its different productions and adaptations. By layering approaches and materials in this way, some narratives and trends emerge brightly while other sections remain murky and uncertain. It is easy to impose personalities on the individual creatives and actors from the tone of their writings and manner in interviews while forgetting that these are only fragments of a public (or private) persona. The portraits I have drawn from correspondence are often joyful and full of indicative traits, but many of these collections reveal only the messages that were chosen for preservation by the author, recipient, heir, or archive. Therefore, this book stands as an interpretation of what I have seen and read, rather than a definitive picture of every fact and person who was involved in the making of *Kiss Me, Kate*. What emerges is a melting pot of characters and levels of experience in making a musical who were differently united in making *Kiss Me, Kate* the best they could.

As is indicated here, my research combines many incomplete fragments to suggest a bigger picture. My reading of the collaborative process also uses these fragments to go beyond the published materials like the script and song lyrics. As with any archival project, there are materials missing and there are likely to be imagined sources that never existed. The individuals involved were each very particular in what they did and did not retain. We know, for example, that Cole Porter worked with a copyist to transcribe songs he wrote at the piano. We do not have a record of when the copyist was present or a traceable understanding of how Porter composed around their sessions. Therefore, Porter may have written some songs that were transcribed quickly after they were composed and some that weren't.

Porter's papers at the Library of Congress contain a substantial number of lyric drafts (handwritten or typed, sometimes annotated) and unmarked copies of songs from his shows. In several bound scrapbooks housed by Yale University, his secretaries kept clippings about his life and work, and he also maintained bound volumes of song sketches. These sketches (often unlabeled) tend to be melody fragments with the occasional chord in the right hand or rhythm of a bass line. However, these do not offer us the meticulously transcribed autograph song sheets that we might hope to find in the papers of Frederick Loewe, Kurt Weill, or Richard Rodgers.

Musical analysis of *Kiss Me, Kate* stems most frequently from the original Broadway rental parts and the published vocal scores. David Charles Abell and Seann Alderking's critical edition also provides us with a comprehensive overview of the other music sources available (e.g., orchestral parts from the original Broadway production) and lists of orchestrations by Robert Russell Bennett and Don Walker. Scholars have therefore focused their discussion almost entirely on the music from *Kiss Me, Kate* that we are already familiar with, delving into the success of the score by highlighting its analytical merits such as quotations from opera or complex harmonic progressions in "So in Love." The practical methodological question has been: "How can we read what we have, especially given that what we have is so well loved?"

In my score analysis, I make no claims to have found new music sources for *Kiss Me, Kate*, and I largely agree that Porter achieved new complexity in this set of songs in comparison to other musicals he composed. Where the music drafts that Porter may (or may not) have produced are lacking, there are pages of memorandums, letters, excerpts of unused script, and the script drafts from the Spewack papers to supplement the picture. These documents offer a possible timeline for the order of songwriting that can be cross-referenced with numerous lyric sheets to provide a suggestion of how the score came together. For example, "So in Love" was, at the very least, titled and placed as one of the penultimate songs of *Kiss Me, Kate* in April 1948. (However, the song disappears from all script materials and song breakdowns until dated drafts appear in early September.) Its second act reprisal is also undocumented in any typed version of the script until the clean copies of the original Broadway show were produced. Alfred Drake, who originated Fred/Petruchio, has simply written "So in Love" in the margin of his rehearsal script (see Figure 1.1).

While the absence of music manuscripts (dated or otherwise) leaves us to speculate on whether Porter spent five months polishing "So in Love" or if the team chose to spotlight a different number "It Was Great Fun the First Time" instead, the script and correspondence materials include similar gaps and mysteries. For example, Sam Spewack did not sign a contract for *Kiss Me, Kate* in early 1948, and he is not named as an author or included as a recipient of correspondence related to *Kiss Me, Kate* until December 1948. After *Kiss Me, Kate* opened, many of the creatives involved refer to the Spewacks as a collective writing team and reminisce about Sam being present at specific moments in the pre-Broadway genesis. However, the correspondence and existing accounts on many sides reveal that Sam had very intermittent involvement in the development of the show. Sam is, for example, noticeably unmentioned in John C. Wilson's account of working on *Kiss Me, Kate* in his autobiography.[50] Similarly, Porter wrote to all the key players in the

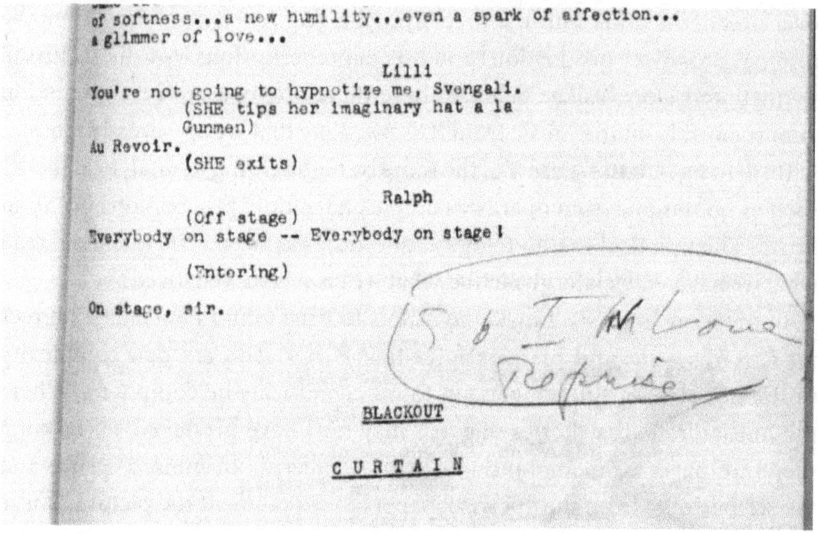

of softness...a new humility...even a spark of affection...
a glimmer of love...

Lilli

You're not going to hypnotize me, Svengali.
(SHE tips her imaginary hat a la Gunmen)
Au Revoir.
(SHE exits)

Ralph

(Off stage)
Everybody on stage -- Everybody on stage!

(Entering)
On stage, sir.

BLACKOUT

C U R T A I N

Figure 1.1 Photograph of annotation on Alfred Drake's rehearsal script[49]

creative team during a stay in California in the summer of 1948. Sam is neither mentioned nor addressed in these writings.

Draft script materials and correspondence from the early writing period help us to place Sam's initial involvement in the first phase of making *Kiss Me, Kate.* Bella notes that Sam attended development meetings for *Kiss Me, Kate* between February and May 1948, but she also rejects a coauthored film project, because Sam was finishing his first novel.[51] In a letter to Walter Kane, she notes that she and Sam would be working separately for the time being:

> As for myself, I have signed contracts on the musical I am doing with Cole Porter. Chances are I will be in California some time [*sic*] in July and will stay through August. I am supposed to deliver the first draft of my work on June 1st.[52]

He next reappears definitively in June 1948, when Porter wired him from Los Angeles to ask him to own credit for this work on the libretto:

> BELLA WRITES ME THAT YOU DONT WANT TO TAKE ANY CREDIT FOR THE BOOK. I BEG YOU TO RECONSIDER THIS DUE TO ALL THE CONTRIBUTIONS YOU HAVE MADE. ALSO IT WILL

> MAKE THE PUBLIC MUCH HAPPIER TO READ QUOTE BOOK BY SAM AND BELLA SPEWACK UNQUOTE WILL YOU DO THIS GREAT FAVOUR FOR ME. MY BEST REGARDS DEAR SAM.[53]

If Porter received a reply, it was not preserved, and Sam becomes otherwise untraceable until "Sam and" is added in pencil ahead of Bella's name on the front of her rehearsal script sometime on or after October 30, 1948.[54] Importantly, the out-of-town reviews for *Kiss Me, Kate* list Bella Spewack as the sole author while the Broadway reviews address the Spewacks, plural.

In Chapter 3, on the adaptation of *The Taming of the Shrew*, I suggest a potential trace of Sam's intervention that distinguishes parts of his contributions from Bella's. However, this is speculative and not corroborated by reassuring examples of named and signed drafts. Sam becomes an active, documented presence once the Broadway production has opened, and he is courted to direct the London transfer. It is very possible that some paper trail of his involvement in writing *Kiss Me, Kate* was lost because he and Bella Spewack were living apart and their respective documents were not combined. However, Sam has such a voluminous presence in the later materials even while he and Bella are on different continents that this does not feel fully satisfactory.

Constructing a Narrative

Using numerous incomplete threads in combination, I connect the existing archival picture of *Kiss Me, Kate* with the published accounts and production materials currently available. Across Chapters 2–5, I present a structured picture of the development process with different phases of activity and collective involvement during, and beyond, the writing of *Kiss Me, Kate*. While the success of Porter's score cannot be underestimated, these chapters place Sam and Bella Spewack, Hanya Holm, Arnold Saint Subber, Lemuel Ayers, and John C. Wilson as other important creative drivers in making the original Broadway show work. In Chapter 6, I also trace how Sam and Bella Spewack controlled (or at least, interfered with) the *Kiss Me, Kate* property as much as they could once it had achieved popularity in New York.

These genesis chapters offer a timeline of script and song materials, based on the process of revisions and dated correspondence and song or script drafts, including the core documents listed in Figure 1.2.

April 1948	*Backstage outline* Untitled script, 12pp.
June 1948	First complete script
August 1948	Interim script
October 1948	October 11 script Rehearsal script
December 1948	Original Broadway script

Figure 1.2 Breakdown of key script documents for *Kiss Me, Kate*[55]

Helpfully, there is substantial agreement about the basic events at the start of 1948, when *Kiss Me, Kate* was first written. By March 1948, the core creative team for *Kiss Me, Kate* had signed contracts, and they began work on the project. This comprised the producers Subber and Ayers (who would later agree to do set and costuming), Bella Spewack as librettist, Cole Porter on the score, and John C. Wilson as director.

In April 1948, Bella Spewack produced the first outline for *Kiss Me, Kate*, which was temporarily titled *Backstage*, and that outline has many overlaps with the musical that we would recognize today. By June 1948, (Sam and) she had produced the first complete draft of *Kiss Me, Kate*, including numerous references to familiar, and unused, songs by Cole Porter. Soon after this was circulated, Porter broke from the group and went to California, where he appears to have pursued his own creative agenda based on the script material that he had access to. Meanwhile, Bella attempted to realize her ambitions for the script and debated how far she intended to rewrite *The Taming of the Shrew* to improve the representation of Katherine's character.

From August 1948, there are more substantial contradictions, including suggestions of a large rift between Bella Spewack and the producers. The alleged fallout is signposted but not explained in the extant correspondence. However, Alfred Drake offers a dramatic, and sometimes vitriolic, account of wrangling Bella, including an alleged staged confrontation on behalf of Ayers, Subber, and Wilson, because they felt unable to reckon with her.[56] According to Drake, the upshot of this midterm tension was that Sam was invited to join the team in order to help Bella to finish the script to mutual satisfaction. An alternative reading of this, which follows the pattern of working earlier in the year, is that Bella consulted Sam and Porter about the script and the contradictory advice she was receiving, and they resolved to address problems together. This would certainly explain why Porter, who worked very separately from the rest of the creative team when tensions appear to have arisen, applied himself to the same crunch points in the script that both Sam and Bella reworked.

When Hanya Holm agreed to choreograph *Kiss Me, Kate* in September 1948, she reviewed two script drafts and provided notes on the staging possibilities and limitations of *Kiss Me, Kate.* Almost all the comments on her script drafts (held in the New York Public Library) and in her notebooks for *Kiss Me, Kate* are interpolated into the rehearsal script or have been realized, consciously or otherwise, in later revivals. For example, there is no record that anyone involved in the Royal Shakespeare Company's 1986 production of *Kiss Me, Kate* was in touch with Hanya Holm or saw her notebooks. However, they used details from the *commedia dell'arte*, including an ornately dressed cart to bring characters onto the stage, which closely resemble illustrations in Holm's notebooks when she was researching how to stage the pageantry in *The Taming of the Shrew* for *Kiss Me, Kate.*

The actual details of the rehearsal period, beginning in November 1948 and presented in Chapter 5, are vague and sketchily documented. According to John C. Wilson and Alfred Drake, Cole Porter and Bella Spewack regularly attended rehearsals and helped address changes as the cast worked. They also made several changes to the end of Act 2, swapping songs in and out until very close to the first preview in December. Porter's biographers and leading actress Patricia Morison (Lilli/Katherine) all suggest that the company were concerned that *Kiss Me, Kate* was not strong because of the subject matter and oscillating edits during rehearsal.[57] Morison also remembers being told to insist that "I Hate Men" be cut from the score: "All the others thought the song would make me look bad."[58] It was assumed that the musical might fail as the process of auditioning for backers had been fraught and protracted. Yet, the opening night in Philadelphia was an enormous success, heralding substantial ticket presales, multiple seasons in New York, on tour, and in translation around the world.

Rooted in this extended genesis, Chapter 6 explores with the involvement of the original creative team in the spread of *Kiss Me, Kate* around the world while highlighting the expansion of its appeal from commercial musical theater venues to publicly funded and subsidized opera companies. Chapter 7 then examines the process of adapting *Kiss Me, Kate* for film, noting that there was considerable interest in producing a professional recording of the original Broadway cast before MGM secured the film rights to translate it into a different medium. In these performance and production analyses, I highlight the appeal of *Kiss Me, Kate* as it balances the familiar but controversial Shakespeare—itself a marketing talking point—with elements of screwball and musical comedy. The theatricality explored in the musical through its references to actors' lives and stagecraft also translates to multiple contexts that have allowed *Kiss Me, Kate* to become a transnational product, simultaneously familiar locally and profoundly American.

Finally, I close with an alternative reading of gender and misogyny as it can be examined in contemporary versions of *Kiss Me, Kate*. As the existing literature is dominated by examinations of *The Taming of the Shrew* emphasizing the role of gendered violence and sexual jokes at the expense of *Kiss Me, Kate*'s female characters, I have inverted this angle. I focus on the significance and construction of Lilli/Katherine within the fabric of this show. Although Fred/Petruchio has more onstage presence, Lilli/Katherine is the heart of *Kiss Me, Kate*. She is the famous actor, the object of Fred's affections, the comedy and disruptive force in the collapse of their *Taming of the Shrew*, and the character in control of the resolution of the show. While there are important and complex concerns about the agency and power of her character in conflict with Fred and the gunmen who hold her in the theater, she offers new life to Katherine while also connecting the gendered struggle in *The Taming of the Shrew* to the lives of women in 1940s America. I suggest that the Spewacks and Porter thought very intentionally about the way in which their heroine is presented in *Kiss Me, Kate* and that the longevity of this musical is connected to the appeal of playing this character in the situations the show contains.

If *Kiss Me, Kate* is Cole Porter and Bella Spewack's masterwork, it is equally the triumph of the wider, and many successive, teams of creatives who have shaped it. At a time when the commercial scope of musical theater was being redefined by works with epic dramas and moral questions, *Kiss Me, Kate* is a paradoxically intimate spectacle. Set over the course of one evening in a Baltimore theater, it reminds us of relevant social commentary in *The Taming of the Shrew*—appealing or otherwise—while celebrating the craft and chaos of mounting a theatrical production. It is melting pot of comedy and bacchanal themes of love, marriage, and sex, scrutinizing the way gender permits and censors the behaviors of differently placed people. At its core, *Kiss Me, Kate* is a remarkable work of entertainment crafted by numerous creative visions. It diverts and amuses while offering sophisticated comment on gender, performance, and the power of charisma in contemporary America.

2

Early Drafts of *Kiss Me, Kate*

Accounts of the development of *Kiss Me, Kate* vary substantially between the author and the audience. Sam and Bella Spewack wrote a lively description of the creative process in the first published edition of the libretto, produced by Knopf, which is subtitled: "How to Write a Musical Comedy: An Esoteric Analysis of a New Art Form."[1] In it, they are playful, providing "How to Collaborate With" guides for William Shakespeare and Cole Porter, depicting the writing process as an open exchange of ideas that calmly flowed into a hit musical. However, in private, Bella Spewack wrote acerbically about the producers Lemuel Ayers and Arnold Saint Subber, noting that she shut them out of the developmental writing process while preparing the first script draft.[2] In his autobiography, producer and director John C. Wilson skirts over the period of writing and rehearsing *Kiss Me, Kate* with noticeable brevity, closing by saying that he fell out with the producers following the Broadway opening, during negotiations for *Kiss Me, Kate*'s transfer to London's West End.[3] The different tones of account may also link to an ongoing disagreement about who conceptualized *Kiss Me, Kate*. Bella Spewack and Arnold Saint Subber both resented sharing this credit.

Broadly speaking, the Shakespeare element, adapting *The Taming of the Shrew* into a musical, is attributed to Saint Subber, but Bella Spewack maintained that the metatheatrical aspect—the musical-within-a-musical device—was her own original contribution.[4] However, this chapter will briefly outline the proximity of *Kiss Me, Kate* to another production of *The Taming of the Shrew* that Subber and Wilson both worked on, suggesting that the idea of a backstage musical was not unique to Bella's conceptualization of the show. This said, there are notable proximities between the backstage details of *Kiss Me, Kate* and the Spewacks' screenplay writing in the 1930s. Therefore, it seems likely that the specifics of the Baltimore scenario were original to Bella, while the situational premise of *Kiss Me, Kate* came from Subber.

Too Darn Hot. Hannah Robbins, Oxford University Press.
DOI: 10.1093/9780190082437.003.0002

The early genesis of *Kiss Me, Kate* contrasts this disagreement about credit with the speed at which the Spewacks and Porter compiled the first draft. Focusing on the early development period spanning late 1947 to June 1948, this chapter presents a timeline of development and revision, using correspondence, scripts, and lyric drafts, focusing on the backstage story and overarching shape of *Kiss Me, Kate*. From late March, the core creative team was formed, and they established their working patterns. Cole Porter and the Spewacks outlined a substantial amount of material for the musical and the producers began to consider viable stars to lead the production. Bella Spewack rapidly finalized the headlines of the backstage plotline, refining the main protagonists Fred and Lilli and linking their intrigues to *The Taming of the Shrew*. Meanwhile, Cole Porter powered through the songwriting, responding to the outlines, song titles, and script pages shared with him, while also considering their potential starring actress. In a period of around ten weeks, the team devised a recognizable draft of *Kiss Me, Kate* with numerous pages of dialogue ready for Broadway and thirteen of nineteen songs ready for public consumption. The feverish productivity of this time highlights how communication and shared understanding between Porter and the Spewacks bloomed even while other working relationships were immediately strained.

First Beginnings

In late 1947, established stage manager Arnold Saint Subber and eminent set and costume designer Lemuel Ayers formed a working partnership to produce a new musical. Subber had grown up on Broadway, working as an office assistant to theater operative Lee Shubert before becoming a stage manager (*Hellzapoppin'* [1938]; *Hollywood Pinafore* [1945]; *Park Avenue* [1946]).[5] Ayers had established himself as an influential Broadway designer, following the success of his sets for the original Broadway production of *The Pirate* (1942). He then worked on three of the most successful musicals of the decade: Rodgers and Hammerstein's *Oklahoma!* (1943), Robert Wright and George Forrest's *Song of Norway* (1944), and Harold Arlen and Yip Harburg's *Bloomer Girl* (1944).[6] Ayers also worked as an art director at the MGM studios. After Ayers had worked on *Meet Me in St. Louis* in 1944 with film musical impresario Arthur Freed, he championed the idea of adapting the play *The Pirate* into a film musical, for which Cole Porter later contributed several songs including "Mack the Black" and "Be a Clown."[7] Neither Ayers nor Subber had experience of producing a musical when they began discussions about *Kiss Me, Kate*, but they both offered firsthand, practical experience, and aesthetic insights into getting new productions to Broadway.

The specific formation of their partnership is partly enigmatic. In his autobiography, John C. Wilson suggests that *Kiss Me, Kate* "was born in a lawyer's waiting room one afternoon" when Ayers and Subber accidentally became acquainted:

> Subber had just come from a summer theater on Long Island, where they had done a musical version of *The Taming of the Shrew* and was enthusiastic about its commercial possibilities. That same afternoon, he succeeded in convincing Lem that they should join forces and produce it on Broadway.[8]

However, there are other variations of this account. For example, in the *New York Times*, Stephen Holden suggests that Ayers and Subber met through a common acquaintance, as Ayers "also had the notion of a musical based on the Shakespeare play."[9] Porter's biographers also avoid addressing this earliest beginning, introducing (by omission) Ayers and Subber as an existing working partnership who approached Bella Spewack to write the book. This ambiguity likely corresponds with their disagreements about the true authorship of the premise of *Kiss Me, Kate*.

John C. Wilson places Subber's idea alongside a recent project Subber had been involved in, but most accounts, including Subber's own, connect the idea for *Kiss Me, Kate* to a major production of *The Taming of the Shrew* (1935) that he had worked on.[10] This *Shrew* starred Broadway favorites (and married couple) Alfred Lunt and Lynn Fontanne and is described by Shakespeare scholar Elizabeth Schafer as a landmark version of the play.[11] In her *Shakespeare in Production* edition of *The Taming of the Shrew*, Schafer highlights the Fontanne/Lunt production as "the big success of the mid-twentieth century."[12] Their version toured the United States and was revived for benefit performances for several years.[13] While working on the play, Subber "observed the quarrels that sometimes ensued backstage between the two stars" and saw potential to make an entertainment from this scenario.[14] According to Porter biographer William McBrien, Subber took the idea to the playwright and novelist Thornton Wilder, but Wilder was too busy to get involved so the idea was left untouched for some time.[15]

As with the producer partnership, there are no detailed reports of how Subber and Ayers then identified Bella Spewack as their potential collaborator. Although McBrien alludes to Thornton Wilder, there is no extant evidence that Subber and Ayers pursued him or any other script writer for *Kiss Me, Kate*. By contrast with the first-time producers, Spewack was an established and successful author of numerous plays and screenplays. Together with her husband Sam, she had written several Broadway successes including the play *Boy Meets Girl* (1935) and the stage musical *Leave It to Me!* (1938), with songs written by Cole Porter. Important to situating *Kiss Me, Kate* is the knowledge that both Porter and the Spewacks had tested themes exploring the relationships between performers, performance writing, and performativity before. In *Boy Meets Girl*, the Spewacks translated their experiences working as screenwriters in Hollywood into a farce about screenplay writers trying to satisfy their talent and accidentally making a newborn baby a star. Titled after a familiar plot formula, the play has lots of moving parts and uses chaos to underpin the interactions between the characters who each conform to specific narrative roles and archetypes. Later, the Spewacks also gained considerable popularity as film writers, garnering an Oscar nomination for the screenplay of box office smash *My Favorite Wife* (1940) starring Cary Grant and Irene Dunne, as well as critical acclaim for their adaptation of Vicky Baum's novel *Grand Hotel—Week-End at the Waldorf* (1945)—starring Ginger Rogers, Walter Pidgeon, and Van Johnson.[16]

In the commentary to Wilson's autobiography, the editors describe the Spewacks as "known for their satirical tone, wisecracking characters, and lively dialogue," which is immediately familiar to anyone who has seen *Kiss Me, Kate*.[17] This style of writing and her previous portfolio of projects, which included adapting texts as stage and screen comedies, placed Bella Spewack as an experienced and commercially viable collaborator for fledgling producers developing new work. Bella Spewack recalled that "the boys" approached her via a mutual acquaintance, theater agent Richard Lamarr, to ask if she would be interested in writing a musical for them.[18] They met in late 1947, and after discussing the concept, she agreed to write the book if they could secure a composer to sign at the same time.

Although omitted from other accounts of the genesis of *Kiss Me, Kate*, Lamarr successfully sued Ayers and Subber in January 1951 for "services rendered" to *Kiss Me, Kate*.[19] He contended that he had facilitated the producers' working relationship and set up meetings and contracts involving Bella Spewack and Cole Porter. In return, he was promised 5% of any profits *Kiss Me, Kate* returned. However, he was not paid these monies and took Ayers and Subber's The Salem Company to court. Lamarr's name is not mentioned in any general correspondence about *Kiss Me, Kate*, although Bella Spewack does mention that she met Ayers and Subber in his office.[20] Interestingly, William McBrien writes that Porter was looped into the project by his agent Richard Madden and does not mention Lamarr as the possible instigator of the approach.

A Songwriter and a Singer

To secure Bella Spewack formally, the producers began searching for a composer and a possible star for the musical. Immediately, she and Subber tussled for creative control. Bella Spewack recalled strongly disagreeing with his preferences for "Sol Caplin[21] [*sic*], Ralph Blane and Burton Lane" to score their show.[22] Subber initially won this debate, and they agreed to approach composer Burton Lane. However, Bella was ultimately triumphant when Lane, who had had recent success with his score for *Finian's Rainbow* (1947), was unwilling to work on songs without a finished script to refer to.[23] Meanwhile, his appointment would have left them in need of a lyricist. Bella Spewack was hopeful they could secure a single person to tackle both needs and persuaded Subber and Ayers to consider her former collaborator and "first choice," Cole Porter, as a suitable match for their show.[24]

Porter experienced mixed professional success in the 1940s. His first four musicals of the decade—*Panama Hattie* (1940), *Let's Face It* (1941), *Something for the Boys* (1943), and *Mexican Hayride* (1944)—were all box office hits. However, Billy Rose's revue *Seven Lively Arts* (1944), for which Porter contributed several songs, including "Ev'ry Time We Say Goodbye," and his subsequent collaboration with Orson Welles, *Around the World* (1946), achieved neither box office nor critical acclaim. While presenting practical concerns about Porter's commercial sense and appeal, both his failed projects hinted at a subtle change in Porter's working choices. Instead of light stories populated with ditties and ballads, he contributed to a collage of material (including original music by Stravinsky) in Rose's revue and a failed musical epic with a major Hollywood star. The admitted failures of these projects mask Porter's exploration of different formats and storytelling than those that are broadly associated with the heights of his success a decade earlier. In fact, they placed him well to start on *Kiss Me, Kate* with more understanding of what does not translate into a Broadway hit.

Biographer Charles Schwartz explains that Porter "immediately rebuffed" the offer to work on *Kiss Me, Kate*, feeling that "the basic plot was too esoteric; his own style would not be appropriate for a Shakespearean musical."[25] Bella Spewack also recalled his reticence suggesting that Porter was "not too sold on the idea of tackling Shakespeare."[26] However, she persisted, meeting Porter twice more to expand on her ideas for the musical and, in their third meeting, she "decided to bring titles for songs which [she] culled from the *Shrew*" to pique his interest.[27] Richard G. Hubler also suggests that she connected her backstage premise to the plotlines of soap operas, knowing Porter was also considering a project linked to his favorite television format.[28]

The producers also tempted Porter with a possible star to write his music for. As Porter was not a reliably bankable name and no one else on the creative team was especially known for delivering hit musicals, they hoped to secure a star to lead the production, entice financial backers, and draw audiences in. It also quickly emerged that the leading actors, interpreting Katherine and Petruchio, would need to be accomplished singers who could also deliver scenes from *The Taming of the Shrew* convincingly. William McBrien and Alfred Drake both indicate that the producers agreed to approach Bella's first suggestion, Czech opera star Jarmila Novotná, before looking at other casting possibilities. Bella and Sam had seen Novotná as Manon in an earlier season at the Met, and she was easily courted during a long stay in New York for the American premiere of Arthur Honegger's opera *Jeanne d'Arc au bûcher* (1935) in January 1948.[29]

Although known for her opera and screen roles, Novotná had also been a contender to star in Kurt Weill's *One Touch of Venus* (1943), and an undated recording of the ballad "Falling in Love with Love" from *The Boys from Syracuse* suggests that she could have been an exciting interpreter of the music later written for Lilli/Katherine. In late January, she met with Bella and the producers and agreed to visit Porter at the Waldorf Towers to discuss their possible plans. According to Novotná:

> Bella told him [Porter] that her idea was to make a play-within-a-play, and because of my accent, the characters would be Austrian. Porter was quite enthusiastic, and he asked Bella to prepare a scenario so that he could begin to determine what kind of music would be suitable.[30]

A document in the "Notes and Worksheets" folder of the Spewack papers agrees with Novotná's representation of events, including an eleven-page script draft that appears to be the earliest version of a backstage scene from *Kiss Me, Kate.*[31] There are also other draft fragments of this scene with "For Novotna" written atop on the same paper and typeface.[32] Notes from a legal deposition (presumably as part of the Lamarr suit mentioned previously) also record that Bella Spewack was enthusiastic about Novotná and wrote a number of things into the script for her.[33]

The first paragraphs of this earliest draft show a heated argument between the leading actors (Fred, Lilli, and Lois) during a stage rehearsal and then transitions to a small exchange at the stage door, which introduces Lois's boyfriend, Bill, who is also a player in the show. The rest of the document presents ten pages of dialogue in the "Dressing rooms of Fredi and Tilli Becura" that has striking similarity to Act 1, Scene 3, of the original Broadway script of *Kiss Me, Kate.*[34] Here, "Fredi and Tilli" are a married couple, marking their tenth wedding anniversary. Fredi notices a card on the floor and watches in horror as flowers he has bought cast member Lois (whom he and Tilli have just been arguing about) are delivered to his wife instead. They are interrupted by a fight between Lois and Bill outside, and the scene ends with Tilli taking the card from the floor and tucking it in her costume for safekeeping.

In another undated draft from late March or early April, *Kiss Me, Kate* begins in their dressing room, and they discuss Fred's choice of *The Taming of the Shrew* for their latest production.[35] He explains that he's always wanted to play Petruchio and that he thinks she will excel as Katherine. She responds:

TILLY: I don't happen to like Katherine.
FRED: This is a helluva time to tell me.
TILLY: Audiences don't like hard, bitten, nasty women with brains.
FRED: Well, I do, my sweet.[36]

While Fred likens Lilli to Katherine in a rather obvious way that was cut from the script, this snippet offers a possible suggestion of how Bella Spewack intended to frame Lilli—difficult and smart—and concerned by the parallels between her and Katherine.

Bella Spewack suggests that she gave Ayers and Subber no inkling of her work-in-progress, talking it over with Sam first, to agree "a yarn" to make the musical work.[37] Sam was not initially contracted to work on *Kiss Me, Kate*, as he and Bella were separated at the time. However, he attended sessions that also included Porter and offered suggestions and steers while Bella worked on the script details herself. It seems that Bella's ambitions to offer Porter a talented singer and tantalizing script material paid off. According to Richard G. Hubler, Porter "read it, liked it, and wrote a single song"—a ballad called "We Shall Never Be Younger" for Fred and Lilli in the dressing room—which convinced him that he might to do the project justice.[38]

Novotná's potential involvement in the show was trailed in a teaser announcement of the then untitled *Kiss Me, Kate* in the *New York Times* on March 17, 1948:

> Although nothing is signed, Jarmila Novotna of the Metropolitan Opera and Jose Ferrer[39] are being spoken of as the leads in that untitled Cole Porter–Bella Spewack musical. The grapevine reports that Miss Novotna (she's no stranger to the Broadway stage having appeared four years ago in "Helen Goes to Troy") recently heard the music and is said to have expressed her whole-hearted approval over Mr. Porter's collection of sharps and flats.[40]

Unfortunately, the collaboration was not to be. Bella documented at least one later meeting with the opera star in May 1948, where she tried out some of Porter's draft music. However, political unrest in the Czech Republic forced Novotná to return to Europe and, with no idea of when and how she might return to the United States, she was forced to turn down the proposition of *Kiss Me, Kate*.[41]

In pursuing Novotná, the creative team recognized that they wanted a singer who could act and that they should, ideally, be a star or to have obvious "star potential." Porter had written for many iconic singers, including Judy Garland, Sophie Tucker, and Eleanor Powell as well as Ethel Merman. Meanwhile, the Spewacks' screwball comedies featured several megastars including Irene Dunne, Ginger Rogers, and Lana Turner. In this context, we can intuit the caliber of person Lilli was situated alongside. These are vibrant, outspoken, and intensely glamorous women who inhabited multifaceted roles with the capacity for rage, jealousy, and silliness, among many other desirable and fun-to-play qualities. Lilli's variety of "pathos and comedy," described by Olivier-nominated actress Hannah Waddingham then starring in *Kiss Me, Kate* at London's Old Vic, has a cinematic but tabloid quality, which resembles the press reception of real-life stars of her era.[42]

While the prospect of Novotná's casting was still likely, Porter and Bella Spewack signed contracts to write *Kiss Me, Kate* together, becoming the producers' first creative partners on the show. Once fully committed, Porter also suggested that his old friend, John C. Wilson, might be a valuable addition to the team, as they had hoped to work on a musical together and Wilson would bring considerable experience and fundraising appeal.[43] Wilson was an established force on Broadway, particularly known for his collaborations with his former partner, Noël Coward. Wilson had known Porter since the 1920s when he and Coward had holidayed with Porter at the Palazzo Rezzonico in Venice.[44] In addition to producing Coward's musical revue *Set to Music* (1939) and the hit musical *Bloomer Girl* (1944), which ran for 654 performances, Wilson had also worked on the Fontanne/Lunt *Taming of the Shrew* in 1935 and directed them in the stage play *The Pirate* (1942), for which Ayers had designed the sets.

According to Wilson, Porter telephoned to ask if he was "still interested in doing a musical together," but Wilson turned down the initial approach to co-produce *Kiss Me, Kate* because he was concerned about encroaching on Ayers and Subber's creative control.[45] Wilson countered Porter's suggestion with an offer to direct, which Porter and Bella Spewack both supported, and on March 9, 1948, the *New York Times* announced that he had joined the project:

> Last night John C. Wilson signed contracts under which he will stage and supervise a new musical, which Cole Porter and Bella Spewack are writing. As yet untitled, the production is based on an idea by Lemuel Ayers and Arnold Saint Subber, who will serve as sponsors of the venture. Reticent about the details of the forthcoming show, Miss Spewack conceded, however, that Mr. Porter's material—i.e. the music and lyrics—is excellent. Miss Spewack, of course, will provide the book.[46]

Later, in June 1948, a rider was added to Wilson's contract specifying that he would not only "direct and stage" *Kiss Me, Kate* but also "completely and solely supervise, both financially and artistically, the production" and its operations.[47] This addition empowered Wilson to oversee every aspect of the show and may have been added to address the emerging differences of feeling between Ayers, Subber, and Bella Spewack. Certainly, Wilson and Porter exchanged correspondence when Porter left New York for the summer to address conflicts about the script and to circumnavigate the others when discussing aspects of the songwriting. Two letters written on the same day in June 1948 suggest that Porter wrote candidly, if playfully, to Wilson and then reframed the contents in a newly solicitous and careful version to Bella Spewack. Porter also shared copies of correspondence about Bella with her, possibly stoking, rather than suppressing the disagreements that unfolded.

Backstage: The Musical

Once Bella Spewack, Cole Porter, and John C. Wilson were all under contract, they began to develop the earliest version of *Kiss Me, Kate*, which was briefly titled *Backstage*.[48] Bella devised detailed profiles for the leading characters Fred and Lilli. These appear in the synoptic materials for *Backstage* and in the first complete script draft.[49] Reconfiguring the Novotná pages, Bella updated Fred and Lilli from a married couple to divorced co-stars with enduring chemistry but fresh wounds from their failed romance and contrasting professional successes. One particularly fun, but incomplete, document provides a very detailed history of Fred and Lilli's relationship before *Kiss Me, Kate*, contextualizing the personal and professional insecurities that drive these characters in the final plot.[50] The description begins after their wedding, explaining that:

> They then tried some little theatre off Broadway productions of Ibsen, Strindberg, etc. on a shoestring and failed so that each began taking parts offered to them separately. He was the better actor of the two, but she had the glamour and so achieved prominence before he did. The marriage oscillated between hate and love.[51]

Spewack describes the end of the relationship falling when Lilli secures a Hollywood contract and then she outlines their lives apart. Of the various exploits that Bella Spewack lists, a reference to Fred's "SYRANO [*sic*] in French in Paris" for which "*The sponsor bowed out*" jumps off the page.[52] Spewack may have incorporated this as a nod to José Ferrer who, according to the Novotná piece in the *New York Times*, was briefly considered as a possible Fred. Ferrer shared the inaugural Tony Award for Best Actor in a Play in 1947 for his portrayal of the iconic character. Pleasingly, a version of this line was incorporated into the first complete script of *Kiss Me, Kate* and is retained in the original Broadway and licensable versions available now:

FRED: Hollywood—swimming pool—avocado ranches. While I—I put every penny I could scrape, borrow, or steal into my Cyrano in Paris. My magnum opus! But I was a huge success.

LILLI: And you closed on Saturday? Four glorious performances![53]

This backstory document also introduces Harrison Howell, "a wealthy elder statesman," as Lilli's latest romantic connection and explains Lois's involvement in *The Shrew*: "Fred, by dropping into a third-rate nightclub, has found Lois Lane, a song and a dance girl, the ideal purity of Bianca. Besides, she's awfully good company."[54]

Bella condensed this background information into a contextual summary at the beginning of a synopsis document for the musical then titled *Backstage*.[55] Dated April 22, 1948, the *Backstage* outline is ten pages, written mainly in prose, including two working song lists of titles from Cole Porter (see Figure 2.1).[56] Its opening paragraph clarifies the narrative connection between "backstage in Baltimore" and the *Taming of the Shrew* performance, explaining that: "The musical is a play within a play, your personal story paralleling Shakespeare's *Shrew*, and at certain points, the action flows right into the action of the other."[57] Spewack also describes *Backstage* as "a story of show business," in which the romantic battle between Fred and Lilli has an intertextual connection with their vocations as actors: "a musical love story of the eternal serio-comic battle of male and female played against the events of an opening night of the tryout of a musical version of Shakespeare's 'Taming of the Shrew.' "[58]

In nine short paragraphs, Spewack explains the relationship between Fred, the failing theatrical impresario, and Lilli, the successful Hollywood actress, highlighting that they have temperamental sympathies with Petruchio and Katherine respectively, and that this reflexivity will carry the musical. Such was the impact of her description that this preliminary draft is included verbatim at the start of the original Broadway script and in most published versions of *Kiss Me, Kate*.[59]

The first act of *Backstage*, as documented in the April 22 outline, resembles the headlines of *Kiss Me, Kate* in general terms although the plot diverges as

Act One

1. Waltz - Lili [sic] and Fred
2. It Was Great Fun The First Time
3. A Woman's Career - Angela Temple, Ballet of the Lonely Bed
4. We Shall Never Be Younger - Solos for Lilli and Fred
5. Another Op'nin', Another Show - Company
6. Why Can't You Behave? - Bianca [sic]

Songs in *The Shrew*

7. A Band of Strolling Players - Lucentio and Mountebanks
8. If Ever Married I'm - Bianca
9. I Sing of Love - Lucentio and Petruchio
10. I've Come to Wive it Wealthily [sic] - Petruchio
11. Were Thine That Special Face - Lili (As Boy)
12. Tarantella - Dance with Petruchio. Reprise - Were Thine That Special Face - Lili (As Woman)
13. Tom, Dick, or Harry

Act Two

14. Too Darn Hot - Negro Trio. Dance number - Bill and Company
15. So In Love Am I [sic] - Lili
16. True To You, Darlin' In My Fashion - Bianca
17. We Shall Never Be Younger - Reprise, Lili and Fred

Songs in *The Shrew*

18. Where Is the Life That Late I Led? - Petruchio
19. Love is a GAME - Battle of Shuttlecock and Battledore (Battle of the Sexes)

Figure 2.1 Songs listed in the *Backstage* overview (April 22, 1948)[60]

the story progresses. As in the finished musical, Fred is conscious that Lilli is seriously planning to marry Harrison Howell while Lilli is threatened by Fred's interest in Lois.[61] They argue on and off stage while also navigating Harrison, who is present in the theater throughout *Backstage* instead of playing a small role in Act 2. Meanwhile, the couple are also dodging a pushy theatrical agent called Leon Blurr, who wishes to discuss a prospect with them.[62] Eventually, Fred and Lilli's altercations heighten and (as in the original Broadway script) an onstage fight ends with Fred/Petruchio spanking Lilli/Katherine in front of the paying audience. Simultaneously, Lois's ne'er-do-well boyfriend Bill signs a gambling IOU under Fred's name and this triggers two gangsters, who are named the gunmen in all versions of *Kiss Me, Kate*, to visit the theater to collect. Seizing on an opportunity presented, Fred uses the arrival of the gunmen to force Lilli to remain in the production even as she tries to leave.

From here, the *Backstage* plot diverges from *Kiss Me, Kate* as we might recognize it. Lilli, who has already changed her clothes to leave the theater, is forced back into her costume by the gunmen, who demand she perform a number from the show for them since they've missed Act 1. Lilli sings "Were Thine That Special Face" "from behind the screen where she is dressing," and Fred joins her.[63] Their dressing room performance segues into the final scene of Act 1 as a scenic curtain, labeled "Ford's Theatre," hides the dressing room. The half ends with "members of audience" wandering about the stage, "whistling, humming and gradually singing" the song that Fred and Lilli have started.[64]

This end to Act 1 was never realized in a script draft of *Kiss Me, Kate.* Yet it compellingly depicts an exchange of material from actors to a captive audience (the gunmen in the dressing room) and then to fictionalized patrons who are enjoying the show. This provides a first indication of how Bella Spewack imagined the metatextuality might function in *Kiss Me, Kate* and prefaces some prominent representations of the theater audience in MGM's film adaptation later. Spewack captures the ambition to catch the audience with a hummable tune within the fictional *Taming of the Shrew* musical, embodying commercial pressures on new musicals as well as the multilayered performances in this version of the musical. The *Backstage* close to Act 1 also affirms the metatextual parallels between Porter's "Another Op'nin, Another Show" (about first-night jitters in Baltimore) and "We Open in Venice" (which situates the *Shrew* musical as part of a fictional touring repertory), both of which are introduced in this draft. Separately, Bella Spewack is much more direct about Lilli's plans to leave and the threat of the gunmen, which are lightened and prolonged in later drafts of the show.

The second act of *Backstage* briefly coincides with the structure of *Kiss Me, Kate* before taking a different and more dramatic turn. *Backstage*'s Act 2 begins with "Too Darn Hot," performed by "Three Negros" who are hanging around the stage door. In most versions of *Kiss Me, Kate*, "Too Darn Hot" is led by Paul, Fred's dresser, but that character and this song were not linked in the *Backstage* overview. Having led the song and started the dance break, the three performers are joined by Bill and members of the chorus to perform a bigger dance spectacle. The party is interrupted by the stage manager calling places for Act 2, but instead of moving straight into *The Taming of the Shrew* as we might expect, *Backstage*'s Act 2, Scene 1, continues with Bill being threatened by the gunmen's boss Mr. Grogan:

> Bill is sure that Grogan will kill him, but Grogan assures him he doesn't pack a gun. He hires others to do that for him. As Bill moves toward the

stage door, Grogan right behind him, two men who have been lounging in the alley, begin firing. Grogan drops.[65]

The gunmen, unaware of this assassination, complain about the heat and step out into the alley to discover Grogan's body and the attendant police officers. They rapidly return backstage, asking Fred if they can hide in the theater. Fred dispatches them to the stalls, and this ends their involvement in the show. They have no comic interventions in the remaining Shakespeare and do not menace Lilli beyond their first encounter in Act 1. Grogan's assassination subplot is a quirk of the *Backstage* outline and is scrapped by the first script draft. However, the idea is preserved in reportage near the close of *Kiss Me, Kate* (Act 2, Scene 6) when the gunmen narrate a phone call, explaining that: "Mr. Gumpy declared a moratorium on Mr. Hogan. His unidentified remains will be found floating in the bay tomorrow morning."[66]

Unlike all scripted versions of *Kiss Me, Kate*, the *Backstage* outline continues after the onstage performance has ended. Lilli informs Harrison Howell that she thinks they should break their engagement.[67] Then, Fred introduces Lilli to a mystery woman (not Lois) who he explains is his ex-fiancée. The woman tells Lilli that she cannot marry Fred because she cannot bear to think of all the lonely nights "as the wife of an actor."[68] (Again, Spewack returns to the realities of the theatrical life as a preface to the final scene and Fred and Lilli's reunion.) After the fiancée has left, Fred and Lilli join the rest of the cast, who are waiting onstage for his notes. They are interrupted as the theater agent Blurr returns with the president of a film company, who wants to discuss making *The Taming of the Shrew* "with Lili [*sic*] and Fred and Lois—but in Padua, wherever that is."[69] Fred asks Lilli what she thinks, and she replies, quoting part of Katherine's final speech:

LILLI: "My husband is my lord, my life, my keeper, my head, my sovereign."

PRODUCER: Huh?

FRED: My wife is simply saying that she wants what I want, and I want it.

(*Agent and Producer exit*)

LILLI: You said, "My wife?"

FRED: (*Quoting Shakespeare*) "Indeed, I did—But what a fool I am to chat with you. When I should bid good morrow to my bride And seal the title with a lovely kiss!"[70]

The route to this ending is quite different to *Kiss Me, Kate*, in which Lilli walks out on Fred and Harrison (as well as the performance) before returning at the last moment. However, the outline shows that Bella always intended to end the musical with a romantic resolution and by intertwining Fred and Lilli's reconnection with the final lines of *The Taming of the Shrew*. This is the only example of intertextuality, demonstrating a relationship between the *Shrew* play text and her original script, that is signposted in this draft. Instead, she notes in parentheses that "We use only the high spots of the Shrew which is, for the most part, treated musically."[71]

A First Complete Draft

The transition from the *Backstage* outline to a full draft of the now retitled *Kiss Me, Kate* appears to have been relatively straightforward. This script includes seventeen scenes in Act 1 (in comparison to only nine in the original Broadway and published scripts) and seven scenes in Act 2. Bella simplified the chaotic interactions between Fred and Lilli suggested in the plot outlines and *Backstage* overview, removing the agent Leon Blurr, and making Harrison Howell a much smaller, feature role. Instead, the Act 1 structure includes lots of alternations between on- and offstage (see Figure 2.2),

	First script draft	**Original Broadway Script**
	1. Stage of Ford's Theatre	1. Stage of Ford's Theatre
	2. Fred and Lili's dressing rooms	2. The corridor backstage
	3. Backstage - stairs/landing area	3. Fred and Lili's dressing rooms
	4. Theatre exterior	
	5. Fred and Lili's dressing rooms	
	6. Fred and Lili's dressing rooms	
		4. Padua
	7. *Shrew* Street Scene	5. Street Scene, Padua
	8. Backstage - in the wing	6. Backstage
Act One	9. Backstage - in the *opposite* wing	7. Fred and Lili's dressing rooms
	10. *Shrew* scene	
	11. Outside Baptista's house	
	12. Backstage - in the wing	
	13. Baptista's Garden	
	14. Backstage - in the wing	
	15. Baptista's Garden	
	16. Fred and Lili's dressing rooms	
		8. Before the Curtain
	17. Exterior Church	9. Exterior Church

Figure 2.2 Comparison of scenes between the first complete script draft and the original Broadway script

reminiscent of the structure of a screen comedy, allowing characters to move rapidly between locations as a chaotic farce is established. This device is particularly similar to a section of the Spewacks' screenplay for *My Favorite Wife* as the main protagonist Nick (Cary Grant) is forced to sprint between his two wives' hotel rooms while attempting to continue conversations with both women at the same time.

In *Kiss Me, Kate*, Bella Spewack places Fred and Lilli in lots of different physical spaces in the theater, including on the stage, in both wings, and in their respective dressing rooms. These scene changes allowed her to punctuate their disagreements with Lois confronting Bill for being absent from rehearsals, him disclosing to her that he has forged Fred's signature to cover his debt, and the arrival of the gunmen to collect the monies owed. Act 1, Scenes 2, 5, and 6, of the first draft were consolidated into a single scene (Act 1, Scene 3) of the original Broadway script, and although short sections, including a one-sided phone call between Lilli and her Afghan hound, Zulcika, were removed, many lines from each appear in the original Broadway script.[72]

In comparison to Act 1, the second half of the first complete script is largely like the original Broadway production, although it features considerably more "Shakespeare" and considerably less music. The act begins with "Too Darn Hot" as a fun cover of the interval during the onstage production of *The Shrew* before playing Katherine and Petruchio's arrival at his house with interventions from the gunmen. As in the original Broadway production, Harrison Howell arrives with an ambulance to extricate Lilli from the theater and Fred subtly rubbishes Lilli's prospective married life. We also learn that Harrison has previously been entangled with Lois, and she sings the celebrated "Always True to You (In My Fashion)" after Bill jealously confronts her about her flirtations with rich and powerful men.

From May to December, Bella Spewack would continuously reconfigure the closing details of Fred and Lilli's romantic reunion, including finding a home for some unexpected music from Porter. In this first script draft, Lilli stays in the production of *The Taming of the Shrew* with threats to quit after the first performance ends. As the script evolved, cutting their reminiscences and sharpening Fred and Lilli's immediate conflict, Bella changed the scenario to give Lilli a more reasonable and less capitulating response by walking out while the show is still taking place. However, she could never part from closing the musical with Katherine (and Lilli) speaking of their commitment to their marriage, even when Lilli/Katherine's rage is more acutely characterized.

Nonetheless, by June 1948, Bella Spewack had found the backstage structure and narrative hit points for *Kiss Me, Kate*. Meanwhile, Porter had also found his feet with the project, drafting more than half of the song lyrics that would be heard on Broadway during this time. By (re-)connecting through this project, imagining Lilli/Katherine for Novotná, and committing to first concepts for their musical, Porter and Spewack realized many of the ambitions that Ayers and Subber had for *Kiss Me, Kate* long before reaching a final draft. The backstage plot was established. The metatheater was embedded in the script and songs. Porter and Spewack had also forged intertextual connections between the *Shrew* and the Baltimore scenario. They were ready to hone *Kiss Me, Kate* to attract backers, a choreographer, and cast that would achieve the box office success and critical acclaim that they each aspired to.

3

Adapting *The Taming of the Shrew*

Having committed to *Kiss Me, Kate* with Porter, Bella Spewack refamiliarized herself with *The Taming of the Shrew*. When interviewed by George Eells for the Porter biography *The Life That Late He Led*, she claimed that she had not looked at the play since school.[1] Although it is not possible to track her precise journey with the text, and the three copies of *The Taming of the Shrew* in the Spewack papers are editions published after the original Broadway production had opened, Spewack has made reference to studying the play before embarking on the adaptation. In 1967, she described spending time researching Shakespeare's life and productions of *The Taming of the Shrew* in the New York Public Library, reading performance reviews by George Bernard Shaw, and this leading her to Samuel Johnson's editions of Shakespeare's plays.[2] She was interested in the context of Shakespeare and performances of Shakespeare as well as the play itself.

In their coauthored introduction to the first published version of *Kiss Me, Kate*'s libretto (Knopf, 1953), Sam and Bella humorously characterize their approach to adapting *The Shrew* in the style of a recipe or crafting guide:

> How to Collaborate with W. Shakespeare
>
> If you want to collaborate with Shakespeare, get two inexpensive copies of any one of his plays. Tear them out of their bindings and spread the pages on a large table or bed or floor, so that you can spot at a glance what you will retain and what you will discard. Take well-sharpened pencil, or pen that works, and so indicate.
>
> Then with shears cut out the parts you intend using, and if you're handy with the paste-pot, paste up in sequence on ordinary copy paper. If allergic to paste or glue, use stapler. If you have no stapler, your lawyer is sure to have one.
>
> Do not throw away discarded pages. Some wonderful ideas for songs may be among them. Or you can run up your own lampshade.
>
> Total outlay: many, many sleepless nights and haggard days; cash $2.50.[3]

Too Darn Hot. Hannah Robbins, Oxford University Press. © Oxford University Press 2026.
DOI: 10.1093/9780190082437.003.0003

Although the tone of this explanation is flippant, it is striking that the Spewacks represent Shakespeare as an active participant in their activities. While he isn't mentioned again, it highlights a trend in *Kiss Me, Kate*'s performance history that productions and creative teams consider how William Shakespeare might be embodied within the musical. This makes its way into the very first draft of Act 1, Scene 1, of *Kiss Me, Kate* when Fred wishes the company good luck for opening night, bantering: "We owe it to Shakespeare, not to mention the six other fellows who've been sitting up nights rewriting him."[4] By the original Broadway script, the scene had been trimmed, leaving this as the final line of the opening scene and the setup to "Another Op'nin', Another Show." While personifying Shakespeare and describing the decimation of a book, the Spewacks loosely summarized their early adaptation process, and this is evidenced by the surviving draft materials. These indicate that they made substantial cuts to *The Taming of the Shrew* immediately (c. April 1948), with a few smaller deletions (and re-insertions) near to opening in November.

Shakespeare's *The Taming of the Shrew* consists of five acts, fourteen scenes, and twenty-two named characters.[5] Figure 3.1 outlines how *The Taming of the Shrew* was cut from over 2,500 lines down to just 320 by June 1948. As is shown in the figure, Shakespeare's play begins with the two-scene Induction, a framing device, in which a nobleman tricks a drunken tinker called Christopher Sly into believing he is a lord. This scene was immediately

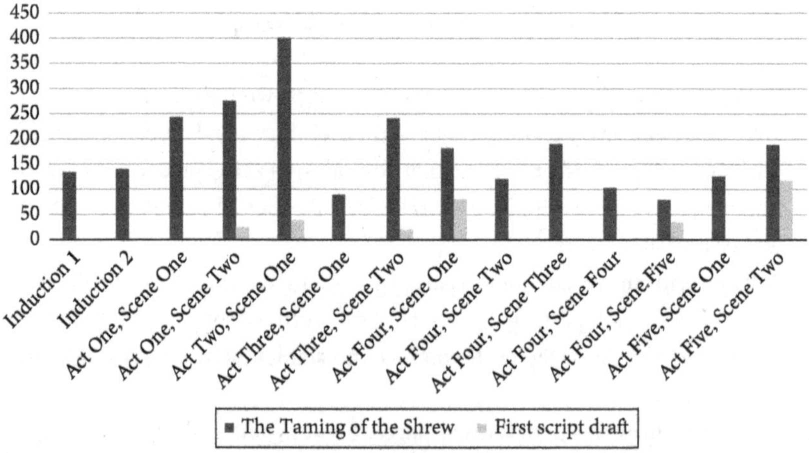

Figure 3.1 Comparison of lines in Shakespeare's *The Taming of the Shrew* and those retained in first script draft (June 1948)

purged from *Kiss Me, Kate*.[6] However, as noted previously, the spirit of this device has been preserved in other ways.

Nominally, *Kiss Me, Kate* follows the structure of *The Taming of the Shrew*'s internal play, hitting the key narrative headlines of Katherine and Petruchio's story. The play focuses on a Paduan nobleman Baptista and his two daughters Katherine and Bianca. Baptista refuses to allow his younger daughter Bianca to marry any of her suitors (Lucentio, Hortensio, and Gremio) until her older sister Katherine is married. Petruchio, a friend of Lucentio, appears in Padua looking for a wealthy bride to make his fortune and agrees to marry Katherine. Baptista agrees and Katherine is forced to wed Petruchio. At the wedding, Petruchio publicly humiliates Katherine and refuses to let her attend the feast with their friends and family. They experience a difficult journey back to his home, where Petruchio begins his scheme to tame Katherine, who is perceived to be difficult and wild. They are recalled to Baptista's house to celebrate Bianca's nuptials and Petruchio displays to the company how he has curbed "her mad and headstrong humour."[7]

In the middle development period of *Kiss Me, Kate* (c. July–October 1948), Bella Spewack reintroduced some *Taming of the Shrew* material to replace her own original "Shakespeare." This was revised again during the rehearsal period when they had confirmed cast numbers and were finalizing the *Shrew* scenes with some concessions to leading actor Alfred Drake. Figure 3.2 maps these fluctuations through the evolving character lists from *The Taming of the Shrew* in *Kiss Me, Kate* from June 1948 to the first Broadway performance. By removing the Induction, the character list immediately decreased from twenty-two roles to seventeen. The first script draft pared this to thirteen, and this was reduced further to eight named characters and three unnamed servants in the original Broadway script.

This chapter uses the adaptation of *The Taming of the Shrew* to illustrate collaborative synergies among the creative team. Although the broader genesis of *Kiss Me, Kate* includes moments of discontent, it is clear that the team found creative sympathies while addressing the Shakespearean aspects of the show. The existing script materials, song lyrics, and correspondence reveal negotiations between different creative priorities and illuminate how individuals co-designed this aspect of the musical in happy dialogue with one another. Together, the team devised a distinct and comic, yet harmonious vision of a Shakespearean production done in fun to serve other dramatic priorities. They also achieved rich intertextuality between

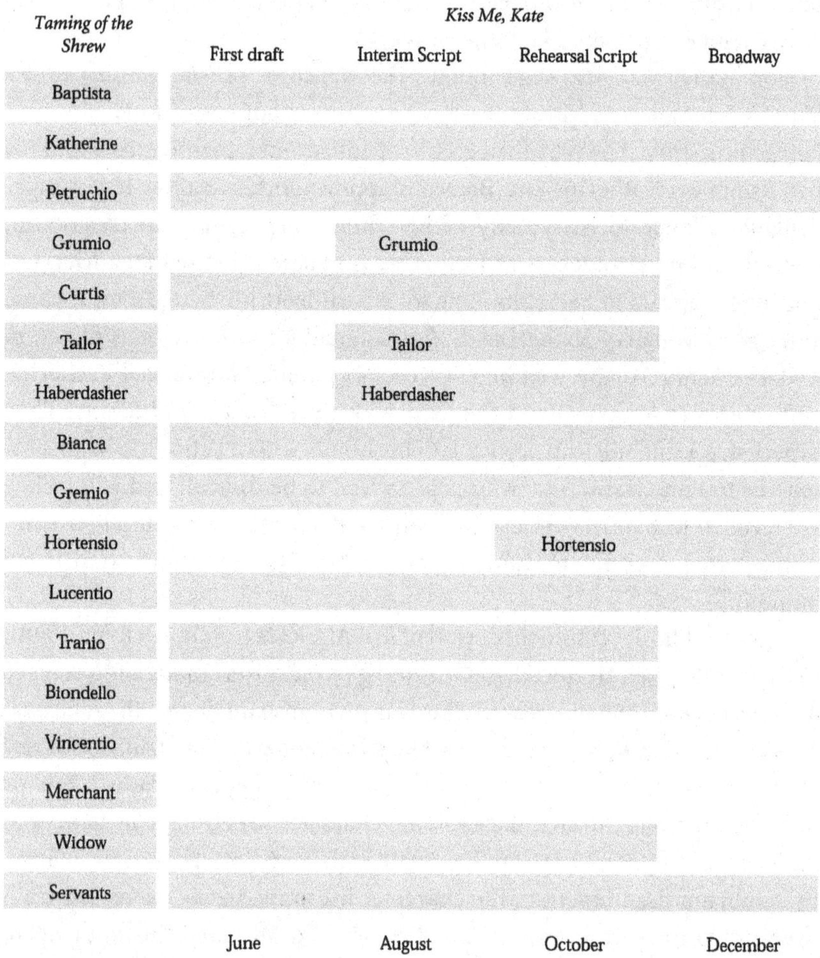

Figure 3.2 Overview of characters from *The Taming of the Shrew* incorporated across drafts of *Kiss Me, Kate*

"Baltimore" and "Padua" so that the boundaries between the two settings and sets of characters become almost meaningless. As outlined previously, Porter was initially skeptical if "a *Taming of the Shrew* musical" might work and hesitated in joining the project. In this chapter, I suggest that *Kiss Me, Kate* succeeds because it is not "just" a Shakespeare musical. Instead, it plays with the importance of *The Taming of the Shrew* while offering a compelling musical comedy that is accessible to audiences familiar or otherwise with the play.

Sam's Shakespeare

As outlined in Chapters 1 and 2, the earliest materials for *Kiss Me, Kate* include the *Backstage* overview, some dated correspondence between the production team, and an untitled draft of the first six scenes, dated April 28, 1948. This nine-page document, produced only a few days after the *Backstage* overview, appears to be written by Sam Spewack and deals very specifically with "the Shakespeare" in *Kiss Me, Kate.*[8] The draft begins "Scene opens as Bella outlined,"[9] summarizing the backstage context in a third of a page and then scripts the dialogue from the first Padua street scene (Act 1, Scene 4, of *Kiss Me, Kate*) until Katherine and Petruchio's first meeting.[10] The passages of Shakespeare used are substantially abridged, and characters, including Petruchio's servant Grumio, are completely written out. Here, *The Taming of the Shrew* begins after "We Open in Venice" at line 48 of Shakespeare's Act 1, Scene 2. This is the same beginning as in the original Broadway and licensable scripts. By contrast, Bella's first draft begins with summative dialogue that she has written herself.[11] The April 28 pages then condense Shakespeare's Act 1 (518 lines) and the beginning of Act 2 (277 lines) into just six pages of script or 177 lines.[12]

This draft of *Kiss Me, Kate* begins with Gremio, Hortensio, and Lucentio attempting to get permission from Baptista to court Bianca. Baptista refuses, and they sing "Tom, Dick, or Harry." Having pressed Baptista again, the suitors set about finding Katherine a husband. Lucentio pines for Bianca to his servant Tranio and performs "I Sing of Love" to Bianca who is standing on the balcony. (Parts of this were retained as the setting for "Were Thine That Special Face" performed by Petruchio in *Kiss Me, Kate* as we know it know.) As Lucentio ends "I Sing of Love," Petruchio arrives and "mockingly sings the refrain."[13] Lucentio puts the bargain to his friend who claims to be looking for a wife and Petruchio performs "I've Come to Wive It Wealthily in Padua." After a backstage scene, the pages return to Padua for edited highlights of Shakespeare's Act 2, Scene 1, where Petruchio introduces himself to Baptista, agrees the match with Katherine, and they meet for the first time.

In the process of discarding more than 600 lines of *The Taming of the Shrew*, the April 28 pages immediately abridge the *Shrew*'s most substantial side plot, in which Bianca's suitors vie for her hand, to a few lines and one song. In Shakespeare's play, Lucentio and Hortensio disguise themselves as tutors to court Bianca without detection from Baptista. Meanwhile, Lucentio's servant Tranio poses as his master and persuades Baptista that "he" (Lucentio) should marry Bianca as long as Lucentio's father guarantees his financial position. The April 28 pages repurpose Shakespeare's dialogue, confirming Katherine as a barrier to accessing Bianca, and then have Porter's "Tom, Dick or Harry" paraphrase the lengthy competition between prospective husbands, never to be revisited. The script then moves focus to the scheme to find Katherine a husband.

The document also offers an early glimpse of the song structure for Act 1 of *Kiss Me, Kate.* Figure 3.3 compares the April 28 song list with Bella's first script draft, and their coauthored script for the original Broadway production. Here, it is apparent that Bella Spewack and the author of the April 28 pages envisaged the musical route into *The Taming of the Shrew* in different ways. Given these traces, the authorship of this document is both tantalizing and easily solved as the pages diverge from other early script materials but are noticeably in tune with the original Broadway script, finalized nine months later. While the abridged Shakespeare in these pages is most proximate to the rehearsal and original Broadway scripts, it does not align with Bella's first draft, the interim script, and the October 11 draft. The order of songs is also close to the original Broadway production but is generally inconsistent with the placement of songs in Bella's materials written at the same time. More broadly, the April 28 pages use alternative spellings and bastardizations of the character names like Freddy, Lilly, and Lola, which appear in some of the other preliminary materials (e.g., character outlines).

Taken altogether, we have the picture of a collaborator who was not involved in every creative discussion that took place in early 1948. Instead, they were working from slightly out-of-date information but were privy to the dramaturgical headlines of the plot and Cole Porter's work in progress. As noted in the last chapter, Bella Spewack always maintained that she consulted with Sam and developed the early concepts of *Kiss Me, Kate* together with him and Cole Porter while cutting out the producers. This document reveals an intimate understanding of the intentions of the script as well as the emerging score. When drawn together with the proximity of this draft to the original Broadway script, it seems very likely that the draft is the work of Sam Spewack. It also makes sense of the telegram from Porter to Sam in the summer of 1948, requesting that he (Sam) accept a writing credit for *Kiss Me, Kate* based on his formative contributions to the show.[14]

What we gain from this examination is a glimpse of three autonomous creative individuals—Bella Spewack, Sam Spewack, and Cole Porter—working on conversational but individual sets of material. The parallels

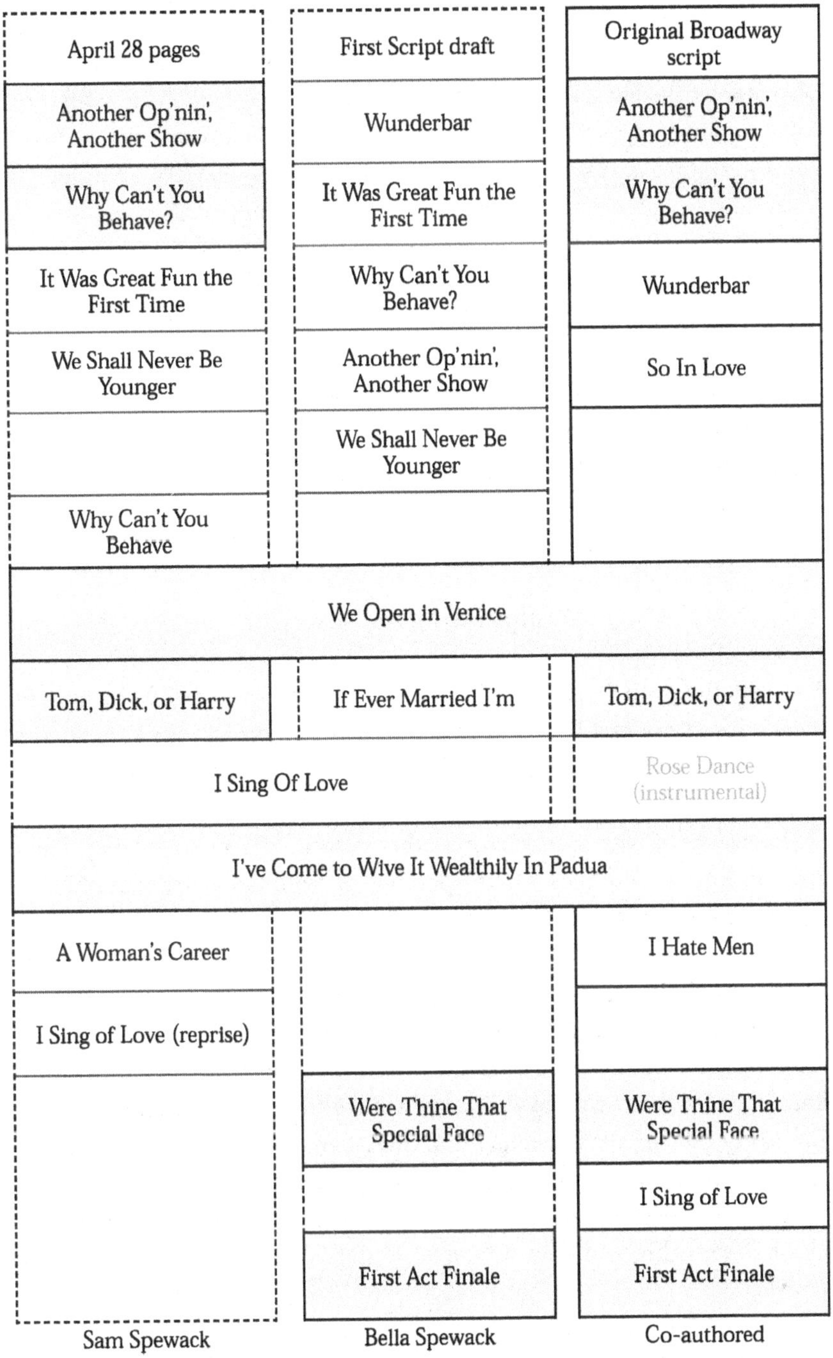

Figure 3.3 Breakdown of music in Act 1, comparing materials drafted by Sam, Bella, and the original Broadway script

between Bella's overarching plot, Sam's adaptation of *The Shrew*, and Porter's song interventions indicate an emerging creative practice where each collaborator worked to a shared brief on their own terms. Significantly, all three collaborators grappled with how to incorporate intertextuality between Baltimore and *The Shrew*. Across all the early script materials, "We Open in Venice" acts a watershed between backstage and *The Shrew*, a second opening number, that allowed the book writers to change tone in the Padua Street Scene. As will be explained, the Spewacks took very different directions in how to manage the first *Taming of the Shrew* scenes, and yet there are obvious agreements about what was to be cut, what was to be retained, and what was to be reworked to make their version of the play. The April 28 pages suggest Sam immediately clarified the interactions between Bella's script ideas and Porter's songs. Through his draft, we get a clear picture of idea making, translation, and creative editing emerging as early as April 1948.

Manipulating the Material

Although the April 28 pages and Bella Spewack's first draft differ in content, there is also considerable overlap in how the two authors abridged *The Taming of the Shrew*. In both documents, a line-by-line analysis reveals a balance of extended quotations, lines that are rearranged or spliced with new script by the Spewacks or with sections from other parts of Shakespeare's play. There are also lots of examples where speeches or sentiments are paraphrased, which matches the Spewacks' representation of the process: "Here and there amongst the omitted passages were lines that we wanted to keep, and these we blithely distributed to the characters that remained."[15]

In Sam's scenes, this tapestry effect is relatively subtle. The first section of "Shakespeare," before "Tom, Dick, or Harry," where the suitors are cajoling Baptista, lifts thirty-five of thirty-eight lines from Act 1, Scene 1, of the *Taming of the Shrew*. The remaining three consist of a paraphrase, an appropriation of line said to a different character, and one original line that merges two conversations together. Here, Sam lightly rearranges the conversation to serve his own flow.[16] Figure 3.4 offers a visualization of how this is achieved.[17]

While this granular analysis simply traces a pattern of moving *The Taming of the Shrew* material around, it becomes more significant in Bella Spewack's first script draft where she introduces her own plot and dialogue as part

Taming of the Shrew	Paraphrased	Appropriated	*Taming of the Shrew*							Sam Spewack	*Shrew*
62-66	76	105	81	79-80	75	77	82-86	92	86-88		94-95

Figure 3.4 Line-by-line analysis of *Taming of the Shrew* adaptation

of "*The Taming of the Shrew*" while also splicing large sections of different Shakespeare scenes together. Using the same approach, much expanded, she created a version of *The Taming of the Shrew* that served her own purposes.

Bella's process of combining original material with disrupted and abridged Shakespeare is best exemplified by the final scene of the first draft. Here, she jigsaws her own fake Shakespeare and Porter's "Were Thine That Special Face" with a merger of the controversial "sun and moon" scene (Act 4, Scene 5) and the close of Katherine and Petruchio's story (Act 5, Scene 2) from *The Taming of the Shrew*. In Act 4 of Shakespeare's play, Petruchio and Katherine are recalled from his home to attend Bianca's wedding. On the way, Petruchio tests whether Katherine has learned to humor him and challenges her to call the sun the moon, or they will return home. Eventually, she capitulates (or according to some readers, chooses to agree to save her peace)[18] and agrees that it is the moon. Petruchio then tests her further by challenging her to call a passing gentleman (Lucentio's father, Vincentio) a young woman. When they arrive at Bianca's wedding, there is some confusion when Baptista discovers that Tranio is an imposter impersonating Lucentio's father, now present, but the marriage has already taken place and that plot is resolved.

Every known draft of *Kiss Me, Kate* omits the plot details that introduce Vincentio to the mix, using the intertextual characterization to signal that Bill's Lucentio will automatically marry Lois's Bianca. These materials also remove a conversation among the husbands and Baptista before the final gesture of the play. Petruchio boasts that he has reformed Katherine, but the others do not believe him so they set a wager that each man will call his wife to him, and they will see which woman is most obedient (Act 5, Scene 2). As Katherine is the only wife to come when summoned, Petruchio wins the bet, and the play closes with a speech when Petruchio asks Katherine to tell the other wives how they should obey their husbands. In the first script draft, Bella Spewack attaches Petruchio's tests of Katherine's pliability in Act 4 as a preface to her controversial closing speech. In its new configuration, Katherine's advocation of obedience and subservience reads as the final phase in a pattern of unnecessary demands from Petruchio, rather than being the closing stage of a campaign of incidents across different scenes. It also interacts with the backstage conflict between Fred and Lilli, who have just had a confrontation with Harrison about the potential boredom of his and Lilli's future lives together.

At the beginning of Bella's scene, Fred (as Petruchio) covers for Lilli, who is changing back into her *Taming of the Shrew* costume, having decided to finish the show rather than leave with Harrison. While waiting, Petruchio tells Lucentio that he has overcome Katherine's "difficult" nature, but he is not believed, and so he uses her arrival to display his "victory."[19] He challenges her to call the sun the moon and then to call Lucentio's father a young woman. When she does, they sing a reprise of "Were Thine That Special Face" and Petruchio is congratulated on his achievement. Bianca is indignant at her sister's behavior and Katherine leads her and the other bride (the Widow) offstage as Bianca goes to confront Petruchio. This sets the scene for the husbands to wager on the respective obedience of their wives, and the scene follows Shakespeare's closing concept.

To achieve this new version of an ending, Bella Spewack patchworked sections together in a much more intricate way than is evidenced in the April 28 pages. She was clearly committed to keeping the end of *The Taming of the Shrew* partially intact in *Kiss Me, Kate*, but she was not particularly concerned about a faithful journey to that close. However, in each subsequent version, Bella Spewack abridged this scene more and more. In the interim script, she marked it into sections, lettered A–E, crossing out the material from Act 4, Scene 5 ("the sun and moon scene") entirely. Interestingly, this loosely coincided with a letter from Porter to John C. Wilson, addressing the same material. Porter wrote:

> I can't for the life of me figure out how I can make a number out of the "This is the moon if I say it is the moon" scene. If you all insist that I attempt this I must have explicit instructions. How much of the scene do you want incorporated into the number? Do you want the number to be literally Shakespeare's words, or do you want me to alter them for the sake of rhyme etc.? Personally, I prefer Bella's first scene in the second act, where Petruchio appears before the curtain and tells the audience that Kate is not able to ride the mule to incorporating the original Shakespeare singing, and if you think it could be strong enough to go in next to closing, I don't agree with you.[20]

Depending on how you interpret Porter's letter, it is possible that they meant to move the material of Act 4, Scene 5, earlier in Act 2. (One throwaway line is retained and delivered from the wings in the backstage scene, Act 2, Scene 4, when Harrison has just arrived.) Bella Spewack hinted also at placing the scene with the mule earlier in the *Backstage* overview when Fred and Lilli "perform the horseback scene from the Shrew"[21] for the gunmen in their dressing room. It is also possible that Bella Spewack hoped that Porter would dramatize of Grumio's speech at the beginning of Act 4, Scene 1—"Tell thou the tale! But hadst thou not crossed / me, thou shouldst have heard how her horse fell and she under her horse"—where the servant recounts their tumultuous journey from Padua to Petruchio's home.[22] Perhaps she wanted Porter to make something different of the scene, maybe introducing a fiery backstage duet in the spirit of "It Was Great Fun the First Time," acting as a similar number for Petruchio and Katherine.

Whatever they imagined, by the fall of 1948, all the material from Act 4, Scene 5, had been abandoned, and the final scene was slashed from nine pages to two. It is impossible to know exactly how Bella Spewack perceived the politics of Katherine's capitulation speech as she uses it to close every version of *Kiss Me, Kate.* Indeed, Chapter 2 quotes its use in the *Backstage* overview when Lilli defers to Fred about the prospect of co-starring in a film.[23] Nonetheless, Bella's first intention, to condense Petruchio's mistreatment of Katherine into one long sequence, sharpens the end of *The Taming of the Shrew*, leaving *Kiss Me, Kate* in a complicated and dark place intertextually. The farcical elements of the backstage plot (and the allegiance against Lilli) lose their comedic qualities when the *Taming of the Shrew* ends with Petruchio relentlessly wearing Katherine down for show. Where Sam appears to focus on achieving narrative cohesion while abridging the *Shrew*, Bella Spewack took a distinctive and unique approach to working with the material and redefining the narrative consequences for her heroine. These differently experimental approaches created an environment for Porter to play with the prompts he was given, allowing him to volunteer some of his most successful material for the score.

Porter's *Taming of the Shrew*

While the Spewacks conceived the recontextualization of *Taming of the Shrew*, Porter worked in close reference to their editorial decisions. Based on subsequent interviews about Porter's creative process, it seems that he and the Spewacks established the optimal working conditions for Porter's creative energies, including his preference to start with an idea, develop a title, and progress from there.[24] (This is explored in greater depth throughout Chapter 4.) In the same introduction that they personified "collaborating" with Shakespeare, the Spewacks also dedicated a section to Porter, beginning:

> *How to Collaborate with C. Porter*
>
> With Porter it is a little bit different. You can't attack him with shears and paste, and you can't spread him out on the bed or the floor. If it's your own play, it's comparatively easy to get Porter to accent the idea. But if it's Shakespeare's play it takes a deal of persuasion.[25]

As Porter was initially reluctant to work on *The Taming of Shrew*, the Spewacks "jotted down song titles" from Shakespeare's own lines, such as "I've Come to Wive It Wealthily," "Where Is the Life That Late I Led?," and "Were Thine That Special Face," to pique his interest.[26] They hoped that Porter would take on what Bella Spewack named the "high spots" of *The Taming of the Shrew*, which would "for the most part, be treated musically" if they could make it sufficiently interesting to him.[27]

Documents dated from April 7 to April 22, 1948, indicate that, once he had found his angle, Porter addressed the entire score rapidly. Eleven of the nineteen songs heard on Broadway were drafted by the end of April 1948 and thirteen by the end of June. Of *The Taming of the Shrew* music, the earliest dated materials are lyric sheets for "I've Come to Wive It Wealthily in Padua," "I Sing of Love," "Tom, Dick or Harry," and "Were Thine That Special Face," as well as the unused "If Ever Married I'm."[28] "Where Is The Life That Late I Led" and "We Open in Venice" were also completed that month (see Figure 3.5 for a full timeline). Almost all these songs are placed in the first half of *Kiss Me, Kate*, suggesting (as is also shown in other chapters) that Porter and the Spewacks focused on establishing and grounding material before resolving the end.

By contrast with the music for *Backstage* score, there were almost no structural changes made to the music of these "*Shrew*" songs, and only a handful of lyrics were refined. Similarly, only one song—"If Ever Married I'm"—was discarded from *The Taming of the Shrew* scenes. However, Porter did not tackle every stimulus he was given, and in his June 16 letter to Wilson (quoted in the previous section), he rejects musicalizing the "sun and moon"

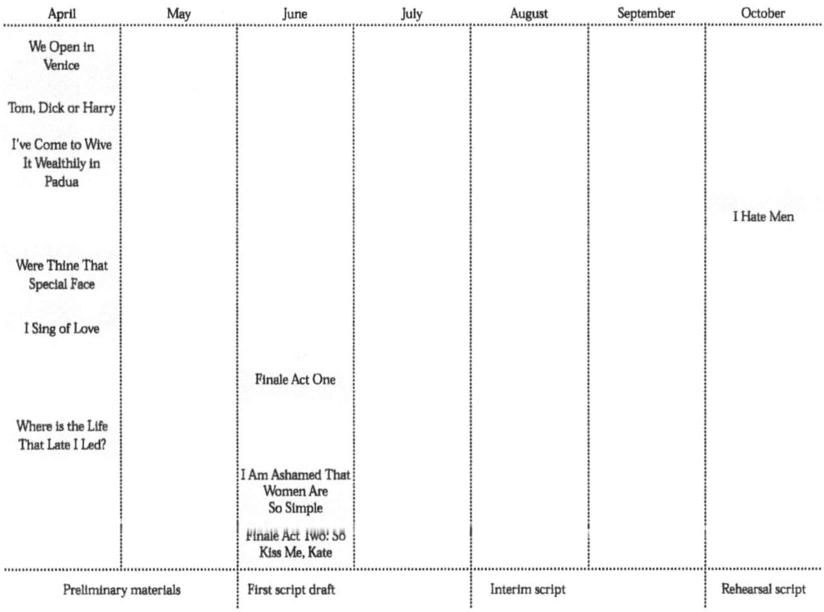

Figure 3.5 Timeline of Porter's *The Taming of the Shrew* songs

scene because he cannot get it to work.[29] It seems, then, that despite his early reticence to adapt Shakespeare, Porter attacked the songs most connected to the play first, before adding the functional music (the Act Finales), leading him last to Katherine's solo music ("I Am Ashamed That Women Are So Simple" and "I Hate Men").

Working chronologically through *Kiss Me, Kate*, we can see that Porter handled *The Shrew* in complementary but sometimes dissimilar ways to the Spewacks. For example, "We Open in Venice" reproduces the spirit of the beginning of Shakespeare's play, which is prefaced by the Induction. However, Porter devised a repetitious musical comedy number that bridges the Baltimore and Padua settings and is reminiscent of Italian traditions of *commedia dell'arte* rather than using an overture or a pastiche of temporally sensitive music. "We Open in Venice" begins with a verse, introducing the four principals, as "a troupe of strolling players," leading to a cycle of refrains in which they sing of their travels and the mundanity of touring theater life, rearticulating the sweat and tears expressed in the first opening number backstage: "Another Op'nin, Another Show."

From the opening verse, Porter collides mock-Shakespeareana (touring players, tavern culture, wenching, etc.) with 1940s references to the film mogul Louis B. Mayer, with whom Porter had worked while in Hollywood, and to the Theatre Guild, who were a major force in producing new work including Rodgers and Hammerstein's hit musicals *Oklahoma!* (1943) and *Carousel* (1945):

> A troupe of strolling players are we,
> Not stars like L. B. Mayer's are we,
> But just a simple band
> Who roams about the land
> Dispensing fol-de-rol frivolity.
> Mere folk who give distraction are we,
> No Theater Guild attraction are we,
> But just a crazy group
> That never ceases to troop
> Around the map of little Italy.[30]

Porter immediately introduced modern sensibilities to *The Taming of the Shrew* by relentlessly reminding us that the onstage performance is also taking place 1940s Baltimore. He continues this in "Tom, Dick, or Harry," which presents the competition for Bianca's hand into a modern lexicon where she is "boy mad," flirtatious, and eager to be partnered to one of three eligible young men. She's also ready to dance.

Where *The Taming of the Shrew* differentiates between Bianca's suitors by age in that Hortensio is generally played as an older man while Lucentio is Bianca's contemporary, "Tom, Dick, or Harry" makes the men interchangeable. Intertextually, Lucentio remains Bianca's preference because he is played by Bill, and we understand that they will be partnered together. However, the song does not privilege him. Instead, the introduction has the three men vie for her attention and then become Bianca's supporting artists in the main body of the song. Not only is Bianca the center of attention here but the song also becomes hers. She is the soloist, leading a lively foxtrot and dance break, rather than the subject of discussion as in *The Taming of the Shrew*. In the narrative progression of *Kiss Me, Kate*, "Tom, Dick, or Harry" also confirms why Fred has cast Lois in his production. She is a charismatic (and savvy) performer perfectly situated to deliver a dance-forward showtune about being flirtatious and sexually available.

Having used musical comedy styles and modern idioms very prominently in the first *Taming of the Shrew* music, we then arrive at Porter's more "traditional" adaptation of Shakespeare in Petruchio's first solo: "I've Come to

Be she as foul as was Florentius' love
As old as Sibyl, and curst and shrewd
As Socrates' Xanthippe or a worst,
She moves me not, or not removes at least
Affection's edge in me, were she as rough
As the swelling Adriatic seas.
I've come to wive it wealthily in Padua;
If wealthily, then happily in Padua.

[...]

Think you a little din can daunt my ears
Have I not in my time heard lions roar?
Have I not heard the sea, puffed up with winds,
Rage like an angry boar chafed with sweat?

Act One, Scene Two, *The Taming of the Shrew*

If she roar like a winter breeze
On the rough Adriatic seas,
If she scream like a teething brat,
If she scratch like a tiger cat,
If she fight like a raging boar?
I have oft stuck a pig before.

I've Come To Wive It Wealthily in Padua

Figure 3.6 Comparison of lines from *The Taming of the Shrew* and the final verse of "I've Come to Wive It Wealthily in Padua"[31]

Wive It Wealthily in Padua." Set over a stately pavane rhythm, Petruchio sings Porter's version of Shakespeare's lines about Petruchio's ambitions to marry whatever kind of woman is rich enough to meet his needs. To craft the lyric, Porter translates a conversation among Petruchio, Hortensio, Grumio, Gremio, and Tranio from Act 1, Scene 2, of *The Taming of the Shrew* into a Shakespeareanesque speech, adapting the imagery from what is said. Figure 3.6 offers a flavor of this process as Porter amalgamates sections from two of Petruchio's speeches (lines 66–73 and 193–196 of Act 1, Scene 2) to produce the last verse of the song.

Porter reinterprets these phrases, originally addressed to Petruchio's doubters, as defining Petruchio's character. Similar to Bella Spewack's reconfiguration of the end of *The Taming of the Shrew*, Porter concentrates long, weaving conversation into a statement of personality and intention. In *Kiss Me, Kate*, we do not deal with sequences of men blustering together. Instead, we are immediately introduced to a Petruchio who is cocky, domineering, and comfortable with overpowering women.

Porter's approach to "I've Come to Wive It Wealthily in Padua" is particularly interesting as one of only two *Taming of the Shrew* songs that directly quote Shakespeare in *Kiss Me, Kate*. Petruchio's other solo music "Were Thine That Special Face" and "Where Is the Life That Late I Led?" refine his character even though they follow the chronology of *The Shrew*. Like "I've Come to Wive It Wealthily in Padua," Petruchio's other songs focus his *Kiss Me, Kate* stage time on the politics and execution of courting women rather than on his interactions with male friends. As a result, "Were Thine That Special Face," a romantic beguine, functions as a seductive ballad that

Petruchio performs to Katherine (hiding on a balcony), casting him romantically for the first time. Then later, "Where Is the Life That Late I Led?," Petruchio's agitated list song, paints him as former womanizer, frustrated by marriage.

In Shakespeare's Act 4, Scene 1, Petruchio ends a scene at his house, where he has teased and frustrated Katherine, with a speech to the audience beginning "Thus have I politicly begun my reign" and explains that he will keep Katherine miserable:

> She ate no meat today, nor none shall eat.
> Last night she slept not, nor tonight she shall not.
> As with the meat, some undeservèd fault
> I'll find about the making of the bed,
> And here I'll fling the pillow, there the bolster,
> This way the coverlet, another way the sheets.[32]

The scene ends with him declaring that he is doing a public service by sharing his methods. However, in *Kiss Me, Kate*, the Spewacks add extra lines to Shakespeare's original language. Petruchio goes to the bedroom door to announce his arrival to Katherine, only to discover that she has locked the door and he cannot execute his plan. Their script gives Katherine a brief upper hand and frames the start of "Where Is the Life That Late I Led?," in which he laments his previously debauched existence in contrast to her successful thwarting of his advances.

The context of the song undeniably evokes Leporello's catalogue aria in Mozart's *Don Giovanni* to an audience in the know, aligning Petruchio with another controversial protagonist known for his mistreatment of women. When Petruchio recounts his past adventures by pairing women with famous Italian landmarks and stereotypical pastimes (like drinking in a palazzo or peddling pizza), Porter situates him as a philanderer well beyond any detail that Shakespeare offers us. He also gives Petruchio characteristics that make him a plausible musical comedy hero, when one might cast the younger roles (Bill and Lois) as more conventional romantic leads. This treads a complex line in adaptation, as Porter does not soften Petruchio's character but does expand his romantic history. "I've Come to Wive It Wealthily in Padua" adds relish to Petruchio's demeanor but also gives Fred a showstopping song that embodies hypermasculine bravado. In other scenes, Petruchio is also given a peppering of romance and cheekiness that is not part of Shakespeare's play text. As each collaborator grappled with how to prioritize *The Taming of the Shrew* in their version of the show, Porter took over characterization of Petruchio in his songs. He provides us with a bawdy backstory to a challenging protagonist who is (in dual narrative) unsuccessfully navigating a power struggle with his wife, and all this stemming from a single line of *The Taming of the Shrew*.

Collaborating on Katherine

While Porter settled many aspects of the *Taming of the Shrew* score at the first stages of working on *Kiss Me, Kate*, he revisited the music for Katherine twice in response to developments in the script. Both he and Bella Spewack agonized over how to characterize Katherine, and the materials reveal several different approaches. The experimentation began when Bella developed a new subplot for Katherine, which Bella felt was a necessary for making *Kiss Me, Kate* suitable for Jarmila Novotná to star in.[33] Interestingly, Novotná was especially known for trouser roles in New York. Although she played a considerable range of characters, almost half of her appearances at the Metropolitan Opera came as Cherubino from *Le nozze di Figaro*, Octavian in *Der Rosenkavalier*, and later as Prince Orlofsky from *Der Fledermaus*. Bella Spewack made good use of this in her script concept, also nodding to a broader Shakespearean trope of cross-dressing actors while celebrating Novotná's fame within the text.

Bella's new scenes (Act 1, Scenes 7 and 11, of the first script draft) therefore have Katherine disguise herself as a boy to meet Petruchio before everyone arrives at Baptista's house. She frames Katherine's first appearance as a boy using her own original scripting:

(At the end of number "I've Come to Wive It Wealthily in Padua," KATHERINE enters reading a book and holding an egg. SHE is dressed as a boy. SHE sits on a bench. HE eyes her curiously.)

PETRUCHIO: Good morrow, lad! What signifies the egg?
(Sits beside her)

KATHERINE: There is a rumor, sir, that the world is round. That a sailor named Columbus has proved this to the Queen of Spain with an egg.
(SHE holds out the egg and absorbedly gazes at it)
Galileo is of the same mind.[34]

She then returns to their established adaptational tactics by repurposing *Taming of the Shrew* dialogue from Act 1, Scene 2, to cover why Petruchio has come to Padua. The exchange, originally between Petruchio, Grumio, and Hortensio (also found in Sam's April 28 pages), allows *Katherine* to introduce the marriage prospect to Petruchio:

KATHERINE: I can, Petruchio, help thee to a wife.
PETRUCHIO: (*Laughs*) Thou, stripling?
KATHERINE: (*Holds up hand to stave off interruption*)
[From *The Taming of the Shrew*]
With wealth enough, and young and beauteous,
Brought up as best becomes a gentlewoman:
Her only fault is that she is intolerable curst,
And shrewd, and forward, so beyond all measure
That, were my state far worse that it is,
I would not wed her for a mine of gold.
PETRUCHIO: Tell me her father's name, and 'tis enough:
For I will board her, tho she chide as loud
As thunder when the clouds in autumn crack.[35]

Here, Bella Spewack disrupts the social structures of Shakespeare's play. She revises the gender and narrative constructions of *The Taming of the Shrew* and poses a considerable change to the intertextuality between Shakespeare's play and the Baltimore storyline. This Katherine is not only aware of the bargain surrounding her marriage but also facilitates Petruchio's interest in her dowry. Later, in Act 1, Scene 13, when Petruchio calls at Baptista's house, Katherine exits the stage and re-enters in her boy's outfit, revealing herself and her contrivance to him.[36]

As part of this experiment in writing "new Shakespeare," we can see that Bella Spewack also explored one of the techniques—layering out-of-context references in his modernizations of the *Shrew*—evident in Porter's songs. In the previously quoted text, Bella incorporates references to Columbus and Galileo, expanding the onstage lexicon beyond *The Taming of the Shrew*. She also attempts something similar in the line prefacing Bianca's discarded ballad, "If Ever Married I'm." Here, she includes a blatant reference to Ophelia (*Hamlet*)[37] in the script:

BIANCA: (*To audience*) I must end my days in a nunnery. My sister, Katherine, will see to that.[38]

This allusion to *Hamlet* might seem superficially comfortable among Porter's modern musical forms and topical contemporary references like making "the cover of *LIFE* and *Time*" in Bianca's subsequent song.[39] However, Bella Spewack employs references that are loosely contemporary to *The Taming of the Shrew* itself. Instead of creating a deliberate collision of eras (using a foxtrot or referring to the fictional collie Lassie), Spewack offers a slightly different tone, handling the period of *The Shrew* with irreverence rather than through a modern lexicon. Instead, her jokes are situated in comedy of information, drawn from a trivial understanding of the context of *The Taming of the Shrew*.

Her ambitions preface Porter's crafty use of the titles of Shakespeare's plays as codes for sexual advances in "Brush Up Your Shakespeare" but does not play the humor in a similar way. Porter's joke requires you to recognize the name of the play and understand its misuse in the song. He uses the conceit over and over allowing the trick to register with most listeners. Instead, Bella Spewack's lines require you to know the plays, the historical context of their era, and to catch fleeting references that are not connected to the focus of the scene. Perhaps because of this contradictory tone, all of Bella's new scenes for Katherine were abandoned after Novotná had withdrawn and the producers demanded change. However, Porter appears to have taken up her mantle, introducing two extra songs for Katherine and making her an important musical force within the tapestry of the *Taming of the Shrew* musical.

Added in June 1948, "I Am Ashamed That Women Are So Simple" solved a writing puzzle for the team, paraphrasing Katherine's forty-three-line speech at the end of *The Taming of the Shrew* into ten phrases of music. "I Am Ashamed" is a notably sparse song, and Porter's setting leaves the lyrics relatively unadorned, allowing Katherine to command the close of the drama. In contrast to almost every other number in *Kiss Me, Kate*, the melody and lyrics have no jokes or diverting ornaments. The song is also distinctive in its lack of other musical humor (pastiche, instrumentational jokes, or quotations of other songs). Here Porter aligned the musicalization of *The Taming of the Shrew* with the conventions of musical theater, allowing the reconciliation of Fred and Lilli—through her return to the performance—space before the closing celebration. In this adaptation, Porter crystallizes Katherine's words into its concluding sentences while providing her with the final solo music of the show. He succinctly brings the finale of *Kiss Me, Kate* and the ending of *The Taming of the Shrew* together by injecting music (rather than speech) as the resolutory act in the scene.

Having settled this moment for everyone, Porter returned to Katherine after the interim script had been circulated. Here he merged multiple agendas into a new musical idea. "I Hate Men" falls exactly in the gap between *Shrew* scenes proposed in Sam's April 28 pages. In that draft, Sam splits the first *Shrew* scene with a backstage interaction between Lilli and an older actress. They bemoan the conditions faced by women, who are judged by their marital status and not by their selves or their achievements, leading to a performance of the unused song "A Woman's Career." Porter does not recreate these sentiments in "I Hate Men," but he fuses the topic of this conversation (misogyny) with Bella's early ambitions to partially emancipate Katherine from her marriage plot.

First introduced to the script in October 1948, "I Hate Men" presents Katherine as fiery, articulate, and incensed by the context she lives in as she churns through its three refrains. Porter also sustains the contrast between Lilli/Katherine and Lois/Bianca through this characterization and uses a contrasting musical setting that is more regal than vivacious. He also offers Katherine new comedy as she quips about the ways in which men are unreliable and mistreat their women. As a result, she and Bianca are polarized in finding men appalling and irresistible respectively, but this does not limit Katherine's desirability, as in *The Taming of the Shrew*. Developing Bella Spewack's earlier concept, Porter allows Katherine space to speak for herself, while connecting Fred's backstage infidelities, Lilli's quick temper, and the power imbalances in both scenarios together into a clever intertextual knot.

From this, *Kiss Me, Kate* allows Katherine her only independent speech—she has none in *The Taming of the Shrew*—and Porter crafts it to validate why she might not be grateful or willing to marry. Regardless of what *Kiss Me, Kate* achieves with her story arc more broadly, in "I Hate Men," Katherine takes center stage and speaks (or rather, sings) for herself for the first time, and this reflects synergies between the creatives working on the adaptation. Porter's final "Shakespearean" song is a welcome addition, developing an idea introduced by Bella and positioned where Sam had previously scripted a conversation about gender inequality. Their collective adaptation of *The Taming of the Shrew* is layered, reimagining the path of the story to make sense of having songs (and later, dance) while appropriating aspects to make a new distilled version of the play, which is enhanced by their modern references and intertexts. In this *Taming of the Shrew*, Katherine, Petruchio, and Bianca become recognizably modern while the musical otherwise deprioritizes the rest of Shakespeare's characters.

4
Crafting the Score

Cole Porter's interventions in *Kiss Me, Kate* were undeniably crucial to the musical's success. As highlighted in the previous chapter, he was receptive and interested in other creative decision making and helped to realize ideas that were not working in other parts of the show. Many of the songs he contributed have remained classics or iconic numbers within musical theater history as well as in wider popular repertoire. Recordings of "Why Can't You Behave?" by Bing Crosby and Frank Sinatra coincided with the musical's early run on Broadway, prefacing numerous, and varied, interpretations of "So in Love," "Too Darn Hot," and "Always True to You (In My Fashion)" across albums, soundtracks, and advertisements into the present day. Perhaps unsurprisingly, the songs associated with *The Taming of the Shrew* have largely stayed in live, theatrical performance contexts, also showcasing *Kiss Me, Kate* as an exemplar of the "Shakespearean musical." In this context, Porter's work on *Kiss Me, Kate* is perhaps the most admired, as well as the most studied, creative contribution to this musical.

Given the unexpected commercial success of *Kiss Me, Kate*, scholars have closely examined the score to place the show among other hit musicals of the era. While histories of Broadway's music are still comparatively few, the ambition to interconnect works from the "classic" era has limited the space to explore many of these scores on their own terms. For example, *Kiss Me, Kate* is consistently placed in dialogue with *Oklahoma!* (1943) rather than with other more tonally similar works like *Annie Get Your Gun*, *Gentlemen Prefer Blondes*, or even *Brigadoon*. The comparison to *Oklahoma!* is used to clarify how Porter changed his writing practice because of the new pressures that Rodgers and Hammerstein introduced to the market, and therefore, to the creative expectations placed on composer/lyricists. In *Enchanted Evenings: The Broadway Musical from "Show Boat" to Sondheim and Lloyd Webber*, Geoffrey Block highlights that Porter drafted a joke about writing songs for the approval (and purchase) of Irving Berlin and Rodgers and Hammerstein into unused lyrics for *Kiss Me, Kate.*[1] The tensions between musicals with serious themes including nation making, community, and

Too Darn Hot. Hannah Robbins, Oxford University Press. © Oxford University Press 2026.
DOI: 10.1093/9780190082437.003.0004

politics and those solely prioritizing romance, comedy, and play are persistent in our approaches to American musicals and have frequently crowded out extended coverage of "lighter" shows that do not map easily on to high sociocultural values.

In this context, *Kiss Me, Kate* is used to epitomize the potential of Porter's creative capacity through the lens of Rodgers and Hammerstein's aesthetic values. Where scholars largely attribute new musical sophistication to their shows, analyses of *Kiss Me, Kate* examine how Porter was forced to consider the relationships between his songs and the rest of the fabric of the musicals that he worked on. This chapter extends already excellent analyses of the *Kiss Me, Kate* score, including those by Joseph P. Swain, Geoffrey Block, Raymond Knapp, Lynn Laitman Siebert, and Michael Buchler,[2] all of whom focus on the original Broadway song list. While Block and Siebert refer to the broader archival picture, their chapter-length accounts must prioritize the most pressing examples in telling their different stories. Here, I continue their unifying arguments that Porter's songs are essential to the success of *Kiss Me, Kate* while acknowledging that this was through the facilitation of other members of the creative team. As Chapters 2 and 3 have shown, Bella and Sam Spewack understood Porter and his working preferences, and used this insight to offer inspiration that happily caught his imagination. As the project evolved, Porter established his voice in the material, determining new boundaries of intertextual and contemporary ideas in his songs, which allowed him to edit the score while supporting Bella Spewack in finishing the script.

I agree with scholars, including Block, Knapp, and Swain,[3] that Porter achieves notable sophistication in *Kiss Me, Kate*, which might seem to move Porter toward writing an "integrated" work (where the music, drama, and dance all speak to one other). Block and Siebert particularly notice how Porter "channel[s] music's power to establish character" in a new way in this musical.[4] However, my account particularly aligns with Knapp's argument that while some of this may be connected to the impact of *Oklahoma!* and other similar musicals, *Kiss Me, Kate* is remarkable because Porter rises "spectacularly to the challenge of setting a property both extremely ambitious and essentially comedic, and extending it in both realms."[5] In this chapter, I suggest that Porter's song score is especially successful because he embraces the material (Spewack and Shakespeare) and then doubles down on his own creative preferences and stylistic idiosyncrasies. Cole Porter's *Kiss Me, Kate* comments on, paraphrases, and emotes aspects of the script more than his songs advance the action. His power in this musical is the ability to combine the contemporary and the Shakespearean with musical theater conventions so that we are simultaneously entertained, provided with given considerable intertextuality between songs, and become aware of Porter and his cleverness at various points in the show.

Although he was reticent about the concept for *Kiss Me, Kate*, we have seen that Porter took to his work with alacrity. Like Bella Spewack, he settled on his initial concepts quickly. By the first script draft, he had finished half the songs that feature in *Kiss Me, Kate* and had written several others that were ultimately discarded. In June 1948, with a script draft in hand, Porter finalized the structure of the score, completing infrastructural numbers like the act finales and "Another Op'nin', Another Show" as well as helping Bella Spewack to refine the final scene of the musical. From then, and throughout the creative process, Porter evaluated the script and his songs, offering several musical interventions that are significant to the character of *Kiss Me, Kate*. First, he reshaped the romantic relationship between Fred and Lilli through his ballad "So in Love." Then, he introduced the unsolicited song "Brush Up Your Shakespeare," fulfilling his creative desire to have a "Porterian" spectacle near the close of this show. Porter's dramaturgical understanding of *Kiss Me, Kate* is essential to his interventions but also empowered him to redefine the songs, offsetting support for the narrative with some of his other creative priorities: comedy and entertainment.[6]

Sourcing the Score

The sources for the evolution of the songs in *Kiss Me, Kate* are patchy and complicated. In total, there are thirty-one song titles associated with *Kiss Me, Kate*. These are tabulated in Figure 4.1.[7] Six are incomplete lyric drafts or micro-fragments of melody, documented by Porter or a copyist. The draft for "If You Love Your Job" offers an exciting glimpse of six couplets set for Hattie, Lilli's maid.[8] Another incomplete sheet, titled "To Be or Not to Be," similarly offers a tantalizing suggestion that Porter pulled on the Shakespearean context for more than one contemporary ballad. Of the remaining twenty-five songs, two—"I'm Afraid, Sweetheart, I Love You" and "What Does Your Servant Dream About?"—are finished piano-vocal scores, but were never incorporated into *Kiss Me, Kate*, and a further four—"A Woman's Career," "If Ever Married I'm," "It Was Great Fun the First Time," and "We Shall Never

Title	Earliest record	Usage
I Sing of Love		
I've Come To Wive It Wealthily in Padua		
Tom, Dick, or Harry	April 7, 1948	Broadway
Were Thine That Special Face		
Why Can't You Behave?		
If Ever Married I'm		
We Shall Never Be Younger	April 7, 1948	Finished but cut
It Was Great Fun The First Time	April 13, 1948	Finished, cut
Always True to You (In My Fashion)		
Another Op'nin', Another Show		
So In Love'		
Too Darn Hot	April 22, 1948	Broadway
We Open in Venice		
Where is The Life That Late I Led		
Wunderbar		
A Woman's Career	April 22, 1948	Finished, cut
Finale Act One		
Finale Act Two: So, Kiss Me, Kate	June 1, 1948	Broadway
Brush Up Your Shakespeare	June 12, 1948	Broadway
I Am Ashamed That Women Are So Simple	June 16, 1948	Broadway
What Does Your Servant Dream About?	July 10, 1948	Finished, cut
I'm Afraid, Sweetheart, I Love You	August 7, 1948	Finished, cut
I Hate Men	October 30, 1948	Broadway
Biance		
So In Love (Reprise)	December 1, 1948	Broadway
Security or Love		
The Trouble With Me Is		
Love Is The Only Thing		
To Be or Not To Be	Undated	Unfinished
How Simple Life Would Be		
If You Love Your Job		

**So In Love' is named in April 1948. The first lyric draft is dated September

Figure 4.1 Complete list of songs associated with *Kiss Me, Kate*, listed in order of writing from available sources

Be Younger"—were incorporated into various script drafts but were cut between June and December 1948. The remaining music comprises eighteen songs and a reprise of "So in Love," which completes the song list for the original Broadway production of *Kiss Me, Kate*. Figure 4.2 presents the songs in the original Broadway score in order of completion.

Broadly speaking, Porter's songs were easily situated in the script and were only moved if scenes were reordered. For example, Bella Spewack repeatedly

Figure 4.2 Visualization of the writing order of songs used in the original Broadway production of *Kiss Me, Kate*

flipped Act 1, Scenes 2 and 3, and therefore "Wunderbar" and "It Was Great Fun the First Time" are switched with "Why Can't You Behave?" in different running orders of the show. She was exploring whether we should progress from the first scene, rehearsing the bows, and continue Fred and Lilli's argument or whether we should receive the plot exposition that Bill has signed Fred's name on an IOU first. However, these scenes are not significantly rewritten from draft to draft.

Of all the songs heard on Broadway, only two—"Were Thine That Special Face" and "I Sing of Love"—were moved or repurposed in any significant way once they were incorporated into the script. "Were Thine That Special Face" always belonged to the early *Taming of the Shrew* scenes in Act 1, but the performer and the exact location of the song changed when Bella Spewack cut her additional material for Katherine and streamlined each scene. By contrast, "I Sing of Love" was originally written as a solo for Lucentio that led to the arrival of Petruchio early in *The Taming of the Shrew*. When the song was repurposed as a chorus number that covered the scene change to the Act 1 finale, it left Bill/Lucentio without a solo number and led to the last-minute creation of "Bianca" to fulfill the contractual rights associated with the role.

Other details of interest include that eight of the songs in the *Kiss Me, Kate* score exist in every complete script draft as well as Bella Spewack's preliminary outline: the *Backstage* overview).[9] Split evenly between the backstage and *The Taming of the Shrew* scenes, these songs are:

Another Op'nin', Another Show
Why Can't You Behave?
We Open in Venice
Tom, Dick, or Harry
I've Come to Wive It Wealthily in Padua
I Sing of Love
Too Darn Hot
Where Is The Life That Late I Led?
Always True to You (In My Fashion)

Of this list, the songs "Too Darn Hot," "Where Is the Life That Late I Led," and "Always True to You (In My Fashion)" are always situated in the same scenes and locations, regardless of the evolving script and, interestingly, they all occur in Act 2, consecutively, without advancing the framing drama of the scenes around them. "I've Come to Wive It Wealthily in Padua" is relocated only once when it temporarily prefaces "We Open in Venice" as the first song in *The Taming in the Shrew* in the interim script. "Another Op'nin', Another Show" was initially placed in the middle of the act before being situated after or at the end of the first scene.

If we amalgamate this into a picture of the emergent musical (see Figure 4.3), it is clear that the infrastructural numbers—"Another Op'nin' Another Show," "We Open in Venice," "Too Darn Hot," and the Act Finales—which involve all or most of the company, combine with the three never-moving songs, and two July additions—"I Am Ashamed That Women Are So Simple" and "Brush Up Your Shakespeare"—to give *Kiss Me, Kate* a very obvious structure by August 1948. Like Bella Spewack, Porter was able to construct most of *Kiss Me, Kate* early in the process. However, he was left with more freedom to tweak lyrics and refine the music while Bella Spewack was still deciding how to get the musical from the dissolution of Lilli's engagement to Harrison and forward to her (re-)partnering with Fred and the finale of the show.

Figure 4.3 Emerging structure of songs by the interim script draft (c. August 1948)

Porter's Process

As well as giving insight into how the songs were placed and the order in which Porter wrote them, the *Kiss Me, Kate* materials affirm Porter's explanation of his creative process in the press. Across the years, Porter was consistent in describing how he developed his songs, and the materials for *Kiss Me, Kate* (as well as *Panama Hattie* [1940], *Can-Can* [1953], and *Silk Stockings* [1955]) all seem to confirm his words. One profile by Howard Taubman, published in January 1949, provides an extended account of Porter's systematic approach to songwriting:

> He works out the whole song before he sets it down on paper and tries it at the piano. The first step is to fix on a central idea; often a title holds the key. Then comes the tune. The lyrics come last. Frequently he thinks of the punch-line first, working backward from the last verse to the first. Occasionally he leaves lines and stanzas blank until the *mot juste* comes. His handy aids are a set of word books: a rhyming dictionary, foreign language dictionaries, medical dictionaries and a volume called "Words—Ancient and Modern." When lyrics are too suggestive for more modest demands of radio and sheet music, he turns out alternative verses. The other day he had at hand a loose-leaf folder devoted to *Kiss Me, Kate*;[10] a little more than half its neatly-typed pages contained the words as they are sung at the Century Theatre, and the remainder the diluted version.[11]

In a subsequent interview, Porter characterized this process again, suggesting that after finding a title and working on a melody, he would approach lyric writing like a problem to be solved:

> First, I think of the idea and then I fit it to a title. Then I go to work on the melody, spotting the title at certain moments in the melody, and then I write the lyric—the end first—that way, it has a strong finish. I do the lyrics like I'd do a crossword puzzle. I try to give myself a meter which will make the lyric as easy as possible to write without being banal. On top of the meter, I try to pick rhyme words of which there is a long list with the same ending.[12]

Porter's description, coupled with what Jeffery Magee describes as Porter's "urbane and polysyllabic" manner of expression,[13] clarifies the nature of his distinctive style, which is layered with rhymes, internal joke schemes, and repetitions of music and language. For Porter, the title is the establishing element, which he then set to music and constructed a verse and/or a refrain around. With the melody secure, he drafted the lyrics to the rhythmic scheme established by the tune, sensible of the peaks and accents in phrasing.[14] The copious lyric drafts preserved in his papers reveal how he experimented with vocabulary, product lists, and pages of optional phrases that he then patchworked into a version of the song he was happy with. On a draft lyric sheet for "I Hate Men," Porter has titled his work-in-progress "Gags unfinished."[15] Figure 4.4 also reproduces a draft of "Too Darn Hot" where Porter experiments with the structure and wording of different phrases.[16] Along the

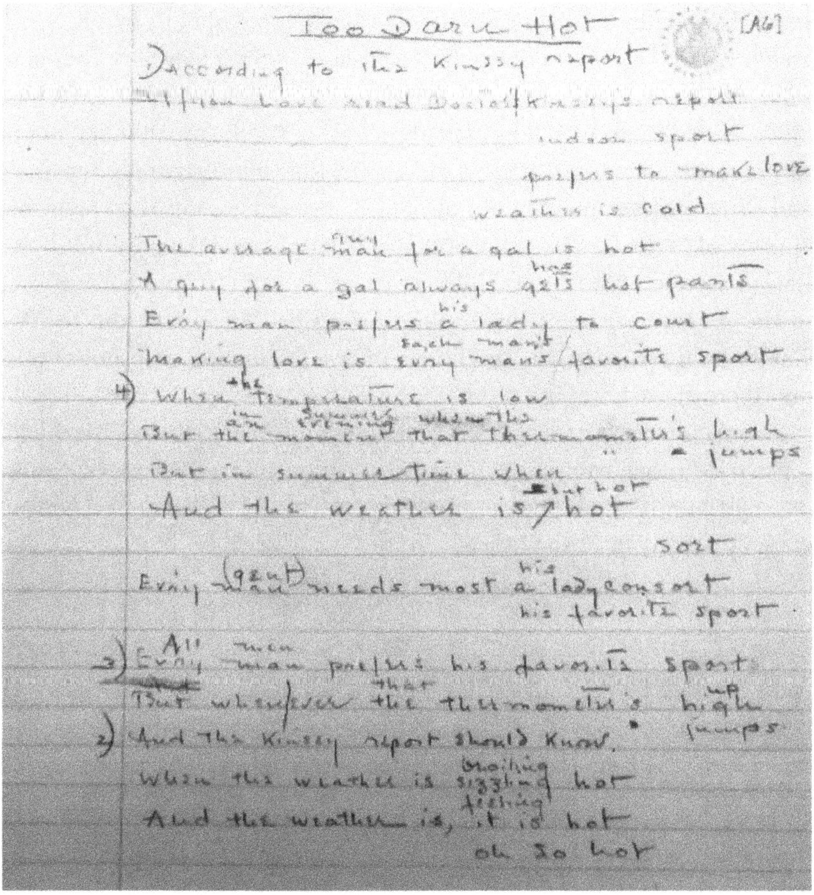
Too Darn Hot
According to the Kinsey report
The average man for a gal is hot
A guy for a gal always gets hot pants
Every man prefers a lady to court
Making love is every man's favorite sport
When the temperature is low
But the moment that the thermometer's high
But in summer time when
And the weather is hot
Every man needs most a lady consort
And the Kinsey report should know.
When the weather is sizzling hot
And the weather is, it is hot
oh so hot

Figure 4.4 Handwritten lyric sheet for "Too Darn Hot" from Porter's papers at the Library of Congress[17]

margin, he has picked out his preferred lines, which, when read from 1 to 4, reveal the familiar lyrics of the verse.

As is noted elsewhere, there are few autograph music materials for *Kiss Me, Kate*. Porter did not leave or, possibly, ever transcribe, the music for most of the songs that make up the score. However, there are two intriguing autograph lead sheets for "I Am Ashamed That Women Are So Simple" and "Finale Act One."[18] For "I Am Ashamed," Porter has transcribed Katherine's vocal line as it is heard in the original Broadway production. By contrast, the double-page spread for "Finale Act One" shows Porter experimenting with fourteen bars of additional melodic material, not seen in any other drafts. This, paired with a lyric sheet dated June 26, 1948, which includes two mini-reprises from "Why Can't You Behave?" and "Another Op'nin', Another Show" (see Figure 4.5), indicates that Porter explored options that have not been preserved in copyist drafts. In this instance, Porter may have chosen to notate "Finale Act One" to negotiate the number of voices singing, which he could not have interpreted himself at the piano. Excitingly, although not in keeping with the musical schema of *Kiss Me, Kate* more generally, the finale lead sheet shows a merging of Lois and Bianca's music together, prefacing Bill's use of "Why Can't You Behave?" to chastise Lois at the start of "Always True to You (In My Fashion)." Bill's return to "Why Can't You Behave?" was added in rehearsals after these mini-reprises had been cut from the Act Finales, so these materials, combined, offer a fascinating snapshot of possible thought processes in action.

Because of the broader absence of autograph materials that we might consult for other composers, any investigation of creative process must reconcile hundreds of notes and lyric drafts with the different iterations of the script and copyist song sheets. In "Secrets of Melody: Line and Design

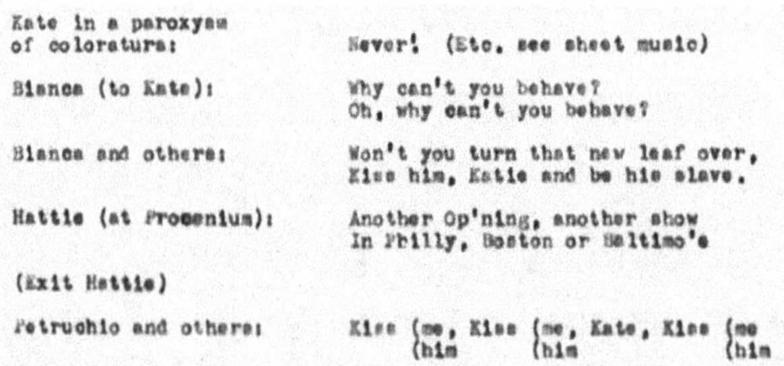

Kate in a paroxysm of coloratura:	Never! (Etc. see sheet music)
Bianca (to Kate):	Why can't you behave? Oh, why can't you behave?
Bianca and others:	Won't you turn that new leaf over, Kiss him, Katie and be his slave.
Hattie (at Proscenium):	Another Op'ning, another show In Philly, Boston or Baltimo'e
(Exit Hattie)	
Petruchio and others:	Kiss (me, Kiss (me, Kate, Kiss (me (him (him (him

Figure 4.5 Excerpt of lyric sheet for "Finale Act One" showing mini-reprises following Katherine's cadenza[19]

in the Songs of Cole Porter," Allen Forte also notes that the musical text is influenced by the roles of the various orchestrators Porter collaborated with and that "the publishers also had various types of arrangements made" for a range of ensembles.[20] However, Forte also notes that the "original music still remained as core structure" and works from piano-vocal scores. Forte then suggests that this is how Porter would have submitted music to copyists for appropriate typesetting.[21]

While Forte rightly acknowledges the role of copyists in this process, it is not certain how often Porter ever handed in complete, or skeleton, piano-vocal music. Instead, the archival materials seem to suggest that he employed one of several copyists to transcribe the music by ear, meaning that the first clean, or "fair," copy was this initial transcription. In examples across his papers, Porter has then written lyrics onto these scores, presumably acting when a typed sheet was not available during the copy process. The lack of autograph scores has also led to some speculation about Porter's relationship to notating his songs, including an implication that he was not capable of transcribing the music himself. Interestingly, a short article from the *Daily Mirror* in 1951 (during *Kiss Me, Kate*'s London run) was accompanied by an image of Porter holding manuscript paper at an unusual angle (see Figure 4.6). It is captioned "Because his mother and nurse disagreed on

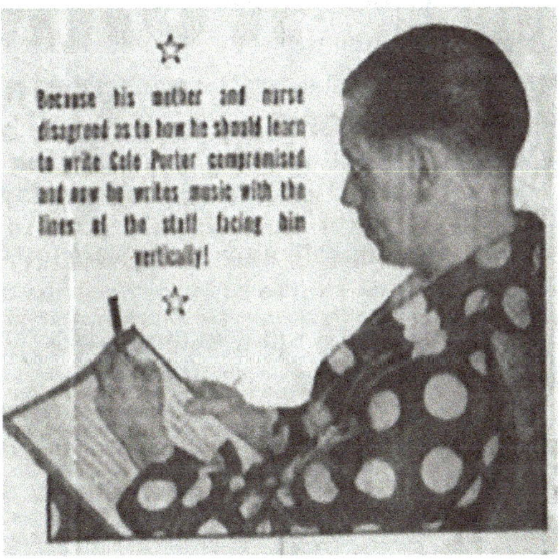

Figure 4.6 Image of Porter working by hand on manuscript paper accompanying a *Daily Mirror* article titled "Shakespeare's 'Kate' Is a Dollar Double-Cross!"[23]

how he should learn to write Cole Porter compromised and now he writes his music with the lines of the staff facing him vertically!"[22] Perhaps, this indicates some conversation about Porter's comfort with a pen beyond musicological analysis.

Despite this, Laitman Siebert and Dominic Broomfield-McHugh have previously demonstrated that Porter was able to work with sophisticated musical notation. Scrapbooks preserved at Yale University reveal hundreds of song fragments, written out by Porter, that show a preference for transcribing the melody and the harmonic arrangement of any accompanying chord but that he did not choose to flesh out these details more than necessary. Some sketches indicate a rhythmic *ostinato*—normally a bar in duration—but do not provide comprehensive piano-vocal sketches that we might associate with Porter's contemporaries such as Richard Rodgers or Frederick Loewe.[24] Broomfield-McHugh has also detailed how Porter "collaborated with others on the music of his songs," offering a brief overview of Porter's working relationship with Albert Sirmay, who was also involved in notating *Kiss Me, Kate.*[25] Marrying previous correspondence, an incomplete manuscript for the opening of "Always True to You (In My Fashion)," and a lyric sheet that perfectly matches the rhythm of the manuscript, it is clear that Sirmay transcribed an unused version of the start of this song for Porter at some point in the fall of 1948.[26]

It is important to recognize (again) that Porter was a committed collaborator who worked on his music with other people. His relationships with copyists are similar to his interpretation of prompts offered by Bella Spewack at the beginning of working on *Kiss Me, Kate.* While this chapter will foreground his creative impact on the musical, it is vital to situate this in the context of his relationships with the other creatives involved. Porter's process was systematic whether working with support or on his own terms. The lyric drafts indicate his rigorous attention to language once he was happy with a melody, and the rest of this chapter will trace how he honed his own writing once the picture of the score was fixed.

Musical Intertextuality

When analyzing Porter's contributions to *Kiss Me, Kate* for pronounced or uncharacteristic sophistication, the role of the score in exploring and extending the intertextuality of the show is the most obvious starting point.

If we accept that the Spewacks and Porter intended there to be ongoing dialogue between the Baltimore scenario and characters and *The Taming of the Shrew* material, then it is easy to see that Porter recognized and acted on this brief. In the words of Laitman Siebert, "the resulting blend is magical."[27] In her brief analysis of the musical, Siebert highlights the layers of "subtle refinement, depth of expression, and inventiveness" of Porter's work by connecting musical analysis of select songs to their impact *in situ*. For example, she explains that the impact of "accent displacement" in "Another Op'nin', Another Show" gives the music a "propulsive drive," fulfilling its purpose as a traditional opening number that is also about industrious activity and theater craft.[28]

Significantly, all scholars and critics agree about the interweaving communication between songs and also between each song and the picture of the score more generally. Several have also argued that this is woven into the granular layers of music throughout the score. For example, in *Enchanted Evenings*, Block expands on Swain's analysis of "the alternation of major and minor modes" in *Kiss Me, Kate*,[29] which "distinguish the Padua songs from their Baltimore counterparts."[30] However, Block suggests that Porter's deployment of these modes "lessens the dramatic contrast between Padua and Baltimore," continuing:

> In fact, it might be said that this device—widely and effectively used by Schubert—not only serves as Porter's way of demonstrating parallels between the *Shrew* numbers and the Baltimore numbers. In the end, it functions primarily as a unifying musical device that shape a musically integrated score.[31]

In fact, the harmonic choices in *Kiss Me, Kate* cannot be distinguished by the section of the score. Like Porter's most classical references and pastiches, they are deployed both backstage and in *The Taming of the Shrew* to different effects. For example, "Wunderbar," a pastiche of a Viennese waltz, is used to show Fred and Lilli's performativity and their undeniable connection *through* their vocation. The heightened, sentimental nature of the song is counterbalanced by the journey the characters take from inhabiting fictional roles to reconnecting as their naked selves. The format of the music allows for performance choices like exaggerated foreign accents that give way to the characters' "legitimate" voices in the final chorus, when Fred and Lilli see one another as they once were and forget the recreation of the performance.

By contrast, the semi-operatic writing in "Where Is the Life That Late I Led?" is employed buffoonishly. Petruchio is made less serious and menacing by the *quasi*-classical vocal writing that adds a feeling of camp exaggeration to his claims of sexual conquest.

In their work, musicologists Raymond Knapp and Michael Buchler have also suggested different but related schemes of musical intertextuality (connectedness and internal dialogue) between Porter's songs. In *The American Musical and the Performance of Identity*, Knapp's thematic analysis looks for musical "*doppelgänger*"[32] across the score, based on a set of criteria evaluating dramatic and musical matching and mismatching in the show.[33] Like those of Swain and Block, Knapp's intertextual analysis is as interested in contrasts as synergies. Building from this, Buchler offers his own set of groupings (after Knapp), looking for thematic musical and textual similarities. Among this, his extended analysis of the pairing "So in Love" and "Were Thine That Special Face," which offers granular insights into the melodic and harmonic construction of both, is especially compelling, and Buchler suggests that "one of these songs was likely patterned on the other."[34] This observation, based on the published score alone, is striking given that "So in Love" was listed early in *Kiss Me, Kate*'s writing and then finished later. Meanwhile, "Were Thine That Special Face" is the only piece, like "So in Love" for Fred and Lilli, that is functionally passed between Katherine and Petruchio (as a love song) in the early script drafts of *Kiss Me, Kate*.

Taking the complete music list together, there are various ways of grouping the score. It is clear that there are infrastructural parallels between Baltimore and the *Shrew* and that Porter neatly solved the merging of plot and character by having unified finales in both halves. As a result, "Another Op'nin', Another Show" and "We Open in Venice" are important sides of the same musical device, and as many have noted, Porter uses overlapping techniques, including cycling the lyrics around a countdown, to create more pronounced links between the two. The Act Finales address two different but connected issues—how to bring the backstage plots and *Taming of the Shrew* together. In Act 1, Porter is juggling Katherine and Petruchio's marriage, the arrival of the gunmen, the entrapment of Lilli, and the functional need to close the act in one musical number. In Act 2, he has to transition Katherine's capitulation with Fred and Lilli's joyful reunion and the end of the show. As a result, it is perhaps unsurprising that he experimented with building a series of mini-reprises, bringing the different parts of the story together at the end of both acts. However, this definitely disrupts the sophistication of other parts of the show, because it achieves inexplicable blurring between the characters who sang the songs, their meanings in context, and the end of *The Taming of the Shrew.*

In addition to the structural applications of songs, Porter also gave his key Shakespearean characters—Petruchio and Katherine—their own character solos, ultimately leaving everyone else in group numbers (including "Tom, Dick, or Harry"). Importantly, Porter writes his character anthems in reference to the dialogue and background the script provides. Because Fred and Lilli recount their backstory in Act 1, Scene 3, they do not need musical introductions or to be better understood. However, the adaptation of *The Taming of the Shrew* removes most of the contextual dialogue about Baptista, his daughters, and about Petruchio as well as the other suitors. In *Kiss Me, Kate*'s *Taming of the Shrew*, Bianca and her suitors are immaterial to the story apart from placing urgency on Katherine's marriage. Instead, we need to get to know Katherine and Petruchio. Cleverly, Porter creates songs exploring fortune-hunting and domination for Petruchio and patterns of misogyny in marriage and romantic relationships for Katherine. Although they do not speak to each other, we are given information about the motivation and politics of these characters, foreshadowing their collisions later in the scene. On top of this, we have a parallel between Fred, attempting to juggle two women to get the production he wants, and Lilli preemptively expressing her hatred of male manipulation before she knows what Fred and the gunman have planned for her.

Drawn from these examples, I have identified three supplementary groups of music that expand on various work already done by other scholars. These groups are Porter's love songs before "Brush Up Your Shakespeare" and "I Hate Men," Porter's love songs after the introduction of these new pieces, and his "manifesto music." In the remainder of this chapter, I offer an analysis of Porter's creative journey in *Kiss Me, Kate.* In the first group, he writes very literal adaptations of Fred and Lilli's backstory as a supplement to the emerging script. This is undone when Porter transitions from accounts of the plot to representations of feeling when it comes to Fred and Lilli's relationship. In "Manifesto Music," I consider the balance of Porter writing interconnected character anthems with his inclination to write for himself. In "Brush Up Your Shakespeare," he returns to the contemporary playfulness that is also apparent in "Tom, Dick, or Harry," "Too Darn Hot," and "Always True to You (In My Fashion)." However, Porter also serves *himself,* imposing a structural feature of his past musicals onto *Kiss Me, Kate* without consulting the other collaborators in advance. As well as asserting his voice in the penultimate gesture of the musical, Porter showcases his writing talent, and the impact of his impish voice as lyricist, on the nature of a musical number. Through the introduction of "Brush Up Your Shakespeare," *Kiss Me, Kate* the smash hit comes into focus as Porter raises his distinctive voice above those of his other collaborators.

Porter's Love Songs

While writing for Novotná, and working from Bella Spewack's character studies, Porter formed a rough concept of Fred and Lilli's musical world early in the writing of *Kiss Me, Kate*. As Knapp explains, Porter's "songs convey both the deep affection and the surface skirmishing that mark the kind of relationships that *Kiss Me, Kate* is built around."[35] Porter experimented with styles to communicate love, connection, frustration, hurt, and rage through different levels of the musical, and his writing for Fred and Lilli characterizes how he evolved his material from the early creative process into the rehearsal period. As highlighted in Figure 4.7, Porter completed at least three of four songs connected to Fred and Lilli's relationship in April 1948, although "Wunderbar" was not introduced to the libretto until the interim script around August. Although listed in the *Backstage* overview (April 22, 1948),

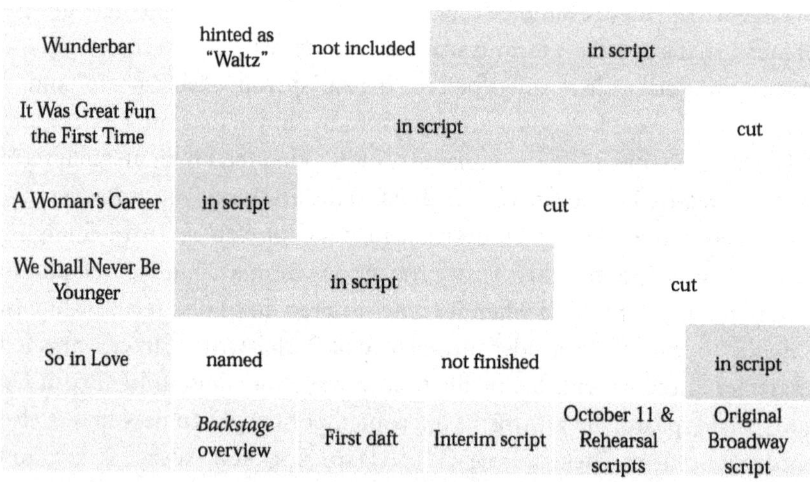

Figure 4.7 Visualization of Fred and Lilli's love songs from April to December 1948

"So in Love" does not appear to have been completed or incorporated into *Kiss Me, Kate* until September.

In addition to these songs, Porter also drafted "A Woman's Career," which was moved around the script before being abandoned. A duet between Lilli and another character (in some instances, Fred and in others, the discarded role Angela Temple), "A Woman's Career" has the beginnings of a Porter "duet of one-upmanship" like "You're the Top" or "Friendship." In it, the characters explain all the personal and professional feats a woman might achieve without overcoming the need to hold down a husband:

SHE: She can act on the screen and be starred in big lights.
She can take home an Oscar to Hollywood Hights
HE: But to live with an Oscar won't liven her nights
If she can't hold her man,
If she can't hold her man.[36]

Like Bella Spewack's fake Shakespeare for Katherine, Porter clearly considered how to represent or address gender inequality in song in *Kiss Me, Kate*. The setting for "A Woman's Career" is relatively stately and sung through. It doesn't allow for the speak-sing flourishes heard across recordings of his more successful competitive duets. Simultaneously, Fred (or Angela Temple) gets the last word in this song, reminding Lilli of the misogynistic scrutiny of her relationships. This is inconsistent with the balance of writing in *Kiss Me, Kate* more generally.

In his analysis of *Kiss Me, Kate*, Raymond Knapp refers to a conscious "doubling"—normally an opposite or a parallel—that is layered through almost every dramatic element of the score.[37] He walks us through the mirrors and inversions in the musical, beginning with the play-within-a-play device, looking at the Baltimore actors and the *Shrew* roles as well as offering a set of musical pairings that encompasses the whole score. Knapp uses musical, textual, functional, and emotive parallels to pair the songs in an effective and compelling account of the sophistication of the score. In his system (working from the original Broadway score), Knapp pairs "Wunderbar" with "Brush Up Your Shakespeare" and puts the two performances of "So in Love" together. The "Wunderbar" pairing highlights comic parody in the music writing of *Kiss Me, Kate*—a romantic Viennese waltz with the quicker Bowery waltz, which G. J. Decker and Michael Buchler describe as "with vamp-like accompaniments and was often used in early Broadway show, vaudeville, and British music-hall numbers of the late nineteenth and early twentieth centuries."[38] Knapp reminds us that Porter's deployed different uses of high- and lowbrow popular culture to comment on our constructions of romantic relationships.[39]

In addition to prompting Buchler's thematic analysis of the score, Knapp's system of "doubles" offers an intriguing opportunity for new consideration of how Porter created and edited his love songs for Fred and Lilli.

Work in progress:

Wunderbar	//	It Was Great Fun the First Time
We Will Never Be Younger	//	So in Love

Broadway:

Wunderbar	//	Always True to You (In My Fashion) *Bianca*
Why Can't You Behave?	//	So in Love

In the first grouping—"Work in progress"—we trace parallels in the function and subject matter of the songs. Both placed in Fred and Lilli's first dressing room scene in Act 1, Scene 3, "Wunderbar" and "It Was Great Fun the First Time" explore Fred and Lilli's relationship before *Kiss Me, Kate*. In addition to the crossover in subject, there are also structural and musical overlaps between these songs that produce a pattern of micro gestures passing between these characters.

Both "Wunderbar" and "It Was Great Fun the First Time" pick up from the dialogue that leads into the opening bars of the song, a complete performance of the refrain, and then a verse and bridge where the competition and disagreements settle in. "Wunderbar" and "It Was Great Fun" use a quickfire, call-and-response bridging passage between Fred and Lilli consistent with the quickfire "skirmishing" identified by Knapp in the *Taming of the Shrew* (see Figures 4.8 and 4.9). Across a familiar and unused song, Porter implemented a simple, yet impactful, musical device to connect the bickering backstage, the quipping onstage, and the limitations of these relationships.

In addition to this overlapping musical gesture, "It Was Great Fun" also provides other details of interest because Porter uses the same numerical, listing device outlined in "Another Op'nin'" and "We Open in Venice." The

Figure 4.8 Excerpt of the vocal lines from "Wunderbar"[40]

Figure 4.9 Excerpt of the vocal lines from "It Was Great Fun the First Time"[41]

Figure 4.10 Excerpt of the refrain to “It Was Great Fun the First Time”[42]

Figure 4.11 Opening melody from “I Sing of Love” (bb. 26–30)[43]

lyrics explain the number of times Fred and Lilli have tested their relationship, and the vocal setting places the numbers on the downbeat, lightly swung (see Figure 4.10), giving each qualifier a special emphasis in the phrase. Meanwhile, the penultimate phrase of the chorus “It was still fun the last time” loosely augments the opening melody of “I Sing of Love” (see the bracketed phrase of Figure 4.10 and the corresponding transcription of the melody in Figure 4.11). Of the numbers written for Fred and Lilli, “It Was Great Fun” provides the most obvious doublings to other sections of the score.

Figure 4.12 Melody from "It Was Great Fun the First Time" (also the closing four bars of Figure 4.9) in "We Shall Never Be Younger"[44]

Like the first grouping, "We Shall Never Be Younger" and "So in Love" characterize a similar yearning nostalgia for the good times, when Fred and Lilli's love was fresh. Set to a slow foxtrot, the lyrics to "We Shall Never Be Younger" regret the passing of time and suggest that Fred and Lilli should embrace their connection and move forward. The music also continues the layers of communication between sections of the score as the verse passingly quotes the call-and-response fight in "It Was Great Fun the First Time" as a flowing *legato* melody (see Figure 4.12). The unused "I'm Afraid, Sweetheart, I Love You" also features this reflective quality. Although less sophisticated in its harmonic details, "I'm Afraid" characterizes a similar tension to "So in Love" set as a slow beguine. "I'm Afraid" also has some passing similarities to "Were Thine That Special Face," although it does not include a direct quotation of that melody. Perhaps this was an interim revision that connects the harmonic and melodic parallels found by Michael Buchler in his pairing of "So in Love" and "Were Thine That Special Face."

In *Enchanted Evenings*, Geoffrey Block reflects on the complicated dramatic impact of "So in Love," commenting that, while "Porter continues the tradition of characters singing songs they're not really supposed to know,"[45] the song "demonstrates a credible bond and a communication" between Fred and Lilli in the dramaturgy of the show.[46] Block suggests that, because Fred and Lilli sing "So in Love" out of each other's hearing, they have no shared history with this music. This distances Porter's writing from the use of shared musical interactions between lovers in other musicals of the time. Examples range from "The Surrey with the Fringe on Top" or "People Will Say We're in Love" in *Oklahoma!*, or "The Heather on the Hill," "Almost Like Being in Love," and "From This Day On" in *Brigadoon* to the initial and reprise performances of "The Girl That I Marry" or "They Say It's Wonderful" in *Annie Get Your Gun*. Unlike the other music tabled for Fred and Lilli or the examples from other hit works of the period, "So in Love" is used to personify the characters' inner turmoil in moments of release (for Lilli) and crisis (for Fred) as their relationship stabilizes and falters.

In my own version of Knapp (and Buchler's) doubles, I pair "So in Love" with Lois (and Bill's) "Why Can't You Behave?" This is because the final song list for *Kiss Me, Kate* shifts from showing what has happened, which the Spewacks achieve in the script, to characterizing the emotional connections and desire between *Kiss Me, Kate*'s two couples. In "Why Can't You Behave?," Lois wishes Bill would be different for the future of their relationship, and this is turned on its head in the opening of "Always True to You (In My Fashion)," when Bill remonstrates Lois for her infidelities. They experience the same insecurities in one another manifested in different ways. Reciprocally, in "So in Love," Lilli and Fred explore the same unspoken connection that continues to flourish between them despite being separated and in conflict most of the time. These are emotive ballads spotlighting different romantic tensions for each couple.

By contrast, "Wunderbar" and "Always True to You"/"Bianca" unmask the fun and effervescence in the two relationships. Here, "Always True to You" and "Bianca" are two halves of one whole, showing Bill and Lois's investment in their partnership despite one another's contradictory behavior. In "Wunderbar," we see Fred and Lilli at their most relaxed, acting together, playing off and against each other's energy, while translating that connection into romantic energy. Porter transitions from "show-and-tell" songs, which set past disagreements to music, to more revelatory and sophisticated storytelling. His songs reveal the inconsistencies of feeling and behavior that underpin the dramatic currents of *Kiss Me, Kate.* By introducing "So in Love" when the song list was already bursting, Porter also indicates his understanding of the demands of the score to enhance, but not expand, the narratives already adequately handled in the script. Rather than setting a Spewack narrative to song, he provides us with clear landmarks in these characters' emotional journeys. This includes their inconsistencies and foibles but does not labor the connections between these songs and the rest of the score to the point of obviousness.

Manifesto Music

Alongside Porter's dramaturgical choices to reflect and serve the core elements of *Kiss Me, Kate*—a play-within-a-play about marriage and relationships—he also evolved his signature "Porterian" style to match this project. As a result, *Kiss Me, Kate* includes several "testament to character" musical numbers that also foreground Cole Porter as the creative voice behind them. In the early development of *Kiss Me, Kate*, "Where Is the Life That Late I Led?" and "Always True to You (In My Fashion)" served as two contrasting representations of sensuality and power that contextualize the other relationship aspects of the show. Musically, "Where Is The Life?" nods to operetta as Petruchio grandstands his conquests in Porter's favorite structure: Introduction followed by repeated Verse and Refrain. In the lyrics, Porter balances stereotypes of Italy with clever wordplay based around the names of Petruchio's previous lovers. He injects *Kiss Me, Kate*'s Petruchio with virality and sexual confidence that is not explicitly discussed in Shakespeare's play text. However, Petruchio's roguishness is pure hearsay and the song foregrounds Porter's forced rhymes more than it (or *Kiss Me, Kate*) demonstrates the character's ability to conquest.

Porter's wit in rhyming examples like "virago" and "Chicago" is at the heart of the number. Meanwhile, Petruchio's ability to brag without us seeing the results is also part of the dramaturgy of *Kiss Me, Kate.* Fred/Petruchio make claims about womanizing, but we have to believe that both characters are invested in Lilli/Katherine above all else. As a companion piece to "Where Is the Life?," Lois's "Always True to You (In My Fashion)" stems from her proven ability to use her beauty to extract the things she wants from the willing men she encounters. While "Where Is the Life?" connects Petruchio's masculinity to his power over women, "Always True to You" clarifies Lois's unemotional smarts about getting what she wants while staying emotionally faithful to Bill. Unlike many soubrettish or gold-digging characters (such as the already cited performance by Marilyn Monroe in *Gentlemen Prefer Blondes*), Lois morphs depending on who she is talking to, and we understand that Fred is simply another target for her. Porter's song positions her as savvy, playful, and, most importantly, in command of her choices. She treats her flirtations like business transactions that she is proud to show off. Simultaneously, Lois's empowerment is communicated through Porter's crafting of naughty little stories that suggest sexual escapades without naming them as such.

Having determined this signature early on, Porter's unsolicited addition to *Kiss Me, Kate*, "Brush Up Your Shakespeare," then embodies the spirit of his score most clearly. Written after Porter left New York for California, "Brush Up Your Shakespeare" turned the non-singing gunmen into vaudevillian wise guys. He first introduced the song to John C. Wilson on June 16, 1948. He wrote:

> I have already taken care of that next to closing spot. I had been looking for that spot for weeks, as I always have had one of those low comedy numbers in practically all my shows, just before the final scene. The number I have written should be sung by the two gunmen just before their final exit, on page 29 of Bella's original second act.
>
> The number is titled Brush up your Shakespeare. Its music is reminiscent of East Side, West Side, i.e., the typical Bowery song of the 1900s, and I firmly believe it will tie up the show into a beautiful knot. The lyrics are a series of gags, and I am almost sure that it will be a showstopper and everyone that I have played it to is crazy about it. No doubt Bella will kill herself when she hears that I have written a number for the gangsters, but it is the type of song that any two vaudeville mugs could put over.[47]

When Porter forwarded the song to Bella Spewack, he adjusted his view on the positioning of the song and showed an interesting engagement with the script:

> In case Jack has not told you, I have written a sock song for the two gangsters. I indicated that they could sing this song on their exit on page 2-6-29 of your book. But now, on further consideration, I think it might ruin the rest of the scene. So I suggest that they enter after the scene is finished in front of the curtain & sing it just before we go into the final Shrew scene.[48]

In addition to recognizing the nature of the song, one written for laughs before the close of the musical, Porter was concerned with how it might be delivered to best effect. Here he fulfilled a creative, and structural, priority of his own. He also perceived that "Brush Up Your Shakespeare" bridged the two sides of the show, playing textually with the works of Shakespeare while continuing the discussions of sex and power that were of particular appeal to him. "Brush Up Your Shakespeare" embodied the most salacious and bawdy aspects of *Kiss Me, Kate*, newly contextualizing *The Taming of the Shrew* in contemporary Baltimore by formally connecting the vaudevillian musical reference points with familiar Shakespearean banter and revelry.

With the repetitive Bowery Waltz as its vehicle, "Brush Up Your Shakespeare" is structured with an introduction, four verses and refrains, and two forced reprises. The song transforms the works of Shakespeare into shorthand for methods of sexual conquest, shoehorning the play titles into a series of jokes about class and sex. For example, Porter successfully incorporates Shakespeare's *Othello* and *Antony and Cleopatra* into a refrain, which requires absolutely no knowledge of the works:

> Just declaim a few lines from *Othella*
> And they'll think you're a helluva fella,
> If your blonde won't respond when you flatter 'er
> Tell her what Tony told Cleopaterer[49]

Porter laughs at the agency of the works of Shakespeare by relegating these play titles to the lexicon of the gunmen while capitalizing on their recognizable cultural capital. Not only does this song offer provocatively comic lyrics about the stereotypical romantic tussle between man and woman, in keeping with vaudevillian songs about seduction, it also incorporates a subtle commentary on our expectations of performance as this "spontaneous" number is obviously contrived.

Here, Porter navigates a very narrow line between shocking comedy about toxic masculinity and actual misogyny in the lyrics to this song. In a typed lyric sheet dated June 12, 1948, Porter completes the first refrain (also quoted above) with a rhyming couplet about violent assault, which was preserved in the script until Broadway:

> If she threatens to call the policy
> Put her wise to the Rape of Lucrecy.
> Brush Up Your Shakespeare
> And they'll all kowtow.[50]

An autograph draft in the same collection of lyrics at the Library of Congress indicates that Porter tested the rhyme of "Lucrecy" in other schemes, including with "And if still she won't say to you 'si, si' / Take a tip from <u>The Rape of Lucrecy</u>."[51] This lyric is included with other play titles (*Timon of Athens* and *The Merry Wives of Windsor*) that did not make it to any formal draft of the song. Porter likely persisted with this most provocative reference because it tied in a topical news item: Benjamin Britten's opera *The Rape of Lucretia* (1946) had its New York premiere at the Ziegfeld Theatre only a couple of blocks downtown and just one day before *Kiss Me, Kate*'s Broadway opening night. Nonetheless, its use—with the other lyric choices in "Brush Up Your Shakespeare"—remains noticeably edgy.

While this unused example is unflinchingly explicit, the finished song continues to play with boundaries of violence and consent, including unwanted contact and physical domination. Although *Kiss Me, Kate* can show its female characters participating in sexual games and violence, in productions that spotlight the misogynistic potential of the musical, "Brush Up Your Shakespeare" is confronting in its apparent trivialization of inappropriate sexual conduct. For some, it will not matter that Porter is critiquing the normalization of this behavior, and the absence of literacy needed to make these jokes, in other vaudevillian repertoire. Then followed by the sober and unfussy "I Am Ashamed That Women Are So Simple," it makes sense that some read these songs as relishing misogyny rather than shining a light to toxic masculinities and the way they feed each other.

Unlike "Always True to You (In My Fashion)" and, to a lesser extent, "Where Is the Life That Late I Led?," "Brush Up Your Shakespeare" is distinctively from the *Kiss Me, Kate* score because it ties vaudeville to Shakespeare without handling the plays in any substance. Unlike more transactional Shakespearean adaptations like *The Boys from Syracuse*, *Kiss Me, Kate* allows its audience distance from *The Taming of the Shrew* while preserving its basic details. It also represents Porter's most compelling creative philosophy in *Kiss Me, Kate*: he uses comedy that references Shakespeare, embodying the riskiest of his speeches (including those cut from *The Taming of the Shrew* in *Kiss Me, Kate*) without using Shakespeare's words, his plot, or his social context.

By using bawdy lyrics in this way, Porter aligned his own writing preferences—and a back catalogue littered with sexual innuendo—with a significant device used in various Shakespeare plays. Meanwhile, he constructs the couplets of "Brush Up Your Shakespeare" without requiring us to know anything about the real plays themselves. The joke is that two lowbrow vaudevillian characters are able to make their crass jokes with an extensive command of Shakespearean characters and play titles. The use of the Bowery waltz places "Brush Up Your Shakespeare" in raucous, extroverted, and crude musical company by comparison with the differently arch tone of "Wunderbar," which satirizes different cultural affectations. Porter amplifies this through the use of vernacular expressions, emphasized by rhymes that draw on dialect, such as the repeated "wow"/"kowtow" in the refrains or by forced rhymes such "flatter 'er" and "Cleopaterer". The lyric writing of "Brush Up Your Shakespeare" relies on a mannered perversion of received pronunciation.

In departing from the collaborative working space of New York for California, Porter came into his own voice and began a journey of clarifying the tone of *Kiss Me, Kate* while keeping command of a vast range of musical styles. In addition to balancing storytelling and characterization, Porter navigated musical lexicons of form and genre (e.g., setting "Why Can't You Behave?," a disappointed love ballad, in a blues style) while referencing *tempi* from Schubert in his draft lead sheet for "Finale Act One."[52] Importantly, Porter transitioned from setting a story to music to offering snapshots of personality and circumstance throughout *Kiss Me, Kate.* He found his own balance of reflecting the drama and keeping his own compositional preferences from musical comedy in the 1930s. As *Kiss Me, Kate* headed toward rehearsal, he placed his own authoritative voice on the score, giving the music an independent character from the script while being tightly on message with its creative aims. As Bella Spewack began to tussle with her contributions to the musical, Porter truly accessed his greatest creative powers.

5

Preparing *Kiss Me, Kate* for Broadway

With a script draft in hand, and Porter away in California, *Kiss Me, Kate*'s production team entered a new phase of recruitment and consolidation. Unaware that Porter would deliver "I Am Ashamed That Women Are So Simple" and "Brush Up Your Shakespeare" along with the finished Act Finales, Bella Spewack began to refine the first script for use when attracting performers to join the production. From June to December 1948, she worked on at least four further drafts: the interim script (summer, c. August 1948), the October 11 script, the rehearsal script (dated October 30), and the original Broadway script. Sam's name is added to the cover sheet of one of the rehearsal scripts and is then represented on the original Broadway typesets, suggesting that he formally re-entered the process after the interim script and casting were complete. When Porter rejoined the team for the winter, he'd also completed "So in Love" and "I Hate Men." Through rehearsals, he made minor structural and lyric tweaks to several of the backstage songs and oversaw text changes for radio and print publications to coincide with *Kiss Me, Kate*'s Broadway launch.

The initial creative and adaptation processes left several questions unanswered, offering different members of the teams their own specific challenges. The book, while on its way, included too many scenes, alongside a sizable score. The likely running time of *Kiss Me, Kate*, before any dance music and choreography was added, was too long. With Novotná unable to play Lilli/Katherine, they needed to find a replacement or reimagine who their leading lady might be, with possible consequences for Porter's vocal writing. Beyond this, the musical needed its remaining cast, a choreographer, financial backing, and to rehearse and tryout successfully before *Kiss Me, Kate* could hit Broadway.

This chapter maps how the creative team delivered *Kiss Me, Kate* to Broadway. It shows how Porter's unsolicited songs forced a change in Act 2 while Bella Spewack wrestled with how to keep the action moving in Act 1. In the end, she and Sam married her initial ideas, his Shakespeare edit, and a balance of slapstick comedy with a backstage romance to accompany their

Too Darn Hot. Hannah Robbins, Oxford University Press. © Oxford University Press 2026.
DOI: 10.1093/9780190082437.003.0005

Taming of the Shrew. Porter's already considerable song list was then made real by the interventions of Wilson and the show's choreographer, Hanya Holm. When Wilson hired Holm, she brought storytelling and staging sensibilities from other dance forms that helped to clarify and edit Spewack's drafts in preparation for rehearsal. Although she was new to musical theater, Holm's previous career enabled her to consider the balance of entertainment, spectacle, and narrative appropriate for *Kiss Me, Kate*. She also introduced her own agenda to locate and create engaging dance moments that prioritized the role of Bill/Lucentio and how he would contribute to the ecosystem of the musical. Leading actor Alfred Drake also made his presence felt when working with Wilson to stage the Shakespearean scenes and pressuring Bella Spewack to cut her original *Taming of the Shrew* dialogue, for which he had no taste.

By December 1948, multiple creative energies and agendas had assembled to make *Kiss Me, Kate* ready for performance. While it was not an exclusively harmonious process, the individuals involved were committed to the principles of musical comedy, including witty humor, physical comedy, recognizable character types, and leaving an audience thoroughly entertained. The Spewacks and Porter produced an appealing metatheatrical romp. Hanya Holm mimicked their writing choices, offering a tapestry of modern and reference dances that drew attention and praise. Meanwhile, Lemuel Ayers designed a sumptuous visual culture for *Kiss Me, Kate*, and especially for its *Taming of the Shrew*, which became a popular part of the marketing of the show and has dominated its branding ever since. The collaborative impact of their work yielded a show with such synergy that *Kiss Me, Kate* is used as both a template for "sophisticated" musical comedy, and as an example of Porter's attempt to write a newly narrative-driven "Rodgers and Hammerstein" type of show. When the musical opened in Philadelphia on December 2, 1948, the team were hopeful but uncertain of what to expect. By the time the first out-of-town notices were printed, everyone understood that *Kiss Me, Kate* would become the next great Broadway hit.

Finding Lilli

Following the loss of Jarmilla Novotná, Porter's biographers George Eells, David Grafton, and William McBrien all suggest that he and Spewack briefly flirted with casting another opera star with a similar appeal and profile: Lily Pons.[1] Pons, a French American coloratura soprano, was the darling of American opera, made numerous records, and appeared in a handful of musical films. With a light but immensely lyrical singing style, Pons (like Novotná) offered considerable dramatic and musical possibilities as well as a popular following. It is possible that Pons's recent appearance in Donizetti's *Lucia di Lammermoor* at the Metropolitan Opera might have inspired a noteworthy musical flourish in "Finale Act One," which happens after Lilli has been coerced back on stage, accompanied by the gunmen. The company play Katherine and Petruchio's wedding scene and their skirmishes are amplified by song as Lilli tries to get away from her captors and Katherine refuses to kiss Petruchio.

Fred/Petruchio begins "So kiss me, Kate / Thou lovely loon,"[2] introducing the closing lines of Shakespeare's play early for symmetry across the two act endings and is supported by the chorus who join the second refrain. Meanwhile, Lilli/Katherine interjects with "no" and "nay," finally stopping the song by calling Fred a "bastard." (This is also an echo of the set-up to "Another Op'nin', Another Show" at the start of Act 1.) The company gasps, and he chastises her: "O, Katey, that's a naughty word / Now, kiss me, kiss me, kiss me,"[3] leading to a cadenza on the word "never" heavily inspired by Lucia's mad scene.[4] This cadenza (see Figure 5.1) offers a short musical hiatus from the action and parodies the famous sequence between flute and soprano in Donizetti's Act 2, Scene 5. In *Kiss Me, Kate*, Porter mocks the high drama of the scene from *Lucia* by characterizing Lilli/Katherine as caught

Figure 5.1 Katherine's cadenza in "Finale Act One"[6]

between a temper tantrum and the thrill of showing off. This is especially ironic to those in the know because Lucia is in the throes of a breakdown, imagining happy marriage with her true love.

In the stage directions of *Kiss Me, Kate*, a chorus member then appears with a bird, embodying the other party in the call-and-response, before the cadenza is cut short as one of the gunmen who, deploying a vaudevillian maneuver, shoots the prop bird and foregrounds the double-sidedness of the song.[5]

To have an opera star, known recently as Lucia, interpret this display, "angrily, in the paroxysm of coloratura,"[7] while representing multiple levels of comic frustration, might have been extremely fun. This writing also demonstrates how Porter began to revisit humor layered with gags and intertextuality in the middle phase of writing *Kiss Me, Kate*. As noted in Chapter 4, the Act Finales become dramaturgically blurry as the boundaries between Baltimore and the *Shrew* are less clear. It is also open to interpretation whether Lilli/Katherine's cadenza is meant to seem rehearsed (as part of a scripted onstage performance of *The Taming of the Shrew* and as would happen in a performance of *Lucia*) or is a genuine ad lib by Lilli continuing to introduce chaos and disruption that is ended by the gunman's shot. With Novotná or Pons in role, the scene might even have played with them forgetting that they are in *Kiss Me, Kate* altogether, breaking character to be seen as the opera stars that they were. Porter introduced extra layers of performativity here, also apparent in "Wunderbar," that pitched the joke to multiple audiences at once.

There is also a subtle parallel that Walter Scott's Lucy Ashton, from whom Lucia di Lammermoor is drawn, is "a very minor role"[8] and that Donizetti makes her and her "inner self" the focus of his opera. *Kiss Me, Kate* addresses the comparatively small stage time of Katherine through Lilli's dominant character and her songs thanks to Porter's musical interventions. Where Susan McClary suggests that "a composer constructing a madwoman is compelled to ensure that the listener experiences and *yet does not identify with* the discourse of madness," Porter uses the quotation from Lucia as a joke to those in the know.[9] While Katherine has been described as ungovernable and unmarriageable, we have seen the beautiful, vivacious, and talented Lilli and also heard "I Hate Men," justifying Katherine's defiance of Petruchio. Where Lucia has "lost touch with outer reality,"[10] Lilli and Katherine are simultaneously reacting (quite understandably) in real time to the predicaments they face. The dynamic is inversed as Fred, and the gunmen, act in wholly fictional and comedic ways forcing Lilli/Katherine to respond in similar—laughably diva-like—terms through this unnaturally polished display of musical virtuosity. However, her cadenza is present, active, and defiant. Whatever we might say about the context she is placed in, Porter offers us a musical literary joke that the only rational reaction to the treatment faced by Lilli/Katherine is to be mad, here meaning angry.

With Pons out of the picture and no other star immediately in mind, the creative team approached the question of casting Lilli more flexibly, exploring a range of vocal talents on the way to their final decision. Bella Spewack, Ayers, Subber, Wilson, and Porter considered several "legitimate" musical theater actresses for Lilli/Katherine, including Nanette Fabray, whom some of the team went to see in *High Button Shoes*.[11] They also courted Broadway favorite Mary Martin, who had made her Broadway debut on the first Porter/Spewack collaboration *Leave It To Me!* In the show, Martin achieved critical acclaim for her performance of Porter's song "My Heart Belongs to Daddy" and then established herself as a star in Kurt Weill's *One Touch of Venus* (1943), also appearing in the less successful *Lute Song* (1946).

In the summer of 1948, Porter saw Martin perform in the national tour of *Annie Get Your Gun* while in California and invited her to read for Lilli. However, George Eells reports that Porter did not feel Martin showed suitable enthusiasm for the show.[12] Martin, by turn, was perplexed that Porter would not release the sheet music for her to take away and learn.[13] Simultaneously, she was pursuing the rights to James Michener's Pulitzer Prize–winning *Tales of the South Pacific* (1947) but was outbid by Rodgers and Hammerstein.[14] Knowing her interest, Richard Rodgers then approached Martin to read for and take the role of Nellie Forbush in their subsequent adaptation, and she decided that "the modern story" and music had "stronger appeal" than what she had seen of *Kiss Me, Kate*.

While this rejection may have come as a disappointment to Porter, he took up the cause of an alternative performer, B-movie actress Patricia Morison, as their leading lady. Morison had not performed on Broadway for four years since being cast in the musical *Allah Be Praised* (1944), which closed after only twenty performances. Previously to that she had played a minor role in a three-act operetta *The Two Bouquets* (through which she had become acquainted with Alfred Drake) in 1938.[15] During the run of *The Two Bouquets*, Morison was headhunted by Paramount Studios and had, with the exception of *Allah Be Praised*, worked solely in film before training for and starring in *Kiss Me, Kate*.

According to Morison, she had no idea about the details of *Kiss Me, Kate*, but, at the request of John C. Wilson, Porter gave her some of the songs to learn.[16] She then heard that Novotná had been provisionally cast and assumed that was the end of her association with it. However, Porter, knowing Novotná was out, promoted Morison's skills to Bella Spewack and Wilson, encouraging them to consider her:

> There are two girls here working like maniacs for the Kate part, 1) Ruth Warwick & 2) Patricia Morison. I don't believe Warwick can sing the part even if she studies all summer because singing is not her vocation.
>
> Pat Morison is, to me, a much more interesting possibility. Apart from her voice which is a high mezzo, she looks like Lynn Fontanne & Kate. As I wired Jack, she is working with Constance Collier on the Kate part. I feel strongly that this is our girl. So much so that I believe we might overnight, create a great new star.
>
> I can picture you putting your hat over your face & squirming in despair as I write you this, but this Morison girl is the one.[17]

Porter hoped for Spewack and Wilson to visit him California and see Morison together but was able to facilitate a meeting when she flew to New York to perform at a benefit with Bob Hope.[18] Morison had just signed contracts to film nine-part crime drama series, *The Cases of Eddie Drake*, for CBS when they decided to offer her the part and there was temporary concern that, after all, she would not be available either.[19] However, the format of making television series was still relatively new and the CBS producers agreed that Morison could film all her scenes, which were contained to a single set, in one session, fulfilling her contract, but also releasing her in time to rehearse for *Kiss Me, Kate* in the late fall.

Creative Tensions

Although Porter expected to welcome Bella Spewack to California, her visit did not happen. Meanwhile, the professional relationships between Bella and the producers became increasingly strained. Throughout the summer, Porter shared several items of correspondence with Spewack between June and August, indicating that she was being shut out of conversations with the other parties. While he does not exclusively defend Bella's work, Porter was largely critical of the script interventions made by other members of the team. This seems to reflect the close creative confidences established between the Spewacks and Porter earlier in the year.

In the same June letter that he introduced "Brush Up Your Shakespeare," Porter encourages Bella to keep him informed about the script and her progress, explaining: "You should write me always when there are book complications. In that way it will be easier for me to back you for I have great respect for your great talent and experience."[20] Three days later, he wired to confirm a (never realized) trip to California and affirm her resistance against other interference:

> I CANNOT = TELL YOU HOW DELIGHTED I AM THAT YOU ARE COMING OUT HERE JULY FIRST STICK TO YOUR GUNS ABOUT YOUR WONDERFUL BOOK AND I SHALL ALWAYS BACK YOU GREAT LOVE = COLE.[21]

By August 1948, Porter decided (motivations unclear) to loop Bella into the correspondence he was receiving about her from the producers. On August 10, she wrote to Ayers and Subber requesting that they allow her to work in her own way and in consultation with Porter before anyone else:

> I read your letter of August 7th to Cole, and greatly resent and take exception to your statement that you and Jack doubt that I will ever apply my full creative powers to the further improvement of "Kiss Me Kate," [*sic*] and that I have been confused, evasive and mentally distraught and will continue to be so. When you told me the changes which you wanted to have made in the play, there were some that I said I would make; there were others I refused to make, and there were still others that I said I would discuss with Cole and would then let you know whether I would make them. [. . .] After I hear from Cole Porter with respect to the changes I am discussing with him, I will discuss with you the changes to be incorporated in my revised script and will then submit same in conformity with my contract with you.[22]

Her letter continues to highlight that the producers have raised $100,000 to finance the production, using the script in its draft state, and they should therefore be satisfied that it is, and will be, of merit. She also warns them against making future changes to her work, indicating she has had sight of a new draft that reworked her script:

> I want to put you on notice however, that you had no right to rewrite my material, you have no right to disseminate the revised version, and you have no right to call in another person to rewrite my material.[23]

It is not immediately apparent what the revisions she is referring to constituted. It is possible that the interim script, which has some noticeable differences from the other drafts, was edited by the producers. However, it seems likely, given that this draft was shared with at least one a cast member and with Hanya Holm, that this version caused the producers alarm and led to their interference.

The interim script (and the October 11 script) are clearly working drafts that were intensely scrutinised by various individuals.[24] The copies preserved in the Holm and Spewack papers suggest that the interim script was predominantly used to respond to immediate feedback and to add the first of Porter's new songs. The October 11 script was intended to move the material on in time for a clean copy to be available at rehearsals. Bella Spewack's interim script is particularly heavily annotated with possible changes and Holm's includes a loose lyric sheet introducing "So in Love" to Act 1, dated September 8, 1948, and placing it slightly later in the revision process.

From the interim script onward, Bella Spewack's original Shakespearean scenes—where Katherine is disguised as a boy—are cut from Act 1, taking it from nineteen scenes to just nine.[25] The interim script replaces this content with the adaptation of *The Taming of the Shrew* found in Sam's April 28 pages, although there are some inconsistencies, unique to this script version. For example, "I've Come to Wive It Wealthily in Padua" is placed (as mentioned in Chapter 4) in its own scene at the start of *The Taming of the Shrew*.[26] Here, Petruchio opens the *Taming of the Shrew* performance before the first street scene in Padua and then "We Open in Venice" is played to an onstage audience as a street entertainment. Figure 5.2 also outlines the rearrangement of music in Act 1 of the *Shrew* that took place across drafts.

To make space for "Brush Up Your Shakespeare," Fred and Lilli's meeting at the stage door in Act 2, Scene 6, including a duet reprise of "We Shall Never Be Younger," was temporarily removed. Instead, the gunmen receive a call to notify them that their boss has been deposed, they void the IOU with Fred,

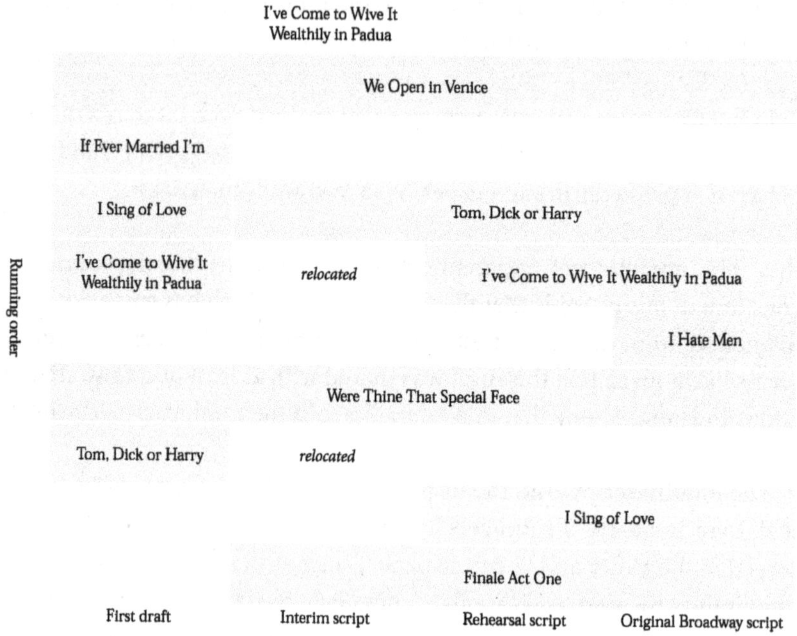

Figure 5.2 Timeline of songs in Act 1 of "*The Taming of the Shrew*" from first draft to Broadway

and go straight into "Brush Up Your Shakespeare," singing to themselves in the corridor. In Hanya Holm's interim script, she questions the sense of this, writing in the margin: "Fred—what happens to him? How about Fred joining in this thing?"[27] The draft offers no stage directions to indicate whether he observes their song (as in the MGM film adaptation) or leaves. As a result of these cuts, Fred and Lilli's plotline leaps from the dressing room scene with Harrison, where Fred belittles their prospective married life, to the finale of *Kiss Me, Kate*, with no reckoning of Fred's bad behavior or Lilli's choice to leave Harrison. Therefore, their reconciliation is confusing and makes the ending of *Kiss Me, Kate* messier than it had been before.

Casting Fred

With the script negotiations ongoing, the production team began to seek an actor able to handle the demands of Fred/Petruchio. They needed a person who could play Fred, the egoist impresario obsessed with his production and his ex-wife, and who could also deliver a compelling, roguish, and arrogant Petruchio while handling Porter's ambitious score. Although options like José Ferrer may have been discussed in early 1948, the producers seriously pursued Alfred Drake for the role fairly immediately. Drake made his Broadway debut in 1935 in the chorus of Gilbert and Sullivan's *The Mikado* before being cast in Rodgers and Hart's *Babes in Arms* (1937), in which he performed the title song.[28] His major break came when he starred as Curly in the original Broadway production of *Oklahoma!* (1943). After the success of *Oklahoma!*, for which he received the inaugural Drama Critics Award for Best Actor in a Musical, Drake continued to perform on Broadway in plays and stage musicals including Duke Ellington's musical adaption of John Gay's *The Beggar's Opera*, *The Beggar's Holiday* (1946), and a revival of Blitzstein's *The Cradle Will Rock* (1947).[29] Despite this experience, Drake's career, although successful, was slow-moving. He did not command the same interest or appeal as did more prominent figures like John Raitt (*Oklahoma!* US tour, *Carousel*, *The Pajama Game*, etc.) or film stars Howard Keel and Danny Kaye who both had successful runs in stage musicals.

In March 1948, Drake was starring in a new play by Allan Scott, *Joy to the World*, about a Hollywood executive who decides to speak out against the impact of censorship, which Subber and Wilson both went to see. They each admired Drake's performance and connected his character Alexander Soren—"also an egotist and also a show-off"—to Fred, concluding that he might be their ideal candidate.[30] After they approached him with the idea, Drake recalled going to the Waldorf Towers to meet Porter and hear him perform some of the songs:

> Cole was an interesting interpreter of his own lyrics and music, and he sang bits and pieces of it as he went along in his nightclubby sort of style. The opening scene was just terrible. Because he was following what Bella Spewack, who was the only writer at that point, had written. But the other songs sounded marvelous. Then I read the script, and I became thoroughly discouraged. You see, I'm afraid that Mrs. Spewack, placed in juxtaposition to Shakespeare, wasn't doing too well. That early script had all kinds of stuff in it that, to me, made no sense.[31]

Drake, like most of the musical's collaborators, was offered the first draft of *Kiss Me, Kate* as a sample of what the musical hoped to achieve. His mistrust of Bella Spewack's abilities permeates his later interviews about *Kiss*

Me, Kate and he places significant recognition with Subber and with Sam Spewack for "saving" the text. In May, the *New York Times* reported twice that Drake was being considered for the role, but Drake initially declined because of his concerns about the script.[32] He was also disinclined to return to musical theater:

> I wanted to go on in straight plays rather than go back to a musical. I always thought of myself as an actor, not as a singer, and I'm afraid I was bit of a snob about musicals, primarily because the characterizations were not fully developed.[33]

Subber and Wilson persisted, keeping Drake in the loop about the script development and sending him a redrafted script (presumably the October 11 draft), and he relented as he had no better offer after *Joy to the World* closed.[34]

In the full transcript of an interview given to *Show Music*, Drake suggests that he attempted to leave *Kiss Me, Kate* when he received the rehearsal script. In his version of events, he confronted Wilson and Subber, saying: "I told them they could go ahead and sue me, but I would not play that script."[35] He suggests that the producers then put him up to telling Bella that he did not like the script and insist that another writer be brought in to assist her:

> I didn't relish what Jack and Saint were asking of me. But <u>they</u> needed help, and so did I. So when I knew Bella would be in Jack Wilson's office, having downed a couple of stiff drinks first to get up the dutch courage, I staged the whole thing, working myself up to a degree of anger where I could say it all, and stormed out of the office. I <u>meant</u> what I said, but I . . . felt odd. I'm not proud of that kind of thing.[36]

According to Drake, the producers were then able to persuade Bella to bring on a second writer to help finish the script and she negotiated that Sam rejoin the project.[37]

The Drake interview transcript is the only account of the interactions between collaborators in late September and October 1948. However, his account is very elaborate and includes several suggestions about the script that reallocate credit for existing ideas to Sam despite them being present in the first draft that he (Drake) rejected. Three pages of transcript detail his memories of rehearsals, and Drake suggests, again, that Subber and Wilson encouraged him to challenge Bella about things he didn't like in the script. Between the letters in August and Drake's recollections of the final months developing *Kiss Me, Kate*, it seems clear that Bella Spewack's request to deal with Porter first and everyone else second was carried into the fall. Whether Drake really advocated for the producers on the scale he suggests or not, there were evident patterns of communication and concern about whether the script would blend effectively with the songs. However, the pressure to make this happen was laid firmly with the script (and not the song) writer.

While Drake's casting was trailed in the press for some months, Morison was only publicly mentioned for the first time on October 16, 1948, in the *New York Times*:

> No contracts have been signed yet, but according to certain parties Patricia Morison is set for one of the leading stints in "Kiss Me, Kate," the Cole Porter–Sam and Bella Spewack musical, which is due here on Dec. 29 under the banner of Lemuel Ayers and Arnold Saint Subber. Miss Morison, say the scouts, will sign the necessary papers over the weekend.[38]

Interestingly, Louis Calta's article is the only published reference to Sam Spewack as a collaborator on the project until late December 1948. Calta also reported that Harold Lang, a "young dancing star," had joined the cast, initially identifying him for the role of Fred/Petruchio, although there is no other evidence that Lang was ever considered for this part.[39] Lang developed his dancing career in the San Francisco Ballet and the Ballet Russe de Monte Carlo before joining the American Ballet Theatre in 1943. There, he originated the role of First Sailor in Jerome Robbins's *Fancy Free* (1944),[40] and solos in George Balanchine's *Waltz Academy* (1944) and Robbins's later one-act ballet *Interplay* (1945), among other important contemporary parts. He made the transition from ballet companies to dancing on Broadway in the following years and was particularly recognized for his role in Lawrence and Lee's *Look Ma! I'm Dancin'* (1948), directed and choreographed by Robbins (once again) and George Abbott with music by Hugh Martin. A friend of Subber's, Lang hoped the secondary lead role *Kiss Me, Kate* would help facilitate his new professional direction, offering him the dominant male dancing part without being too demanding in other areas.[41] In his contract, he was promised a solo song and the rejigging of music that reallocated "I Sing of Love" to the ensemble left him waiting for something to do.

With Fred, Lilli, and Bill all formally contracted, the remaining roles were finalized by the end of October 1948, just in time for the start of rehearsals. Lisa Kirk had performed in fundraising auditions for *Kiss Me, Kate* with Lorenzo Fuller, and they formally took their roles as Lois and Paul in the opening company.[42] Kirk had recently made her Broadway debut in Rodgers and Hammerstein's *Allegro* (1947), and Fuller had previously been a member of the original Broadway cast for *Finian's Rainbow* (1947). Next, Harry Clark and Jack Diamond were cast as the two gunmen.[43] Clark and Diamond were also known for their previous small character roles. Indeed, Clark changed careers from being a factory worker to a performer following his role in the union-sponsored revue *Pins and Needles* (1937). He had also had more recent success in the revue *Call Me Mister* (1946) as well as in the minor role Stanley in *One Touch of Venus*.[44]

The original Broadway cast of *Kiss Me, Kate* brought together a balance of young and relatively new performers with reliable but largely unexciting names. The producers were not able to secure a star, and it impacted on their ability to sell the show, delaying rehearsals while finances were secured.[45] In *The Cole Porter Story*, David Ewen represents these commercial concerns, explaining:

> If there were doubts about the capabilities of the young and inexperienced producers to mount a successful show, or about the willingness of Cole Porter to submit to the requirements of the new integrated kind of musical comedy, there were even greater ones inspired by the casting.[46]

Ayers, Subber, and Wilson had secured a leading actor who was uncertain about starring in a musical and had no respect for the book's author. He was starring opposite a moderately successful screen actress who was not known for her singing. Harold Lang was a rising dance star in dance, but Bill was not significant enough a character to guarantee the show's success. The prospect of this musical was simultaneously intriguing and full of risk.

Choreographing *Kiss Me, Kate*

With casting underway, the producers also addressed recruiting a choreographer. Discussions about the "right fit" began in June or July 1948, with Porter, Wilson, and Subber taking the lead in approaching and negotiating with the two contenders. The pattern of events indicates that, although they approached choreographers Agnes de Mille and Hanya Holm simultaneously, there was a strong preference for de Mille if she were interested. De Mille had developed a portfolio of Broadway hits alongside her work in contemporary ballet, gaining prominence in musical theater via her choreography for Rodgers and Hammerstein's *Oklahoma!* (1943), including the iconic "Dream Ballet" sequence. From *Oklahoma!*, she worked on *Bloomer Girl* (1944) produced by Wilson with set and costumes by Ayers, *Carousel* (1945), and *Brigadoon* (1947). In this instance, Porter led the negotiations, meeting with de Mille to play her some of the songs in development before departing for California.[47] After Porter left New York, Wilson continued conversation with de Mille through August, but in September, she told Wilson that she would not be available for *Kiss Me, Kate* because she had been offered the chance to do her own revue in London:

> I think you have without any question the score of the year and after talking to Saint this morning I am convinced that you also have a story with charming and effective theatre possibilities and one that would be considerable fun to work on. But the review [*sic*] gives me the opportunity of doing three numbers I have been wanting to do for ten years—just simply that. I have worked so hard and so long that I feel that I had better do what I want to do and not strain to dig up material where I have no spontaneous enthusiasm.[48]

The commercial advantage of securing de Mille, whom Wilson described as giving "enormous style, elegance, cachet and to put it bluntly, box office," might have helped their ongoing fundraising.[49] Regretful but charming Wilson responded rapidly: "We are now searching around for a Substitute with a capital 'S' but I completely understand and respect your choice and I think you know how sincerely I send you my fondest best wishes for the enterprise that you have embarked on."[50] Undeterred, Ayers, Subber, and Wilson immediately reconnected with German dancer and choreographer Hanya Holm, who had been away from New York in the summer, and she signed a contract to join the production on September 30, 1948.[51]

By contrast with de Mille, Holm had no experience of choreographing a Broadway musical before 1948. However, she enjoyed an extremely diverse and celebrated career that made her a viable and appealing option. Having arrived in America in 1931 to train as a dancer, Holm had developed an important reputation as one of "leading exponents" of dance in the United States.[52] When she made her New York debut in a historic production of a social protest piece *Trend*, *New York Times* dance critic John Martin wrote:

> here is a creative talent of the first magnitude to be reckoned with. Miss Holm brings to the business of composing a point of view totally different

> from that of any other of our major choreographers, and opens up a new vista for the production of great dance dramas.[53]

Holm ran her own dance company, which won numerous awards, designed ambitious works for her dance students, and in 1948, began to transition into commercial choreography, contributing to the four-act piece *Ballet Ballads* by Jerome Moross and John Latouche and movement in the play *Insect Comedy*.[54]

According to accounts amassed by Andrea Kraut in *Copyrighting Choreography*, Holm favored an improvisational route into creating her routines, providing dancers with a stimulus and developing the dance based on their instinctive movements.[55] For *Kiss Me, Kate*, she brought an experimental approach that challenged the classically trained dancers who did not welcome developing their own steps. In fact, Holm's early technique of developing dances favored the Black dancers cast to perform "Too Darn Hot." Fred Davis, Eddie Sledge, and Lorenzo Fuller (who was cast as Paul) had come from tap, vaudeville, and cabaret backgrounds and were experts in the dance styles they performed. Therefore, they were able to showcase their own moves and preferences (under Holm's name) in the dance extravaganza that closes the Act 2 opener.

As Holm got to work, she undertook a detailed review of the interim script and offered practical suggestions and some acerbic commentary in the margins. For example, she wrote "How did <u>he</u> get in here?!" when a *Taming of the Shrew* character randomly materializes without an entrance or a role in the scene.[56] Strikingly, Holm also wrote: "Too Goddamn much slapping!" next to the moment when Fred overpowers Lilli during their *Taming of the Shrew* skirmish.[57] Throughout the script, she noted clarifications about staging and identified potential locations for choreography beyond the dance breaks in Porter's songs. For example, she noted but crossed through "Choreograph transition time for change for gunmen" ahead of the final scene of Act 1.[58] Next to it, she had written and circled "Harold alone before tarantella," representing a feature moment for Lang before a company section to cover the offstage practicalities.[59] This allowed the gunmen to appear in *Taming of the Shrew* costumes, having just finished the previous Act 1, Scene 7, in their suits.

At all times, Holm was thinking about where everyone might be on the stage and why. Across the scripts in her papers,[60] Holm suggested changes to help the performers to move into dance in more logical ways. She particularly lobbied to showcase Harold Lang as the primary dance talent, often referring to "Harry" rather than "Bill" in her lists of characters where other actors remain anonymous. It's clear that she mapped out every potential opportunity for Lang to dance, noting Bill/Lucentio's character trajectory as she went, and thinking about how to capitalize on his abilities while servicing the script.[61] Among her notes on *Kiss Me, Kate* is one typed sheet on headed Hanya Holm Studio notepaper, which exclusively tracks Bill/Lucentio's involvement in the interim script. No similar records remain for the other characters. In one of several lists of planned choreography she made, Holm noted under "Why Can't You Behave?": "If possible, Another Op'nin' underneath (Song not good to dance to) but Harry should dance, it is his dance," and in another she labeled Lois's song: "Dance of Harold Lang."[62] While this ambition went unrealized in *Kiss Me, Kate* for Broadway, her suggestion is made good in the extended sequence starring Tommy Rall (a friend and contemporary of Lang who successfully broke into Hollywood as a feature dancer) following "Why Can't You Behave?" in the MGM film.

By contrast with this shift in focus, most of Holm's smaller suggestions were incorporated into the rehearsal script. In the first *Taming of the Shrew* scene, Holm combined these creative and practical instincts, noting that "Harold has to meet or see Bianca—both love at first sight."[63] It is not clear where exactly Holm felt that this interaction might happen or if it should be part of the choreography. However, there is a new stage direction added to the first *Taming of the Shrew* scene after Holm joined the production: "During dance, Bianca sidles forth, carrying a red rose, followed by Gremio and Hortensio carrying nothing. Lucentio tags along carrying books."[64] This detail ties together Bianca and Lucentio's first meeting with the subsequent "Rose Dance," Lucentio's solo exhibition of love for Bianca after "Tom, Dick, or Harry." When Holm was making her notes, the "Rose Dance" was an unrelated chorus number that had nothing to do with the suitors' plot. She recognized an opportunity to affirm the intertextuality in *Kiss Me, Kate* and demonstrate that, regardless of the message of "Tom, Dick, or Harry," Bill and Lois will also be united in the end.

Holm also attempted to embellish musical numbers including a narrative dance sequence for the instrumental break of "Were Thine That Special Face." In some of her diagrams planning out Act 1, she noted: "Cole wants to insert a dance—too risky to drag at this point."[65] Picking up on Porter's instincts to sexualize (and perhaps even romanticize) Petruchio, Holm designed a short sequence in which Petruchio is tempted by a dancer who embodies the mysterious woman imagined in the lyric. She also wrote and refined descriptions of the different women named in "Where Is the Life That Late I Led?," giving each person imagined characteristics. This included:

VENETIA: society type—talking much, loves drinking, always dewy eyed
LUCRETIA: young and gay—scandalous with the face of innocence
LISA: emotional, romantic
REBECCA: streetwalker. Tough—cold—hardboiled
MOMO: common. lower class. *Billig + willig. Geht mit jedem, tut alles für einen reichen Lieb haben.* [cheap and willing. Goes with everyone and does everything for a rich lover]
FEDORA: uncontrollable. Sex maniac. Nymphomaniac.[66]

After three pages of refining these descriptions, Holm then narrativized these personalities into an unrealized fantasy sequence titled "5 women."[67] In a handwritten outline, Holm describes Petruchio dropping his address book of names at the end of singing "Where Is the Life That Late I Led?" and entering the bedroom with Katherine as a translucent curtain falls across the scene. When lit from behind, the stage reveals five women in "odd positions" who are "all very surprised to find themselves in such a situation."[68] They "laugh it off," step through the curtain, and take it in turns to dance toward the bedroom door before Petruchio emerges to reclaim the book and returns (in his nightclothes) to bed.

Although this concept did not ultimately appear in *Kiss Me, Kate*, it gives an important indication of the process Holm undertook. In her notebooks, there are various snapshots of her plans for songs. For example, she envisaged dancers populating the stage during "Another Op'nin', Another Show" as commonly found stereotypes of dance rehearsal rooms including: "somebody deep breathing in Buddha position" "the over emotional—hysterical type," "the one who goes over passages marking it out," and "the comedy girl."[69] She also planned sections of movement, writing out rhythms, drawing diagrams of movement across the stage, and describing gestures that were then translated in person. For the "Rose Dance," she broke the movement into eighteen sections with an accompanying map of the stage tracking where Lang should end up at specific points. She also used the ambiance established in the setup of "Too Darn Hot"—noting "Boys play dice, cigarettes lighted + smoke coming up"—to establish how the dancing should be divided. Across six pages, she reworked the split of dancing in various ways, assigning different lengths of solo and combined dance windows, all measured in full or half verses and refrains, for Davis and Sledge and Lang.

In the reception to *Kiss Me, Kate*, Holm's choreography was routinely praised for its variety, bringing formal ballet aesthetics into conversation with styles including jazz, swing, and jitterbug. She embraced the different periods and energies of Porter's songs while attempting to incorporate classical, jazz, and contemporary features with different blending depending on the context. This was particularly noted in "Too Darn Hot," which Holm clearly demarcated as a "piece in itself" that "could stand alone" from the rest of the scene.[70] One review in (American) *Vogue* captioned an illustration of the sequence by Vertès as "*Kate*'s best number": "a big full-stage exciting production in which Harold Lang, Fred Davis, and Eddie Sledge dance with force and abandon against an imaginative stage-door alley in blues and brick-mauve."[71] Holm responded to the mixture of contemporary and traditional that Bella Spewack and Porter were chasing. Her success in interpreting their aims, and the popularity of her work in *Kiss Me, Kate* led Holm to hire an expert in dance notation in order to pursue the first ever certificate of copyright for dance in an American musical, which she achieved in 1952.[72]

However, Andrea Kraut also offers an important insight into the erasure of the dancers involved in the experiments that led to the final choreography of *Kiss Me, Kate*, explaining, for example, that the Labanotation for "Too Darn Hot" does not include movement for the three featured dancers. Instead, it provides the steps for the backing chorus. As such, the dancers who shaped one of the most successful spectacles of the musical are both absent and uncredited in the records of the choreography. The distinction of labor between the African American dancers who are referred to as "three Negroes" without character names throughout the script, by comparison to the white chorus members who are referred to as "Dancers," is stark, given what Holm contributed to the staging of *Kiss Me, Kate* before rehearsals began.

The Rehearsal Period

Rehearsals for *Kiss Me, Kate* began on November 1, 1948, and Wilson staged the production scene by scene with Drake's assistance and reference to Hanya Holm.[73] In addition to this, both Bella and Porter attended rehearsals frequently, with mixed effects on the show. Spewack noted that Porter was significantly more engaged with the production process of *Kiss*

Me, Kate than he had been during *Leave It to Me!*: "Cole attended practically all of the working sessions. He knew exactly how he wanted 'I Hate Men' to be staged. He was absorbed with every phase of the production."[74] Patricia Morison remembered that Porter had been inspired by a scene in an operetta by Victor Herbert "featuring a fellow who sang the line 'I want what I want when I want it' and then slammed the table."[75] He was determined that his reference point would be retained in the staging as well as the music in that moment.

Alfred Drake suggests that Bella Spewack's contributions to the rehearsal process were not so well received, complaining that she would talk over and undermine Wilson's instructions: "There are people who direct the directors. Bella did it a couple of times. She obviously didn't know what she was talking about."[76] Drake is noticeably critical of Bella Spewack whenever he refers to her, and it seems likely that she was also attempting to protect her work while finishing edits to the script with Sam. As noted previously, the earliest materials for *Kiss Me, Kate* make clear that she had a strong vision of the final musical that Drake refuses to credit her with. Simultaneously, correspondence between Bella's lawyer Edward E. Colton and the producers reveals that she was monitoring every aspect of the show's development. If Drake's attitude toward her is an indication of Bella Spewack's later working environment on *Kiss Me, Kate*, this caution seems entirely proportionate.

On November 11, Colton wrote to raise alarm that she was not receiving appropriate billing in the advertising for the show:

> Gentlemen:
> Bella Spewack saw a proof of an ad you are planning to run in which the name of John Wilson [*sic*] is in the larger type than her name. We are surprised at this and assume it is an error. The director's name is never larger than that of an author, particularly an author of the standing of Bella Spewack.
>
> Will you also call your press department's attention to the fact that on all forms of advertising and publicity without limit, wherever authorship credit is given to Cole Porter, credit should also be given to Bella Spewack. This also applies to radio broadcasts.
>
> Very truly yours[77]

Possibly, Bella sensed, even at this rehearsal stage, that once *Kiss Me, Kate* had opened to the public, the marketability and popular appeal of Porter's songs would surpass any critical acclaim the book might achieve, leaving her work behind. Certainly, Drake's assertions that the producers did not give her credit for the conceptualization of *Kiss Me, Kate* would have understandably put her on guard. Later, in 1950, Colton wrote to the producers again, expressing frustration about the continued need to raise this matter:

> Gentlemen:
> Bella Spewack has just seen some of the signs and posters for the road company of *Kiss Me, Kate* and notes that credit to Sam and herself is not in type at least 75% of the size of type in which the name of Cole Porter appears.
>
> Why there should be this continual trouble about size of credit is something I cannot understand. Won't you please look into the matter and give instructions to whoever is responsible for ordering this printed material to see that the Spewacks are given the credit provided for in the Production Contract.
>
> Will you please confirm that the improper posters and signs will be promptly corrected.[78]

Evidently, Bella Spewack was forced to survey material connected to *Kiss Me, Kate* to ensure that her (and Sam's) credits were not overlooked or limited in comparison to Porter and Wilson, who were both more easily recognized figures at the time. The letters quoted here form part of a wider campaign of recognition she was forced to instigate after *Kiss Me, Kate* had opened. Her hypervigilance has an uncomfortable symmetry with some of patterns of behavior her heroine is forced into, suggesting that while she worked affably with Porter, the conditions that Bella Spewack experienced toward the end of staging *Kiss Me, Kate* were increasingly hostile despite her significant impact on the show.

Among the cast, Lang appears to have inspired affection and annoyance in equal measures. Patricia Morison described him as a "lovely artist, naughty but loveable."[79] William McBrien suggests that Lang was keen to attract attention and once provoked the company by appearing "onstage with an excessively large codpiece. When Cole told Saint [Subber] to remove it, Saint said he was leaving that to Porter."[80] Lang was particularly frustrated that his solo song ("I Sing of Love") had been removed, and insisted they give him a replacement. Porter's last addition to *Kiss Me, Kate*, "Bianca," has a silly quality as Bill complains about Lois's affairs and then declares he loves her anyway. In style and tone, "Bianca" belongs with "Tom, Dick, or Harry" and

"Always True to You (In My Fashion)" as lightly arch showtunes with comic content that places Bill/Lucentio and Lois/Bianca firmly in the modern era. While there is no indication that it was tried in Act 1, it is telling that the refrain of Porter's song could happily slot in the opening *Taming of the Shrew* scene where Lucentio's solo had previously been. Porter added a verse, making "Bianca" about Lois, at some period after circulating the music and lyrics for the song's two refrains.

The final details of the production hinged on settling the songs for Fred and Lilli's backstage romance. As noted in Chapter 4, Porter pushed *Kiss Me, Kate* away from songs outlining reminiscence and toward demonstrations and expositions of feeling instead. Figure 5.3 shows how different iterations of songs that they considered would highlight the trajectory of the relationship once the space for dialogue was squeezed by a new scene for "Brush Up Your Shakespeare" and the later addition of "Bianca" to Act 2, Scene 4. Despite its early listing, and inclusion on flyers for fundraising performances, "So in Love" only entered consideration for this journey just before the rehearsal period. As noted previously, the first dated lyric sheet is from September 8,[81] and the song is introduced via pencil annotations to the October 11 and rehearsal scripts but only formally written into the original Broadway script.

Figure 5.3 Breakdown of songs in Act 2 across *Kiss Me, Kate* script drafts

Dramaturgically, "So in Love" replaces Porter's earlier duets between Fred and Lilli that look backward in their lives. Instead, they each perform the same song, reflecting on their connection to the other, in moments of heightened emotion. In Act 1, Lilli believes that Fred's gift of her wedding bouquet is a sign they will get back together. In Act 2, Fred knows he has ruined their reconciliation as Lilli leaves the production. "So in Love" tidies the Spewacks' script by musicalizing Fred and Lilli's connection when they are apart from one another, reflecting the evolution of the script from *Backstage*, where Fred and Lilli are still married and in love, to the original Broadway script where their emotional connection does not temper the way that they treat one another. Porter used his creative instincts to define almost every scene of Act 2, including the trajectory towards *Kiss Me, Kate*'s romantic resolution.

Visualizing *Kiss Me, Kate*

In imagining *Kiss Me, Kate*'s visual identity, Lemuel Ayers reflected Bella Spewack's boundaries against external intervention while working on the designs for the set and costumes. According to William McBrien, Ayers refused to show Subber his work until it was complete.[82] Subber was concerned that Ayers was attempting to stylize *Kiss Me, Kate* as "modern, à la Matisse" and not introduce appropriate contemporary and period designs that Subber felt fitted best.[83] One of Ayers's concept paintings for the set remains in the New York Public Library, suggesting that he in initially approached the backstage design impressionistically, with moody colors and a cluttered set (see Figure 5.4).

Certainly, descriptions of the original Broadway production design highlight that he used color in artificial and moody ways to contrast the dark and messy backstage from noticeably stylized and precise designs in *The Taming of the Shrew*.

However, it seems that Subber otherwise fretted needlessly as production photography from the original Broadway production includes naturalistic sets for busy dressing rooms and empty corridors opposing the boldly graphic mock-Tudor aesthetics in *The Taming of the Shrew*. Images by Will Rapport, Eileen Darby, and Stanley Kubrick were widely used in the publicity for *Kiss Me, Kate*, allowing publications to amplify Ayers's designs.[84] This allows us to see how Ayers also explored opportunities with the height

Figure 5.4 Concept art for the backstage set design of *Kiss Me, Kate*

of the stage, keeping the Baltimore backdrops simple and low and then using increasingly tall and angular shapes through the *Taming of the Shrew*. Holm had hoped that they would build a multilevel set to stage Bianca's wedding and the finale. Ayers clearly suggested or embraced this idea, designing vast geometric arches that tower over the company who are partially arranged on steps, creating a striking set piece to close the musical. Meanwhile, his use of contrasting color featuring large 2D black shapes backed on off-white, fabrics (harlequin-like and similar to costumes associated with the *commedia dell'arte*) became a staple of newspaper illustrations and the visual merchandising for the show. The backstage costumes also featured softer block colors and understated patterns allowing the visual culture of the *Taming of the Shrew* to sing.[85]

Holm and Ayers also shared an exploration of sixteenth-century Italian theater for the original Broadway production. For example, Holm thoroughly researched the *commedia dell'arte* as an integral influence for the *Taming of the Shrew* staging and dances.[86] Penny Gay outlines references to the *commedia* in *The Taming of the Shrew* in *The Cambridge Introduction to Shakespeare's Comedies*.[87] In her overview of *The Shrew*, she maps Petruchio, Baptista, Bianca, Lucentio, and the servants onto the typical characters of the *commedia* (e.g., Baptista as a Pantalone character, one of the *vecchi* or old men), separating Katherine's character as the notable exception.[88] This connection was clearly recognized by Holm, who hoped to construct a dance sequence around the characters of the *commedia* in parts of the Padua Street Scenes (Act 1, Scene 4, and Act 1, Scene 9). She sketched an image of "a pageant wagon of Florence (c. 1580)"[89] as part of her research, and later in her notes she incorporated this into her vision for *Kiss Me, Kate*, writing: "Players in Parade, Riding on simple cart + itinerant players follow by foot."[90] Holm's idea has been realized in several productions of *Kiss Me, Kate*, including at the Royal Shakespeare Company in 1986, where the leading actors arrive on a wagon very similar to Holm's drawing before "We Open in Venice."[91] Meanwhile, Ayers drew inspiration from images of touring minstrels and acting troupes in the shapes of his *Shrew* designs tying this vision together.

Testing a Hit

Kiss Me Kate had its first complete run-through at the New Amsterdam Roof on 42nd Street on November 30. With "[n]o costumes, no sets, no props or orchestra; only a rehearsal pianist," the cast were perturbed by the state of the show.[92] George Eells suggests that Subber hid playwright and director Moss Hart in the audience to listen to the performance, but Hart was not impressed by what he heard.[93] Similarly, Eells recounts that "the program concessionaire was so pessimistic that Dorothy Ross and her former husband George, who were the show's press agents, offered to buy the program man's share."[94] Indeed, George Ross was so discouraged that he also sold half of his share to the show's stage manager Ben Francis.[95] The short rehearsal process and last-minute changes to the show, including fixing "Bianca" and the "So in Love" reprise at the end of Act 2, did not improve expectations. Meanwhile, Alfred Drake had had a fall, injuring his knee, and had not been able to walk through the staging once they reached the tryout theater in Philadelphia. There was a prevailing worry that the content of the show and rehearsal outcomes were not strong enough to make a commercial hit. Patricia Morison remembered attempting to insist that "I Hate Men" be cut from the score: "All the others thought the song would make me look bad."[96] However, Porter was adamant that it would play well.

Despite this context, not everyone shared this outlook. Wilson wrote effusively to Porter's wife, Linda, before the company traveled to Philadelphia, for *Kiss Me, Kate*'s opening "out-of-town":

> Darling Linda,
>
> Who could have forseen [*sic*] on the Lido in 1925 a Cole Porter Kiss Me Kate [*sic*] staged by John C. Wilson?!! Not Princess Jane not even Elsa [Maxwell] and certainly not John C. Wilson.

> I am so proud and happy about it all and Cole aside from simply being a genius is the sweetest kindest person in show business.
>
> Good luck tonight—and even if some of the lights don't work—they will by Saturday![97]

In due preparation, Porter and Linda also traveled to Philadelphia, installing themselves in the Hotel Barclay to attend the first performance. Their suites, prepared by Porter's assistant, (also) Paul, were furnished with "a dozen boxes of Kleenex [. . .], a piano and such favorite paintings as a Dali, a Grandma Moses, and a Picasso."[98] Linda Porter's health was continually declining but she was determined to attend Porter's opening night as she had always done before.[99]

Kiss Me, Kate premiered at the Shubert Theatre, Philadelphia, on December 2 to hugely positive reviews. *Variety*'s out-of-town reviewer suggested that a few cuts to the show might be profitable for time's sake, but praised the unity between *The Taming of the Shrew* and Baltimore as well as the songs: "The dovetailing of the modern story has been so shrewdly done, and the Porter score is so consistently Grade-A that trimming will come hard."[100] Edwin H. Schloss, a friend of Bella Spewack's, also praised the first performance, describing the show as "brilliantly entertaining, charming and completely beguiling."[101] He continued:

> In an imperfect world, no one has the right to look for perfection in—of all places—a theatrical opening. But after getting off to a somewhat tentative start last night the production fairly rocketed to gay distinction and it's going to take a thesaurus-full of superlatives to give you a working blueprint of a delightful evening. [. . .] if you have any breath left add that Bella Spewack has contributed a witty and diverting book to hang the show on. [. . .] You will find no references to the First Folio, however, in Porter's lyrics which crackle with that elfin sophistication, highly spiced mockery and stylish nostalgia of which he is a master.[102]

Here, Schloss draws early attention to lack of Shakespeare in *Kiss Me, Kate* as well as the playful character of Porter's score, foreshadowing aspects of the critical reception to the original Broadway production. He later amplified his review when he wrote to Bella Spewack on December 8:

> I am writing this to you because I don't know whether Sam is with you or you are living in solitary sin. In either case, please thank him for the book

> which now occupies a prominent place on my "autographed by the author" shelf.
>
> I am not going to bother you with calls because I know you must be very busy these days arranging for the investment of that fortune "Out of Shakespeare by Spewack."[103]

Strikingly, Schloss's review and subsequent acknowledgment of the show's success to Spewack is one of the few instances in which a critic positively highlights the musical's libretto. Her insecurity about her intellectual property may also have developed with wider criticisms of the script in the Philadelphia reviews, which were subsequently reiterated after the Broadway opening. For example, Jerry Gaghan wrote in the *Philadelphia Daily News* that "the show needs speeding in the early sequences and the second set has stretches of sag. These are largely book faults, which Bella Spewack can remedy. Some of her gags and situations also need artificial respiration and they would be better dropped."[104] Maurie Orodenker also commented that "whatever comedy creaks in the Spewack lines and situations, the Clark and Diamond combo does more than make up for it with the high hilarity of the 'Brush Up Your Shakespeare' number. 'Stopping the show cold' is merely lukewarm wordage for their wit here."[105] The latter review specifically suggests that the performers and score compensate for problems with the book, an opinion that has been subsequently repeated by Ethan Mordden, in his survey of the 1940s: "It's my contention that *Kiss Me, Kate* is a show we love not despite its sloppy realism and irrelevant hunks of Shakespeare but because the score is so good that the rest doesn't matter."[106]

The collaborative labor that shaped *Kiss Me, Kate* is easily downplayed in the critical reviews of the show, although there is praise for all the creative team if you look hard enough. While the Spewacks would continue to be recognized for their role in the triumph, the musical cemented Cole Porter's place as one of the great musical theater songwriters and lyricists. However, the genesis I have constructed demonstrates the numerous and varied creative inputs that informed the development of *Kiss Me, Kate* and amplified Porter's songs. Ayers and Subber imagined the concept. Bella Spewack breathed life into the characters, while she and Sam juggled the Shakespearean adaptation. Cole Porter excelled with the stimulus he was given, enabling Wilson, Ayers, and Holm to define the visual culture of *Kiss Me, Kate* before it reached Broadway. Porter's score is undeniably exciting in its diversity and sparkle, but *Kiss Me, Kate* is rich because of the many brains that brought every aspect to life.

6

Kiss Me, Kate after Broadway

When *Kiss Me, Kate* reached Broadway, there was widespread admiration for the musical, and it became one of the tickets of the season. After nineteen months, the producers were able to relocate the production from the New Century to the Shubert Theatre, taking *Kiss Me, Kate* from West 58th Street, out of the way of most of the major theaters in Manhattan, to West 44th Street, just moments from Times Square. However, Porter's songs continued to attract more column inches than the contributions of the other creatives involved. Headlines such as "Cole Porter and Shakespeare Collaborate in *Kiss Me, Kate*,"[1] "Cole Porter Tunes Click in *Kate*,"[2] "*Kiss Me, Kate* Porter's Best, a Terrific Hit,"[3] and "Of Sweet Kate and Mr. Porter"[4] indicate the centering of the songwriter in the show's early write-ups.

In the *New York Star*, John Lardner referred to Porter as "the true star of the show," continuing: "The composer has provided songs without stint. His score is a skillful and curious mixture of Shakespearean words, airs, and notions with standard Porter songs."[5] Meanwhile, the *New Yorker* opened its review with "Any man who will rhyme 'Cressida' and 'ambassador' is capable of practically anything."[6] While this early reception was widely positive, with only minor criticisms of the Spewack book, initial press for *Kiss Me, Kate* is underscored by two main themes: *Kiss Me, Kate* has no bad songs and it is quintessential Cole Porter, executed perfectly. It is perhaps this unevenly weighted acclaim that encouraged Bella and Sam Spewack to invest considerable energy in the future life of the stage show, protecting their rights and intellectual property very cautiously.

With a rich and diverse international performance history, a chapter on *Kiss Me, Kate*'s life on stage since 1948 might include very many stories. In the decade following its Broadway opening, the musical had a brief revival in New York (1952), was taken on national tour twice (1950 and 1955), and was staged in numerous international locations including London (1951), Melbourne and Sydney (1952), Stockholm (1952), Frankfurt (1955), and Warsaw (1957), making it the first American musical to be licensed in Soviet-allied Poland. As a result, this chapter might trace the process of locating

Too Darn Hot. Hannah Robbins, Oxford University Press. © Oxford University Press 2026.
DOI: 10.1093/9780190082437.003.0006

translators and reimagining the complex idioms of this musical across decades and continents. The Spewack papers have a fascinating trail of correspondence, addressing rights and translation priorities across nearly forty years of productions. This includes tantalizing glimpses of the fraught pursuit of poet Louise de Villmorain to create a definitive French translation of the musical and disagreements about local radio and television rights to *Kiss Me, Kate* that were not referred to the Spewacks for script approvals.

Instead, this chapter spotlights three productions of *Kiss Me, Kate*, which reveal how different members of the creative team stayed with, and departed from, the performance history of *Kiss Me, Kate*. Spanning 1950 to 1970, I consider the politics of control over the property and in securing *Kiss Me, Kate*'s stage legacy until the death of Sam Spewack in 1971. Porter and Wilson quickly moved on to new projects after *Kiss Me, Kate* hit Broadway, using lawyers and light touch interactions where they were consulted. Meanwhile, Sam and Bella Spewack paid close attention to the musical's international spread and reputation, making interventions about directorial choices including staging and casting as well as any proposed changes to the script. From the original London production (1951) to the second London revival (1970), we see how the Spewack's involvement preserved aspects of *Kiss Me, Kate* in its subsequent stage life. Simultaneously, the Vienna Volksoper production (1956) and the second London revival illustrate how *Kiss Me, Kate* lent itself to opera companies seeking new commercial repertoire. This broadened the musical's programming appeal, securing multiple kinds of audiences for decades beyond its original Broadway run.

To establish the environment for this history, the chapter begins with the conflicts between the Spewacks, the Broadway, and the West End producers of *Kiss Me, Kate*. In this section, we see negotiations between financial pragmatism and creative and commercial instinct from three different perspectives. Then, we move to the 1956 production at the Vienna Volksoper, which introduced *Kiss Me, Kate* to the repertory of opera and operetta companies around the world. The Viennese approach of merging their "house style" with American influences contrasts with the violent disagreements during the 1970 Sadler's Wells revival, which returned *Kiss Me, Kate* to the first London theater it had appeared in. Through numerous draft letters and the formal correspondence between company management, the production director, and Sam Spewack, we see how a more traditional approach to Shakespeare interrupts a production of *Kiss Me, Kate*, including reimagining sections of the songs.

Kiss Me, Kate in London

With a US tour in hand, Ayers and Subber began considering a UK transfer for *Kiss Me, Kate*, and in 1950 British theater producer Jack Hylton flew to New York to negotiate the exclusive stage rights for a London production. Hylton had established himself in the 1920s as a prominent bandleader, recording artist, and savvy businessman. He was an early advocate of the Decca record label, turning down the option to sign with the established HMV in the early 1930s. At the outbreak of the Second World War, his band dissolved when many of the players were called up to serve. However, Hylton built a second career as a manager and producer in British theater. Before securing rights to *Kiss Me, Kate*, Hylton had previously produced a successful revival of *Irene*, the London transfer production of *High Button Shoes*, and a hit production of *Annie Get Your Gun*. He was therefore a reliable person to trust with the British version of *Kiss Me, Kate*.

From early in the process, Hylton experienced frustration with the American producers who renewed their roles for the London production. As part of the negotiated contract with Hylton, they also committed to providing the West End *Kiss Me, Kate* with a director. Hylton indicated John C. Wilson as a first preference to maintain as much continuity between London and New York as possible. However, his wishes were thwarted when the producers refused to negotiate terms to match Wilson's contract (a 2% royalty) on Broadway. Wilson describes the conflict that took place in his autobiography, explaining:

> I had neglected to insert in my original [Broadway] contract that my fee for any London engagement would automatically be equivalent to my New York percentage. Lem Ayers took advantage of this and insisted that as it was my third job on Kate, I should settle for half of my previous royalty. I must say that Jack Hylton was for me all the way, but Lem was firm and I was firmer.[7]

This separation from Wilson was unwelcome, especially as the producers had previously been on very cordial terms. It also forecast the tension of priorities between sides during the later running of *Kiss Me, Kate*. Selma Tamber, secretary to Ayers and Subber's The Salem Company, came to refer to Hylton as the "Inspector General" in his dealings with the American parties.[8] However, Ayers and Subber were also juggling several concerns including that, by June 1950, *Kiss Me, Kate* on Broadway was beginning to run at a loss.

In a private memorandum about her relationship with the producers, Bella Spewack also noted that disagreements were emerging between Ayers and Subber in private. She suggested that Subber was keen to engage Sam Spewack to replace Wilson as the London director, given his proximity to the Broadway production, but that she "feared" that Ayers hoped to fill the role himself while Sam's mother was ill and he might reject an offer if it were made.[9] According to Spewack, Subber emphatically rejected supporting Ayers as director and that it would only happen "over his dead body."[10] This disagreement laid the groundwork for the dissolution of Ayers and Subber's working partnership, which happened in the months following the opening of Porter's next musical, *Out of This World* (1950). Ayers and Subber had continued on with Porter, as had Hanya Holm as choreographer, Pembroke Davenport as musical director, and Robert Russell Bennett as orchestrator. They also secured Agnes de Mille with overall responsibility for staging. This transition indicated the hopes of starting a rolling collaborative outfit in the forward movement from *Kiss Me, Kate* to *Out of this World*, but neither the team nor the new musical thrived during this second endeavor.

Eventually (and after the opening of *Out of This World*), Sam agreed to direct *Kiss Me, Kate* in London in December 1950, subject to Wilson's being credited with the original staging. Following the insistence of Bella Spewack and the hopes of Hylton, the producers also signed Patricia Morison to star alongside Julie Wilson as Lois and Bill Johnson as Fred. Wilson was a popular choice with the Americans, having briefly performed in the US tour and on Broadway while Johnson was a known quantity to both Hylton and the Americans, having led a production of the Spewacks' *Boy Meets Girl* and Hylton's *Annie Get Your Gun*. In contrast to the tentative interest in *Kiss Me, Kate* before it previewed in America, the British press were thrilled by the import of two glamorous American actresses. This dominated the post-opening publicity and allowed Julie Wilson to cement a career in London after the production closed. Happily for Morison, her role in the London production became an important selling point for Hylton, contrasting with the overall reticence about her return to musicals when she was cast for Broadway.

The appeal of the American actors and the hype surrounding *Kiss Me, Kate*'s surprise success on Broadway meant that the London production was hotly anticipated. It received widely positive reviews in tryouts, with the *Daily Telegraph* highlighting the attendance of Princess Margaret at the first preview performance as additional endorsement.[11] The *Daily Mirror* also reported that eager audience members had queued at the Coliseum for up to twenty-two hours in order to purchase tickets.[12] This anticipation became a focus point of several of the West End reviews.[13] For example, *The Times*' reviewer prefaced their column on *Kiss Me, Kate* by noting that:

> It has been for some time in the public minds that this renowned American musical was bound to succeed in London—a tribute, it is pleasant to think, to the potency of travellers' tales rather than to skilful advertising. However, memory recalls no audience more murmurously confident before the curtain rose of being about to enjoy itself, and the boxes on either side of the house toasting each other and the occasion in champagne lent an unwonted sparkle to the impression.[14]

Public anticipation in London was responsive to the American reviews, which highlighted *Kiss Me, Kate* as a sparkling night of carefree entertainment. London reviewers celebrated Morison's performance as central to the production's success: "Miss Morison sings excellently, and is a shapely and harmonious creature, wholly worthy of the praises lavished on her in America."[15] There was also universal praise for the costume design and for Holm's choreography: "The contribution by Hanya Holm, famous American modern dance creator to *Kiss Me, Kate* is considerable. Her dances are the decorative cement that binds the show together."[16] However, there were some criticism of the humor in the backstage script.[17]

The behind-the-scenes environment continued to bubble as the factions—the producers vs. the Spewacks vs. Hylton—solidified. In May 1951, Bella Spewack discovered an advertisement for a Columbia recording of the London cast for which she, Sam, and Porter received no royalty. She felt that Ayers and Subber had monopolized *Kiss Me, Kate*, asking the others to "participate in their losses—not their profits."[18] There is little correspondence about the fallout of her discovery, but documents from the time show that Lemuel Ayers was the last person to have his royalty cut when they were attempting to salvage the finances of the original Broadway production.[19] Meanwhile, by June 1951, the producers feared that the London *Kiss Me, Kate* had lost its luster, with Selma Tamber confiding to Bella Spewack that although Hylton was visiting New York, he had not met with Ayers and Subber. In July, Bella's attorney confirmed that the production was experiencing considerable losses. However, Hylton, undeterred, approached the American creators to pitch a ninety-minute radio version of *Kiss Me, Kate* to air on the BBC in August 1951. Despite the express encouragement of her legal advisers, Bella Spewack (and Sam) flew to London from Europe to stop the recording from taking place, with one newspaper article quoting them as saying: "We will allow no adaptation unless we write it."[20]

Hylton had hoped to put together some scratch marketing to keep the show interesting to British audiences in London before a planned tour. However, the Spewacks' insistence that no radio adaptation could happen unless they developed it was just the start of their conflict. The Spewacks entered fraught exchanges with Hylton about keeping Morison in the production after she had asked to leave. He wrote to them on October 5, 1951, to say he had done all he could to keep her in the show but had replacements including Morison's ultimate successor, Helena Bliss, ready for them to approve.[21] Hylton eventually managed to persuade Morison to stay in the role until Christmas while organizing private coaching for Bliss with Sam before she joined the production in London. However, Bella Spewack fretted that the English replacements for American cast members would not carry the intention of the show over to the audience, and she wrote to Hylton to demand additional rehearsals led by Sam to bring the new cast up to scratch:

> It's therefore my wish—and Lem and Saint and Cole all feel the same way—that it be b- [missing text] if you asked Sam to get over to London about the same time as Miss Bliss gets over. No stage manager, no matter how good, can direct. You know that. So let's pull together, please. There's a property at stake.[22]

Hylton, who becomes noticeably terse after the failed radio production, responded to Bella's request with great irritation, explaining that Bliss was planned to shadow Morison before taking over as Lilli and that Bill Johnson who was "giving a splendid performance" as Fred would be staying in the company to ease the transition.[23] His letter ends:

> You must forgive me saying, Bella that perhaps unwittingly you give the impression that we are altogether stupid and unintelligent on this side. It seems, therefore, necessary to remind you that I have much more at stake that [*sic*] you have and am not likely to **neglect** it. The production is looking absolutely "bang up to the minute" and much better than any "Kate" productions I saw on your side.[24]

In the end, Hylton chose peace, capitulated, and Sam held a handful of rehearsals with the new company before the winter changeover. Although the new casting led to a small spike in ticket sales, the producers were dismayed to hear critical reports of the new cast's performances. Selma Tamber relayed these concerns to Bella, writing:

> I do hope [. . .] you are able to beat Hylton's brains in—I have heard lots of reports on the English company and know that he hasn't done a thing to keep the show the way it should have been, etc.—I agree with you about the billing and program—he could be forgiven anything in [*sic*] the replacements were good.[25]

Whatever view the Americans took, Hylton maintained to the last that he would never facilitate the failure of a commercial project or sabotage a cast. However, Bella, fueled by Tamber's secondhand reports, maintained that Hylton did not care about the continued success of the show.

The West End production of *Kiss, Me Kate* closed after a very respectable 501 performances and was followed by a popular national tour, which Hylton invested considerable marketing in. This included trailing "return performances," meaning that *Kiss Me, Kate* played a second fixture in venues like the Manchester Opera House, as "bowing to popular demand." Such energy directly counteracts the fears expressed about Hylton's commitment to the musical, but the details of his relationship with the Spewacks as directors, authors, and interested parties provide the first glimpse of the scrutiny of negotiations that took place as *Kiss Me, Kate* was marketed to producers across Europe and in Australia. Even as a successful and experienced producer took on their property with guidance from Sam and support from Hanya Holm who adjusted her choreography for the stage at London's Coliseum, Bella Spewack and the producers became distrustful of Hylton's creative and commercial investment in *Kiss Me, Kate*. By blocking the radio broadcast, it is possible that they actually shortened the life of *Kiss Me, Kate* in London. By contrast, Porter dealt with the production through his lawyers unless contacted by Holm. She submitted some brief notes to him when the production was being rehearsed and couriered a handful of minor lyric changes back to Hylton. Otherwise, Porter retreated from the life of *Kiss Me, Kate* on stage as he moved on to new musicals. One letter in the Spewack papers suggests he discussed making *Can-Can* with Bella and Sam, but ultimately this marked the end of their close working relationship.

Kiss Me, Kate in Vienna

When *Kiss Me, Kate* was first suggested as new repertoire to the management of Vienna's world-renowned Volksoper, Austria had just gained independence from occupying Allied forces. The decision to incorporate an American musical into their season was suggested by Marcel Prawy as an innovative way to reinvigorate box office sales as the city was rebuilding itself for the future. Prawy felt Cole Porter's songs (especially "Night and Day" and "Begin the Beguine") were sufficiently well known in Vienna for the music to appeal. Meanwhile, Shakespeare was a staple in Viennese theater repertory and, as J. Daniel Jenkins puts it: Prawy "believed that the Shakespearean cachet might lessen any objections that the musical was too 'low culture.' "[26] It also aligned with a cultural policy agenda introduced to rehabilitate American work for Austrian audiences.[27]

His proposed production was met with significant resistance from the opera house staff, including members of the orchestra who wrote to management in protest about the introduction of frivolous, commercial material to a cultural center. In a retrospective interview, Prawy suggests that management agreed to the experiment as a possible box office opportunity as well as a strategic alliance with the American delegations who were resident in and near the city.[28] Prawy began rights negotiations for *Kiss Me, Kate* in mid-1954 while other German-language negotiations were also taking place. However, the Volksoper scheduled a noticeably short preparation period to organize the production once it was confirmed.

On December 25, 1955, Prawy secured Heinz Rosen to direct and choreograph the production, even though Rosen had never seen or read *Kiss Me, Kate*. Instead, Prawy described the musical to him, and Rosen agreed, setting the show's premiere for February 14, 1956.[29] Together, Prawy and Rosen shared the task of designing and rehearsing *Kiss Me, Kate* across just six intervening weeks despite its being a new undertaking for the venue.[30] According to Jenkins, "no rehearsal space at the Volksoper was made available for *Kiss Me, Kate*," so Prawy was forced to improvise at local hotels and restaurants to bring the production together.[31] Meanwhile, he hosted lectures and concerts of songs from American musicals in order to prepare the local appetite for a change in musical style.[32] Prawy also prepared an essay for the program placing American musicals within the history of operetta and connecting it to the prestigious authors like Voltaire (*Candide*) and Shaw (*My Fair Lady*), who had inspired many of the relevant hit shows.[33]

Conscious of the unfamiliar musical styles in sections of *Kiss Me, Kate*, the Volksoper recruited three American singers, Brenda Lewis, Olive Moorefield, and Hubert Dilworth, to perform Lilli, Lois, and Paul. Brenda Lewis, an American soprano and regular star with the New York City Opera, had interpreted many operatic and operetta roles, including performing *The Merry Widow* alongside Jan Kiepura on Broadway (1944) and Rosalinde in *Die Fledermaus* for a TV broadcast filmed at the Metropolitan Opera (1954). In 1954, she was one of the original Broadway cast of the musical comedy *The Girl in Pink Tights*. Following the success of *Kiss Me, Kate* at the Volksoper, she returned to star in their second musical *Annie Get Your Gun*, highlighting the versatility of her voice to interpret a Cole Porter song or a Berlin ballad alongside key operatic leads like Carmen and Salome.[34]

As Lilli was interpreted by an American, Prawy cast the Austrian baritone Fred Liewehr as Fred to make the intercultural layers of his vision manifest. However, he looked to America again to cast Paul, and then Lois, acknowledging that their musical demands required different kinds of voices. Like Brenda Lewis, African American baritone Hubert Dilworth (cast as Paul) sat between both classical and musical theater environments, appearing in *Carmen Jones* (1943) on Broadway, and in multiple versions of *Bloomer Girl* (1944), including the original Broadway cast, the national tour, and the City Center revival (1947) while also delivering solo recital performances of music ranging from Scarlatti to Schumann and Rachmaninoff. Dilworth was able to swing the role while having a voice in character with the other performers.

Alongside Dilworth, Olive Moorefield, also a Black actress and singer, broke boundaries in this production when she was cast as Lois. Moorefield had sung in some of Prawy's preparatory concerts and was familiar to the local audience, so that he felt able to dismiss concerns about colorblind casting in the internal *Taming of the Shrew* production.[35] Aged just twenty-four, Moorefield was the first Black actress to take on one of the four leads in *Kiss Me, Kate*, extending the limited representation Porter and the Spewacks had originally written into the show. After the Volksoper success, she leveraged this break and continued to sing Lois in productions in Belgium, France, and Germany as well as in a television adaptation made for Italian audiences. Making several returns to the Volksoper, she also co-starred with William Warfield in the Volksoper's premiere of *Porgy and Bess* in 1965, before becoming a popular performer on variety television, especially in Germany.

With the American contingent secured and tasked with learning *Kiss Me, Kate* in German as quickly as possible, attention turned to finalizing other components of the production. For example, he invited Austrian-American conductor Julius Rudel to return to Vienna for the first time since Rudel had emigrated to the United States in 1938. Rudel had previous experience of musical direction of *Show Boat, Carousel,* and *Brigadoon* on Broadway and undertook a ruthless selection process of "the youngest, most attractive, and slimmest" members of the Volksoper chorus, who were then drilled in ballet.[36] Meanwhile, the house ballet dancers were also taught to sing in order to provide the musical with a viable, and substantial, chorus. Rudel reflected that: "To have singers moving and dancers singing was a revolution in Viennese production."[37] Rudel and Prawy were also concerned with doing the music full justice, so they recruited additional musicians from Viennese dance and jazz bands to encourage the house players to become comfortable with the swing and rhythm sections of several songs.

The substitutions and musical adjustments required six orchestral rehearsals for forty-five players, in contrast to the Volksoper's usual two. Reciprocally, the external musicians faced their own struggles in passages of the score that included stylistic nods to more classical forms.[38] However, the extra rehearsals allowed the two sides to collaborate, facilitating a free-style section for the band musicians during the dance break of "Too Darn Hot" ("S'ist viel zu heiss!"). Through their combined force, the Viennese production featured an orchestra that was nearly double the size of the original Broadway pit, pairing inexperienced opera performers with versatile singers familiar with musical theater. This was matched by a substantial set and costume budget that allowed the house builders to construct a real wall with a working fire escape as part of the set, making real the different heights imagined by Lemuel Ayers.

On opening night, Prawy's *Kiss Me, Kate* was described as a sensation, with the *New York Times* reporting that:

> The enthusiastic first-night audience in the Volksoper applauded stamped and cheered. The most notable success of the evening was the Austro-German Ballet, with the dances that, since they needed no translation, produced major audience reaction. The costumes were eye-filling.[39]

The success prompted broadcasters to cover the production, introducing (at least according to Prawy) television cameras to the Volksoper for the first time.[40] Because of the early concerns expressed by many of the house staff and artists, Prawy was surprised and pleased to discover that the reception of *Kiss Me, Kate* also had a positive impact on the company, which became hugely enthusiastic about the show. A letter from US Cultural Affairs Officer Sam H. Linch to conductor Rudel especially praised the orchestral playing, closing by highlighting how the audience responded to the skill of the players: "The information has come to me that some of the orchestra members are quoted as saying that this is the first time that they have ever really heard such applause for their efforts."[41]

The combination of support by the production team, performers, and audiences solidified *Kiss Me, Kate* in the Volksoper repertory and led Prawy to mount a touring production with Moorefield beginning as Lois and closing as Lilli. Although Prawy also considered *Annie Get Your Gun* as a possible launch work for this new direction of programming, it seems that *Kiss Me, Kate* offered a fine balance of music that would be both familiar in its classical modes and different in its jazz idioms, while being a viable option for the house to stage itself. With the Volksoper resources, they were able to rival if not surpass the production values on Broadway, using the set piece nature of *Kiss Me, Kate* (and *The Taming of the Shrew*) as a vehicle for audiovisual spectacle. The comedy of the book also lent itself to local interpretation, with Prawy securing permission to allow the comedians playing the gunmen absolute freedom to ad lib, as was the house custom for similar roles in operetta. Therefore, *Kiss Me, Kate* presented a challenging but interesting possibility to house and audience alike. Prawy foresaw that a production done with sufficient investment (if not time) could offer something new and desirable where more traditional opera venues were unwilling to engage with the themes and sounds of new opera being developed at the time.

Prawy revived *Kiss Me, Kate* at the Volksoper in 1957 and then organized openings in Brussels and in Trieste, where he briefly pursued casting Patricia Morison opposite Jan Kiepura. He wrote to Bella Spewack in late 1957, asking her to have patience with the early European negotiations and celebrating the first revival of the Volksoper production as proof of *Kiss Me, Kate*'s longevity in the company's programming: "It is grand that we have really succeeded in making 'repertory' out of your wonderful *Kate*."[42] Two years later, Bella Spewack wrote effusively to Porter about the ripple effect of Prawy's vision in Europe:

> Your orchestra numbers 55!
>
> Ours will be the first American musical to play the opera house in English or French.

> It will mark KATE's thirteenth language!
> If it's at all like the Vienne [*sic*] Volksoper production, it'll be dreamy.[43]

Her enthusiasm for the Viennese version of *Kiss Me, Kate* is significant because it did not reproduce the original Broadway production and included several "local" editorial changes to satisfy the Volksoper's management and resources. Equally, she and Sam were not involved in the rapid development and rehearsal of the first Volksoper production. Prawy's *Kiss Me, Kate* confirmed that they could trust the musical to new creative minds, when they were sympathetic to the musical, and therefore, she and Sam encouraged Prawy to sell his production to anyone who would like to use it. Over a decade later, European journalists would continue to remember the impact *Kiss Me, Kate* achieved in its opera house adaptation, using the legacy of the Volksoper *Kiss Me, Kate* to trail a staging by Sadler's Wells opera company in London.[44]

Returning to London

As a result of the Viennese triumph, and the hugely profitable productions that followed in Europe, *Kiss Me, Kate* held firm in the minds of publicly subsidized companies that specialized in opera and operetta. After *Kiss Me, Kate*, the Volksoper incorporated other "suitable" material including *Candide*, *My Fair Lady*, *West Side Story*, and *Porgy and Bess* into their programming, setting a trend for other companies to dabble in some "appropriate" musical theater.[45] Their risk-taking had proven that a popular and adaptable work could meet the commercial imperative to connect opera companies with new and disengaged audiences, improving ticket sales to support other programming innovations.[46]

Earlier, in 1952, a disagreement broke out in the *New York Times* after the commercial and entertainment value of *Kiss Me, Kate* was edified in comparison to the musicals of Rodgers and Hammerstein. Richard Rodgers himself felt at pains to defend their work against an opinion piece, "Down with Sense," authored by Fred Lounsberry.[47] In it, Lounsberry complained that musicals with "realism or meaning or depth" were crowding out the "brilliantly entertaining" "fluff" musicals from Broadway.[48] Rodgers responded that:

> The theater as a whole has come on hard times. It isn't the picnic it used to be by any means and at this moment the only truly healthy segment of the

> living theater is its musical wing. The healthiest and most successful portion of this wing is to be found in comparatively serious efforts. These are doing by far the biggest business so, perhaps if Mr. Lounsberry loves the theater so much and wishes it to stay open so he can have his nights of carefree goofiness, he might do well to support what he calls the serious musical and stop thinking of it as a menace.[49]

Rodgers dismisses Lounsberry's suggestion that his musicals—specifically *South Pacific* and *The King and I*—were not entertaining while arguing that these successes sustained stage musicals as viable commercial projects and allowed other "carefree goofiness" to run alongside them. It is striking that, while *Kiss Me, Kate* is perceived as modest and less commercial in this exchange, its broad appeal, including the use of *The Taming of the Shrew* and the diversity of its score, made it an important show in financial models of other performance arenas.

However, the success of the Viennese production also facilitated less well-received methods of experimentation when adapting *Kiss Me, Kate* for classically trained artists and their audiences. When artistic director Stephen Arlen wrote to frame Sadler's Wells's proposed production in September 1970, he described *Kiss Me, Kate* as "something of an innovation" for the English opera house:

> The operatic canon included DIE FLEDERMAUS about ten years ago, albeit reluctantly. We pushed it a little further with THE MERRY WIDOW and that too got acceptance; and now we think it is time to take the next, rather longer, step into the great era of the American Musical.[50]

Arlen indicated that they planned to premiere *Kiss Me, Kate* as "a special Christmas attraction" before incorporating it into the core repertoire for annual and touring performances. Like Prawy, he saw *Kiss Me, Kate* as the next step in programming development for Sadler's Wells as they looked beyond opera and operetta for sympathetic music that might appeal to a new contemporary audience.

However, Arlen also deemed *Kiss Me, Kate* a risk, identifying the dated orchestrations of the original Broadway production as a potential trouble.[51] His worries were not ill-founded, as music critic Peter Heyworth raised concerns in a long feature on the opera company in *The Guardian*. Published only days before *Kiss Me Kate* reopened in London, Heyworth suggested that the programming might represent a sign of desperation, and curtailed artistic ambition, in difficult financial circumstances:

> Their [Sadler's Wells Opera] success is well earned. But it represents a narrow basis for Mr. Arlen's claim that the tide has turned for the Coliseum operation. It could equally be said to bear out the fears originally expressed by opponents of the move to St. Martin's Lane, that pressure to fill the Coliseum would inevitably lead to a preponderance of massive productions of popular works which would, in their turn, result in less varied and enterprising fare than we got at Roseberry Avenue. That these fears are not unjustified is borne out by the fact that the theatre is about to be devoted to a month's uninterrupted run of "Kiss Me, Kate." (I am not opposed to the inclusion of operettas and musicals in the repertory, but to perform one to the exclusion of all else during a period that represents more than a ninth of the entire season is surely something that can be justified only by acute financial pressure.)[52]

Later, Heyworth also notes the inclusion of *Kiss Me, Kate* and a now obscure work *Lucky Peter's Journey* (1969) as one of only two pieces written in the previous fifty years programmed since Sadler's Wells had moved from smaller premises to the iconic Coliseum. While the public narrative could have been about returning *Kiss Me, Kate* to its London home, instead there were worries about what this meant for the business of British opera companies.

Under the direction of Peter Coe, the Sadler's Wells production starred Emile Belcourt and Ann Howard and reimagined *Kiss Me, Kate* in 1940s England. The production included a wrought-iron set but combined this new modern aesthetic with costumes that emulated Ayers's original designs. Their blended approach also led to some superficial changes such as replacing "American" names like Harrison with Lindsay, stripping topical comments on American politics, and amending location names in various places. As a result, the second line of "Another Op'nin', Another Show" replaced "Phili, Boston, or Baltimo'" with "Glasgow, London or Tokyo" and the framing dialogue to "Wunderbar" depicts Fred and Lilli playing at the Theatre Royal in York while living over a fish and chip shop.[53] Despite these fairly stereotypical choices, Coe requested no alterations to the lyrics of songs like "Tom, Dick, or Harry" or "Too Darn Hot," leaving deliberately idiomatic vernacular American (e.g., "Howdy,

Pop!" or "A G.I. / For his cutie-pie") to stand against dialogue about life in Britain.[54]

While Coe allegedly believed he had ongoing approval from the Spewacks to revise the script, they became increasingly alarmed by the pervasive changes he intended for the *Taming of the Shrew* scenes and entered a lengthy exchange of views with Coe and Stephen Arlen about Coe's approach. Above all, Coe was concerned that *Kiss Me, Kate* presented *The Taming of the Shrew* in a bad light that would not land with British audiences. In November 1970, he wrote to the Spewacks to outline several changes he felt were crucial to improve these scenes and lists three reasons for revising the Shakespearean text:

> 1. It has been seriously mangled. Twenty years ago this may not have mattered so much as today. Now he [Shakespeare] is a pop author in this country and a major film has been made of *the Shrew*. The play will be running at the same time at the National Theatre. [. . .]
> 2. Inventing lines for Shakespeare is more difficult than one can imagine, and the invented lines stand out like old fashioned sore thumbs. I have eliminated as many as possible. [. . .]
> 3. Three of the songs within the Shakespeare are badly motivated. "I Hate Men" has a little scene specially invented for it which seems unnecessary. . . . The scene between "Tom, Dick and Harry" [*sic*] and "I've Come To Wive It Wealthily in Padua" seems unnecessary . . . & "Were Thine That Special Face" comes in the most unlikely place, but unfortunately there seems to be no other place for it.[55]

Coe's disapproval of Porter and the Spewacks' approach to *The Taming of the Shrew* was forcefully matched by Sam Spewack's fury that Coe proposed such substantial changes. The Notes and Worksheets' folders of Spewack papers indicate that Sam drafted numerous responses to the note and includes a copy of an undated telegram to Arlen that summarized his sentiments:

> APPRECIATE YOUR COMING CLOSER TO ORIGINAL KATE BUT CAN ACCEPT NO CHANGES IN SHAKESPEARE TEXT STOP BALANCE PERSONAL STORY SONGS DANCE AND SHAKESPEARE CAREFULLY TIMED AND WE INSIST KATE BE PLAYED AS ORIGINALLY WRITTEN STOP SEE NO ADVANTAGE IN SEMIAMERICAN [*SIC*] COMPANY IN LONDON STOP THIS IS AMERICAN MUSICAL STOP ONE HUNDRED AND SIXTEEN

> GERMAN PRODUCTIONS AND THIS WILL BE FELIX BLOCH EBEN BIGGEST YEAR YET STOP GERMANS PLAYED IT EXACTLY AS WRITTEN AFTER LONG AND DETAILED CONFERENCES WITH US STOP IF YOUR DIRECTOR WILL DIRECT AND NOT WRITE AND LISTEN TO ME I WILL COME OVER STOP EITHER DO IT OUR WAY OR FORGET IT REGARDS.[56]

During this time, Bella Spewack flew to London to sit in rehearsals and observe how the material was being handled so that Coe (and Arlen) were dealing with opinions in person and via correspondence from both authors. Days after Coe's note about the "badly motivated" Shakespeare, Sam received word from the Spewacks' agent Adza Vincent that Bella was very dissatisfied with what she had seen but that they needed to prioritize salvaging the libretto:

> Bella, very rightly, longs for so many things to be changed in the production—but with only one week to go Sam, I am trying to persuade her that the most important matter is your script. Everything she says is absolutely right, but it becomes too frustrating beating one's head against a wall where Coe and his production are concerned.[57]

Despite the numerous concerns raised, Coe pressed on with his vision of *Kiss Me, Kate*, outlined in a letter he sent that detailed further minor changes including reordering and abridging lines of the script.[58] Along the left margin, Sam Spewack has marked up the requests with many receiving a "no!" At the top, he has written: "For heaven's sake. Will he stop tampering with dialogue! This show has been played!!"[59] Certain that Coe had overreached even what was in writing, Sam Spewack attended a January 1971 performance of *Kiss Me, Kate* at the Coliseum unannounced and was dismayed by what he saw. He wrote to Stephen Arlen in vehement terms that "outrageous changes" had been made by Coe who had "very carefully shoveled back his garbage dialogue we shoveled out."[60] He continued:

> One thing I will say for Mr. Coe however—KISS ME KATE [*sic*] has hitherto been indestructible. He has managed to murder it. Surely, to cite one of the many atrocities, you as a Producer must realize that WUNDERBAR was written as a satirical number. Mr. Coe plays it straight. It's all dull, dull, dull.[61]

Although advance bookings for *Kiss Me, Kate* were strong, with the Coliseum achieving a reported £28,000 in early ticket sales,[62] critical responses to production were generally subdued. Felix Aprahamian of *The Sunday Times* was one of few wholly positive reviews:

> I am less concerned with whether or not our second opera-house should have any truck with Cole Porter and musical comedy and more with registering profound admiration at its versatility. With a bare handful of extra musicians, the Sadler's Wells Opera Orchestra give Marcus Dods all the musical zing and zest this amusing piece, after—a long way after—Shakespeare's "The Taming of the Shrew," needs.[63]

However, the *Guardian*'s Philip Hope-Walla described it as "an updated and Englished production, which does not quite disguise the fact that two different traditions, Broadway and Merrie England, are here not quite happily yoked together."[64] Interestingly, Hope-Walla also prefaced this review with a comment on the programming choice:

> The notion is that if you play Gilbert and Sullivan and "Die Fledermaus" you can also extend the repertory to include musicals as they do in Vienna. I hope the venture pays off although I must say I see it as a downward extension of the repertory, but that if it heals the break between the public which likes a musical but might be shy of a real opera, it's a worthwhile experiment.[65]

Yet it was not simply the problem of *Kiss Me, Kate* playing in an opera house that attracted critical disapproval. Benedict Nightingale offers an extensive dissection of the ambitions and execution of Coe's production in *New Statesman*, particularly targeting the limited delivery of *The Taming of the Shrew* and the physical comedy required in this work:

> How can a musical with no fewer than two plots possibly fail? It can, and does if mistakenly cast, as it is here. The production within the production is prettily dressed, with the whole company frolicking up and over what looks like a spindly metal gazebo; but the effect of such artifice has been to make their Shakespearean acting yet more abominably stilted, and at times, coy. It is impossible to the believe—the implication of the Spewack book—that it is all a roaring success, likely to bring our divorced coupled

> together again. They are played by Emile Belcourt and Ann Howard, the former a dapper, elegant figure, the latter strapping and lanky. She may not literally loom over him, but she certainly seems to do so; and though a formidable Katherine is to be welcomed, we must also believe her essentially weak enough, and Petruchio strong enough, for the "taming" to take place. This time, we don't—and (worse) where is the comedy? Both players are in good voice, but they play the funniest scene in the musical—in which private violence spills over into Shakespeare—as though it was a long, perilous patch of sedge. They move deliberately forward, like cowards in gumboots. The American musical, especially this one, needs speed, verve, attack and a deadly instinct for comic timing: such things are not seen at the Coliseum.[66]

Clearly, the impact of such reviews was felt at the company and, in a letter dated April 6, 1971, Stephen Arlen confirmed that Colin Graham had been asked to take over control of the production with refreshed staging that would return *Kiss Me, Kate* closer to the original Broadway production. This was a preface to requesting future permissions securing the compromise version as part of the company's regular repertory. However, the press reception remained cold to Graham. One *Daily Mail* headline proclaimed: "Kate's Kiss Is Not So Hot," continuing:

> Kate got to kiss yet again at the Coliseum. But not exactly in a way to knock your hat in the air. More a chaste, not to say sterile, peck somewhere not so sensitive. Colin Graham has seen fit to retain all the updating and misplacing Peter Coe brought to Sadler's Wells Christmas production. Which is a pity. What Sam and Bella Spewack's front stage story of a divorced couple bickering through a bizarre performance of *The Taming of the Shrew* needs is the innocence of the forties which spawned it. As a result the near perfect score of Cole Porter is dimmed.[67]

In lots of ways, this reception is in dialogue with the concerns Bella Spewack felt more than twenty years previously. In defending her (and Sam's) credit for developing *Kiss Me, Kate*, she became aware that the songs of the show and public familiarity with Porter would accelerate his contributions. In this 1970 version, the press reception frames Coe's revisions as to the detriment of Porter or as unsalvageable despite Porter's talents. This is all while the Spewacks were present and determined advocates, championing their work, and resisting the changes they felt undermined the musical as a whole.

Through their frustrations with Coe, Sam and Bella were also pushed to characterize the essence of *Kiss Me, Kate* in order to challenge his decisions. Unlike the Viennese production, which scaled *Kiss Me, Kate* up, Sadler's Wells wanted the musical because it might adapt to their pre-existing forces. Arlen planned to cast affiliates of Sadler's Wells throughout *Kiss Me, Kate* to make it viable as core repertoire for the company. His concerns were financial and practical. However, this was complicated by Coe, who rightly identified the irreverent handling of *The Taming of the Shrew*, but did not like it. Because Coe felt this was a significant flaw rather than a feature of *Kiss Me, Kate*, it is understandable that he felt some lack of sympathy with parts of the score as well as with the humor of the musical more generally. However, it distanced the Sadler's Wells production from Prawy's imagining of *Kiss Me, Kate*, which hoped the comic appeal would register with fans of light and comic opera as well as operetta.

From 1948 onward, the Spewacks considered how they exercised control over *Kiss Me, Kate*. Where they felt that the new creatives involved with their work did not understand the musical or did not show appropriate investment, they were willing to be present and demand what they felt would make new productions a success. Although not detailed in this chapter, their papers indicate that they supported and encouraged the proliferation of *Kiss Me, Kate* globally and attempted to appear at productions wherever they could. Despite the emphasis on Porter's songs, which were able to live beyond the confines of stage productions, the Spewacks showed care and investment in keeping *Kiss Me, Kate* working and relevant to audiences on their own terms. The Volksoper production successfully translated *Kiss Me, Kate* into an expanded market that has persisted since 1956. As a result, the Spewacks were able to see their work thrive beyond musical theater venues and to appraise versions that did not honor their musical with clarity.

The model of using *Kiss Me, Kate* to expand the performance remit of a specialist organization was also tested by the Royal Shakespeare Company (RSC) in 1987. Again, coinciding with a period of financial trouble—the RSC faced a reported deficit of £1.1 million[68]—the RSC aimed to test the viability of "Shakespeare musicals" with their audience. Their production of *Kiss Me, Kate* began in Shakespeare's hometown, Stratford-upon-Avon, before embarking on a UK tour and a short run in London. Once more, *Kiss Me, Kate* was seen as the least risky option for the company to explore—it was internationally popular and known for its accessible appeal.[69] In contrast to Coe's censorious views of the Shakespearean material, the RSC version wholly embraced the irreverent dealings with *The Taming of the Shrew* as well as its musical spectacle, adding bonus visual jokes about the works of Shakespeare, and quoting famous stagings (e.g., Hamlet talking to a skull) within the direction of the script.

However, the production received equivalently lukewarm reviews to the Sadler's Wells version. For some reviewers including Irving Wardle of *The Times*, the production was perceived as a limited commercial exercise. Under the headline "Just in It for the Money," Wardle was discouraged by the underuse of the ensemble, "banal" choreography, and that the fun costuming did not translate in matching performances: "Like *Les Miserables*, its manifest aim is to earn the RSC some much-needed revenue. I hope it succeeds: but there is little sign of any other purpose."[70] In *The Telegraph*, Francis King praised the music, the sets, and the cast but remained critical of the book: "The result is that, as long as there is singing and dancing, the show is a delight; but that at other times only the vigour of the performances and the surprises of William Dudley's constantly changing sets ward off tedium."[71] Strikingly, the production received most press attention when Sarah Ferguson, then the Duchess of York, attended a performance in a remarkable outfit that featured a "full puffball skirt in orange, pink, yellow, and brown"[72] and ostrich feathers in her hair.[73] On the *Daily Mirror* front page, her attendance was rather ironically billed "Anything You Can Do, I Can Do Better" (after Irving Berlin's *Annie Get Your Gun*), speaking specifically to a fashion "rivalry," contrived by the British press, between Ferguson and Diana, Princess of Wales.

In both these Sadler's Wells and RSC examples, the appeal and challenge of *Kiss Me, Kate* is in its accessibility to a spectrum of audiences outside of traditional musical theater goers. While the Spewacks' tussles for control may have limited aspects of the proliferation of *Kiss Me, Kate*, their stewardship and commitment to their musical was significant in keeping the show onstage for decades after it opened on Broadway. However, the later reception (and subsequent hit revival in 1999) identified their script as the limitation of the work. What emerges is a fraught creative context for the writers who invested in and nurtured this musical as Porter moved on to other projects, then retiring from public life before his death in 1964. Sam Spewack's correspondence with Coe illuminates their conceptualization of the property, hinted at throughout the genesis period in 1948. It confirms a synergy between Porter's irreverent impositions on the score and their vision of *Kiss Me, Kate*, connecting what we can see of their original creative process together.

Above all, these last case studies reveal how, at core, *Kiss Me, Kate* was designed for musical theater practitioners, and presented complications to different kinds of performing companies. The need to have directors, choreographers, designers, and performers with capacity to handle the American 1940s romantic comedy *and* a disrupted musical version of *The Taming of the Shrew* was harder than many imagined. It remains a persistent challenge of translating *Kiss Me, Kate* for modern audiences, and underscored the drawn-out process of recreating the musical on screen.

7
Kiss Me, Kate on film

Where the Spewacks maintained creative control over the details of as many stage versions of *Kiss Me, Kate* as they could, they were unable to exert the same influence over its adaptation to film once they had signed contracts with MGM. Having produced many of the most influential film musicals of all time including *The Wizard of Oz* (1939), *Meet Me in St Louis* (1944), and *An American in Paris* (1951), MGM's Freed Unit had remarkable production experience as well as a roster of directors, musicians, choreographers, and a considerable list of stars available to make their version of the musical. MGM also had previous relationships with Lemuel Ayers, who had worked in the costume department and directed a short sequence "Love" in *Ziegfeld Follies* (1946), and with Cole Porter, having produced film adaptations of his musicals *Panama Hattie* (1942) and *Du Barry Was a Lady* (1943), commissioned new work or used his songs in films including *Born to Dance* (1936), *Broadway Melody of 1940* (1940), and *The Pirate* (1947), and produced a musicalized biopic of Porter's life, *Night and Day* (1946).

By the time, *Kiss Me Kate* went into production, Ayers and Subber's Salem Company had dissolved, John C. Wilson and Hanya Holm had moved on to new projects, and Porter, who was well known to the studio and well accustomed to Hollywood, became the main representative of the original Broadway creative team during production. This left the MGM film adaptation of *Kiss Me, Kate* in the hands of producer Jack Cummings, who made his name producing Porter's film musical *Born to Dance*, and director George Sidney (*Annie Get Your Gun* [1950] and *Show Boat* [1951]), who contracted screenwriter Dorothy Kingsley to oversee the adaptation process. Kingsley began working for MGM in 1942, adapting the Gershwins' 1930 musical *Girl Crazy* as a Judy Garland and Mickey Rooney two-hander. She was associated with many film musicals across the 1940s and especially with those featuring former Olympic swimmer Esther Williams.

Kiss Me, Kate's producers received a range of film offers before settling contracts with MGM in 1952. In the three-year period between the Broadway opening and MGM signing the film, prospective buyers proposed

Too Darn Hot. Hannah Robbins, Oxford University Press. © Oxford University Press 2026.
DOI: 10.1093/9780190082437.003.0007

similar plans for adapting this theatrical material—performatively and environmentally—in an engaging way for screen. In 1950, New York–born director and producer Joseph Lerner proposed to make a film from the original Broadway production of *Kiss Me, Kate*, creating one of the first commercial documentations of a live stage musical.[1] Then, a more protracted bid in 1951, led by Sir Alexander Korda, proposed to record a live performance of *Kiss Me, Kate* from London but featuring the original Broadway cast.[2] One outlying offer mentioned Rita Hayworth as a possible casting for Lilli if the picture rights were bought by Columbia.[3] However, when Porter got news of the option, he telephoned Hayworth to ask it were true and she immediately denied approaching any film studio with the idea of starring in *Kiss Me, Kate*, as she felt that the role of Lilli/Katherine demanded too much singing.[4]

These tentative offers highlight two important concerns for filmmakers tackling *Kiss Me, Kate*: how to tackle its conscious "stageiness" and how to cast stars appropriately equipped to perform (and especially, to sing) these roles. It is striking that the first film proposals intended to record or adapt a stage performance of *Kiss Me, Kate* rather than imagine it for screen anew. They both retained the original casting while avoiding adapting the locations for studio sets altogether. This approach reflects a specific challenge in producing *Kiss Me, Kate*: there is no consistent boundary between what is "onstage" and what is "backstage." Although backstage musicals were already popular on screen, many featured "non-narrative" stage performances that were isolated from the backstage plot. For example, in MGM's *Easter Parade* (1948), the songs "I Want to Go Back to Michigan," "Shakin' the Blues Away," and "A Couple of Swells" are onstage numbers that do not relate to the emerging relationship between Don (Fred Astaire) and his new dance partner Hannah (Judy Garland). Its other songs (about the characters and their romantic lives), such as "Easter Parade" and "A Fella with an Umbrella," are performed at distance from the stage and the rehearsal room, in "everyday" environments, like walking on the pavement or getting dressed to leave the house.

Kiss Me, Kate offers specific challenges because the backstage plot progresses during *The Taming of Shrew* scenes, preventing similar separations between "on-" and "off-" stage. "Another Op'nin', Another Show" sits in its own realm because it is about the staging of a musical and not about an exploration of character or relationships ("So in Love" or "Why Can't You Behave?") or the progress of *The Taming of the Shrew* ("I've Come to Wive It Wealthily in Padua" or "Tom, Dick, or Harry." Then, "Brush Up Your Shakespeare" is non-narrative in a different way—nothing is learned or changed through this song—and yet, the material hinges on being, simultaneously, part of a performance across the fourth wall and within a production about a Shakespeare play. The exploration of producing theater, of staging Shakespeare, and of intertextuality between the Baltimore plot and *The Taming of the Shrew* forces messy collisions throughout every version of *Kiss Me, Kate.*

This chapter explores the MGM film adaptation, tracing the intersecting concerns this material provided its producers. Beginning with Kingsley's screenplay, it highlights how the MGM adaptation considered the framing of the film through devices proximate to *The Taming of the Shrew* and Bella Spewack's early drafts of *Kiss Me, Kate* in the spring of 1948. Then, it considers the implications of the star casting and how this interacts with the changes Kingsley introduced to the script. With a script and a cast in place, I outline the adaptation of the song list (covered more extensively in my chapter in *The Oxford Handbook of Musical Theatre Screen Adaptations*)[5] and the impact of screen censorship on Porter's lyrics. The chapter closes by examining the role of technology in making *Kiss Me Kate* (note there is no comma in the film title; 1953). I emphasize that the film's creative team experimented with play and spectacle in making their film adequately theatrical and true to the spirit of the original Broadway musical. I also acknowledge that many of the (subtle) adaptive changes imposed in the production process have led to a newly conservative version of *Kiss Me, Kate* with different politics to its stage iterations.

Framing *Kiss Me, Kate* for Screen

Between the summer of 1952 and March 1953, Dorothy Kingsley worked on the screenplay, focusing prolifically on the opening and closing scenes of the film and how to frame the musical's key plots. The drafts suggest that she was particularly concerned with addressing the role of Shakespeare in the musical and in setting up the relationships between Fred, Lilli, and Lois more explicitly than is achieved in the original Broadway libretto. By September 1952, she had produced two script drafts, prefacing a version dated November 29, which introduced a completely original concept to start the film. In this November 1952 version, the movie opens on a cloud, where

William Shakespeare and his wife Ann Hathaway are observing the contemporary scene below. It begins:

> Twinkling lights proclaiming "KISS ME KATE" is opening tonight. THE CAMERA TRAVELS SLOWLY UPWARD—past big stars, little stars, the Milky Way—the various credits etched against the star-spangled background.
>
> Following the director's card, there is an additional credit:
>
> Lightly Based On A Story
> By WILLIAM SHAKESPEARE[6]

The card fades to the "large, fleecy"[7] cloud where Hathaway is reading news clippings to Shakespeare. She informs him that someone is making a musical of *The Taming of the Shrew*, and he responds:

> SHAKESPEARE: A musical, eh? Who dost the sonnets?
> ANN: 'Tis Cole Porter.
> SHAKESPEARE: (*nods*) Ah, yes—Cole Porter—I know him well. (*Hums "When The* [sic] *Begin the Beguine"*) Prithee, Ann—how wouldst they start a musical?[8]

Ann then sings the first chorus of "Another Op'nin', Another Show" and the camera drops to theater where the song is picked up by Fred and Lilli with the company of *Kiss Me, Kate.*

Kingsley's embodiment or perhaps her fictionalized personification of Shakespeare and Hathaway is striking in its own terms (as is the faux-Shakespearean syntax, including incorrect conjugations similar to those Bella Spewack tested and removed from the original Broadway script). Kingsley's new beginning also plays with the idea that William Shakespeare has become an omnipresent figure in adaptations of his work and is invoked by the *Kiss Me, Kate* text. She also solves the positioning of "Another Op'nin', Another Show" by reframing it as a song given to the company by Shakespeare and his wife! In this spirit, Kingsley toyed with having Shakespeare reappear at the end of the film. In a change page dated January 13, 1953, Shakespeare joins the cast on stage during the bows and shares their applause, taking a share of the credit for the night's entertainment.[9] In a January 17 version, Shakespeare reappears from his cloud in heaven as the camera pans up from the finale to reveal him "now flanked on either side by the two departed gangsters in their Shakespearean costumes" who then sing an encore of "Brush Up Your Shakespeare" to close the film.[10]

The January 17 version also develops the opening conversation between Shakespeare and Hathaway to discuss Fred and Lilli's divorce:

SHAKESPEARE:	Divorced? Why, they were scarcely wed two years. How long have we been married?
ANN:	Let me see—about 371 years.
SHAKESPEARE:	They didn't give it a chance (*Frowns*) I don't like it, Ann. All the great Shakespearian teams have been happily married. Sothern and Marlow—Lunt and Fontaine [sic]—Olivier and Leigh.[11]

The joke here, that none of these acting couples was peaceably married, foreshadows the drama to come while being very much in the humor of Cole Porter who loved society gossip, wrote lyrics about his friends (often removed before work was made public), and once invented a society couple to toy with newspaper gossip columnists. Kingsley's expanded dialogue also reintroduced Lunt and Fontanne as a reference point for the 1953 American audience who may have been aware of the theatrical couple, potentially reminding viewers of their *Taming of the Shrew*, and (for a select few) formalizing the connection between the various references and debts that *Kiss Me, Kate* owed their production. In these examples, Kingsley explored a comedic revision of the Induction from *The Taming of the Shrew* in which Christopher Sly is browbeaten by his wife. In her draft screenplays, she personifies Shakespeare as a creative and narrative voice in *Kiss Me, Kate* while also including comment on the making of a musical, the "Shakespeare Trade,"[12] and on the state of marriage before the main plot of *Kiss Me, Kate* begins.

Clearly, Kingsley felt that a film audience needed some broader context to opening night than is possible in the Spewacks' "slice-of-life" libretto. Having put aside Shakespeare and Hathaway as characters, she also experimented with original, (earthly) scenes to preface the evening in the theater. In the January 13 draft, she starts the film with a press preview of *Kiss Me Kate*'s opening night. The scene outline reads:

> 1. OPENING—TELEVISION STATION IN BALTIMORE
> Lois is being interviewed by a local commentator about the musical version of KISS ME KATE, which is opening tonight. We learn about Fred

> and Lilli—their broken marriage—and that Lois thinks Fred is just too wonderful. We go to: 2. INT. THEATRE Fred and Lilli looking at program. Fred beaming, Lilli obviously annoyed. We show a kinescoped version of the number Lois, and her partner were doing in a nightclub when they were discovered by Fred, who decided she was just the type to do Shakespeare.
>
> NUMBER: TOO DARN HOT (Lois and Bill)
> At the finish of the number Lois says she must hurry back to the theatre for the final run-through with that marvelous producer-director, Fred Graham.[13]

Here, Fred takes Lilli to see Lois perform before their production begins. This is the first record of "Too Darn Hot" being resituated from an Act 2 ensemble number to a diegetic spectacle performed by Lois. At the end of this draft, Kingsley also tweaks the final scene. Here, Lilli quits the production as normal, and the gunmen perform "Brush Up Your Shakespeare." Then, Fred returns to the stage believing that Jeannie, Lilli's understudy, has taken on the role of Katherine and will appear on a balcony to close the play. He sings a short excerpt of "Were Thine That Special Face" as the figure appears, but it turns out to be Lilli.[14] They finish the song together and the company sing the "Finale Act Two." In this version, they do not finish *The Taming of the Shrew*, and we do not see its controversial ending.

Across these drafts, there are some noticeable parallels between Kingsley's contextualization of the songs and different draft versions of *Kiss Me, Kate* from 1948. The existing sources do not map how Kingsley made these choices, but it is striking that she tested the same device—of using songs like "Another Op'nin', Another Show" and "Brush Up Your Shakespeare" to transport us between characters and places—that Bella Spewack explored in the first outline of *Kiss Me, Kate* during April 1948.[15] It is also noticeable that Kingsley places the reprise of "Were Thine That Special Face" in almost the same place as in Bella Spewack's first script draft.[16] As outlined in Chapter 2, the song is set within a patchwork of dialogue from *The Taming of the Shrew*. However, it also serves as a duet between Fred and Lilli that leads to the resolution of the show. Perhaps Porter, who was regularly consulted on the use of the music and had uncharacteristic involvement in the politics of the stage script's development, recalled these examples or provided access to some of the discarded material. The existing files do not clarify whether these trends are conscious re-investigations of Bella Spewack's ideas or merely coincidences of working on material informed by those initial ideas. The parallels are especially intriguing because, in this draft, Kingsley then scraps the end of *The Taming of the Shrew*, resolving one of *Kiss Me, Kate*'s most enduring controversies.

The opening of *Kiss Me Kate* (the film), as we recognize it, is first traceable in a temporary incomplete script dated February 3, 1953:

> INT. SMART CONTEMPORARY APARTMENT
> CLOSEUP—PORTFOLIO OF MUSIC
> The title tells us it is the score of "KISS ME KATE," lyrics and music by Cole Porter. CAMERA PULLS BACK and we see the score rests on the music rack of a highly polished concert Grand.[17]

This description matches the opening frames of *Kiss Me Kate* absolutely and leads into a first scene in Fred's apartment where he and the (now fictionalized) "Cole Porter" are waiting for Lilli to arrive. Unexplored in the stage version, Kingsley uses this scene to explain that Fred and "Cole Porter" have solicited Lilli's interest in the show, and the scene shows her refusing to perform with Fred, before reconsidering when she fears Lois will take the lead role.

This script offers two differently interesting additions to MGM's *Kiss Me Kate*. The first is that Kingsley rebrands the internal musical from *The Taming of the Shrew* to *Kiss Me, Kate*. At several points in the finished film, we are shown the name of the musical, with and without comma, on books, boxes, and outside of the theater in the transition from Fred's apartment to opening night as well as from Fred and Lilli's dressing room (see Figures 7.1 and 7.2 for examples). Kingsley's new opening scene also promotes an active rivalry between Lois and Lilli, unique to the film version, as the women think they are competing for material as well as for Fred's attention. The apartment meeting ends, as in the finished film, with Fred ripping a score in half and handing half to each woman before the scene cuts to the theater (see Image 2 in Figure 7.3), continuing with dialogue very similar to Act 1, Scene 1, of the original Broadway production.

Kingsley's adaptation makes it clear that Lilli and Lois are in competition with each other, and this recurs in ongoing sniping about Lois's shallowness and Lilli having unattractive knees in subsequent scenes of the film. The addition, which runs at almost ten minutes including two songs ("So in Love" and "Too Darn Hot"), has a significant structural consequence, leaving

Figure 7.1 Stills of the opening frames of *Kiss Me Kate*, which feature a binder titled "Cole Porter's *Kiss Me, Kate*" and Fred (Howard Keel) looking at the binder

Figure 7.2 Stills of the sign advertising *Kiss Me, Kate* outside the theater being switched on for opening night

Figure 7.3 Lilli (Kathryn Grayson) and Lois (Ann Miller) fighting for their roles in *Kiss Me, Kate* in Dorothy Kingsley's new apartment scene

a considerable imbalance between the screen time of Acts 1 and 2 as they happen in the film adaptation. In the 2D print of *Kiss Me Kate*, Act 1 takes 75 minutes of 110-minute running time, leaving the whole of Act 2 at a third of the length. However, the relocation of "Too Darn Hot" into this opening scene also purged the interval from *Kiss Me Kate*, removing the sense of being "halfway" through in the film imagining of the show.

Casting *Kiss Me Kate*

As Kingsley finished the screenplay, Cummings began to arrange the film's casting and immediately settled on Kathryn Grayson in the role of Lilli. Grayson was an established MGM star and recording artist, known for her soprano voice. She had recently starred as Magnolia in Sidney's *Show Boat* and in the MGM remake of Harbach and Kern's *Roberta* (1933) titled *Lovely to Look At* (1952), which was also produced by Cummings.[18] Grayson had strong working relationships with both men and brought many of the characteristics that Porter, Bella Spewack, and others had investigated while developing the role of Lilli. Not only could Grayson perform the score in the register it was originally set, but she had also trained as an opera singer. She later spent some of her post-MGM career performing key roles in productions of *The Merry Widow*, *La bohème*, and *Madama Butterfly*. *Kiss Me Kate*'s musical arrangers, (a twenty-something) André Previn and Saul Chaplin, incorporated her skill into their versions of Porter's songs. Most notably, they added a decoration for her, setting the main theme of the *Die Fledermaus* waltz, in counterpoint with Howard Keel, who carries the tune in the final refrain of "Wunderbar."[19] The film uses the same language of quotation, including the pastiche of *Lucia di Lammermoor*, as the original Broadway production, this time linking Grayson, the real-life star, with the character of Lilli, and adding to her star persona in the film adaptation.

They had similar ease in securing a fun and playful actor as Lois, seeking a star who could offer a comedic but contrasting performance to Grayson's. Ann Miller was also established name with box office appeal, known for her secondary lead roles and tap extravaganzas. She made several hit films throughout the 1940s although she was, perhaps, best known for her roles in *Easter Parade* and *On the Town* (1949). She had also starred in *Lovely to Look At*, playing a vamp against Grayson's more wholesome romantic lead, and the producers recognized their different but complementary appeals for *Kiss*

Me Kate. Miller, like Grayson and Lilli/Katherine, was particularly suited to her role. Lois offered a vivacious and likable character with an accessible singing load and lots of dance potential. Because Miller's prowess as a tap dancer suited Lois's song list (and the newly transposed "Too Darn Hot") particularly well, the film is able to emphasizes the stylistic changes between "classically inspired" music like "Wunderbar" and the swinging showtunes like "Tom, Dick, or Harry," making it a point of difference within the tapestry of competition between Lois and Lilli.

Casting Lois as a dance specialist offered new possibilities when Miller was paired with dancer Tommy Rall as Bill. Rall appeared on stage and screen throughout the 1940s, taking on Harold Lang's role in stagings of *Fancy Free* when Lang had moved on, before enjoying a handful of more prominent screen roles after *Kiss Me Kate.* Like Lang in the original Broadway production, Rall offered choreographer Hermes Pan additional creative options in the making of *Kiss Me Kate.* Pan was a known force in screen musicals, particularly celebrated for his work with Fred Astaire, meeting on *Flying Down to Rio* in 1933 and collaborating often, including on the hit films co-starring Ginger Rogers *Top Hat* (1935), *Swing Time* (1936), and *Follow The Fleet* (1937), until the film adaptation of *Finian's Rainbow* in 1968. Pan had also worked on *Lovely to Look At* and, although no longer at the cutting edge of film choreography at the time, was an undeniably safe pair of hands with a musical comedy heavily informed by 1930s values.

Pan was able to maintain the collage of styles in Holm's work by exploiting Miller's range for tap, swing, and show styles, and accenting them with extra balletic details. Therefore, Rall was given his own spot in the extended instrumental close to "Why Can't You Behave?" His routine is characterized by acrobatic leaps, pirouettes, and spins, which showcase his ability to reach heights, lines, and shapes that other performers could not achieve. Rall and Miller are particularly well matched in this, and other, sequences, because they both combine athletic dancing and notably expressive faces. There is obvious agreement (and fun) between them in numerous close-up shots throughout the film when they mirror each other's scornful, annoyed, or flirtatious expressions. The credibility of their connection underpins this adaptation of *Kiss Me, Kate* where Fred is more petulant than commanding, and Lilli's agency is reframed.

By contrast with the ease of casting Lilli, Lois, and Bill, the search to find a film actor for Fred presented Cummings with several concerns. They needed a singer able to match Grayson in style, if not skill, and someone who could stand alongside her with plausible box office appeal. In the first instance, the studio auditioned an emerging favorite, Howard Keel, who was gaining traction as a romantic baritone in film musicals including *Annie Get Your Gun* and opposite Grayson in *Show Boat* and *Lovely to Look At*, but Cummings did not feel he was well suited to the material and decided to explore other options.

Alongside Keel, Cummings invited Alfred Drake to Hollywood to take a screen test in case he was right to reprise his Broadway role on film. Drake later reflected that the studio offered a "fantastic contract" with "a splendiferous salary," which would still allow him to travel to and from New York to keep other commitments on track.[20] However, he also recalled that the test itself was not an auspicious beginning:

> when I got to Hollywood, I had a screen test. I was clean shaven, so they put makeup on me and a little beard, like a goatee. The test consisted of turn left, turn center, turn right, look this way, look that way. That was all.[21]

It seems that Drake was never a serious prospect for the film adaptation, having been listed as one of 151 individuals with suspected communist sympathies in the notorious *Red Channels* pamphlet in June 1950. Drake's television contract, which had prevented him from accompanying Morison to London when *Kiss Me, Kate* transferred, was canceled, and he was left out of work for a short while before returning to Broadway to replace Yul Brynner in *The King and I* (1952). Drake claims that he was asked to write a statement on his attitude to America for the studio to assess, and he suggested his answer was used as a leverage to revoke the contract, which had unfavorable terms for the studio.[22]

There's little documentation of the other candidates considered for Fred/Petruchio. However, Howard Keel recalled the "trauma" of being rejected, left to sit around while everyone at the studio knew he'd been passed over, and then used as a "last resort" when no one more suitable was found. In a radio interview later in his career, he explained:

> They were thinking of Danny Kaye and all sorts of things. They were thinking for a while of getting Olivier over and having somebody sing for him. Or to have him sing himself, you know. The producer on the film, Jack Cummings, said when my name came up said you put him on the film, and you take my name off it. Finally, they just couldn't find the right person to

> do this part so finally the studio forced Jack Cummings, they said: "Look you use Keel or that's it: nobody else." So, I went in to see Jack about it, and I said: "Jack, I know I'm not the ideal person for this part." I said: "But nobody is. You are looking for an Olivier that can sing like Lanza or a Lanza who can act like Olivier and there isn't anybody."[23]

Keel's anxiety drove him to work exceptionally hard at the part, although he felt he never really understood it during filming, and he became an iconic interpreter of the role. This led British television broadcaster the BBC to invite him to star against Patricia Morison in a special recording of the musical for the opening night programming on BBC2. The contrast between Keel's shallow film star and slightly malevolent buccaneer in MGM's film with the battle-worn thespian whose schemes backfire in the BBC version also offers a tantalizing insight into how he grew into a role he felt unready and unsuited to some decades earlier.

The four leading actors placed MGM's *Kiss Me Kate* in a new position. Unlike the original Broadway production and previously proposed films, Keel and Grayson were known entities with very recent successes in Sidney's screen adaptations of stage shows. Ann Miller, supported by Tommy Rall, promised exciting and spectacular dance sequences, with already famous routines in the public consciousness. While the performer roster was not made of MGM's most celebrated names, these were reliable artists with known working relationships and dependable performance styles that lent themselves to the musical as Kingsley had reshaped it. Significantly, the casting of Grayson and Miller, born only months apart, reinforces Kingsley's changes by situating Lois and Lilli as accomplished peers of different molds. Grayson and Miller's star personas mapped onto their roles while removing the tension of Fred (Keel was also contemporary in age) pursuing a younger actress early in her career. In MGM's film, Grayson and Miller's characters jostle for star power as much as for Fred's attention.

Adapting the Songs

Like most aspects of *Kiss Me Kate*, a superficial examination of the film suggests that there is very little variation between the original Broadway song list and the vocal music in the film soundtrack (see Figure 7.4 for comparative song lists). By contrast with MGM's film adaptations of *On the Town*

Broadway song list (1948)	Broadway song list (1948)
Another Op'nin, Another Show	So In Love
Why Can't You Behave?	Too Dam Hot
Wunderbar	Why Can't You Behave?
So In Love	Wunderbar
We Open in Venice	So In Love (Reprise)
Tom, Dick, or Harry	We Open in Venice
I've Come To Wive It Wealthily in Padua	Tom, Dick, or Harry
I Hate Men	I've Come To Wive It Wealthily in Padua
Were Thine That Special Face	I Hate Men
I Song of Love	Were Thine That Special Face
First Act Finale	First Act Finale - abridged
Too Dam Hot	I've Come To Wive It Wealthily in Padua (Reprise)
Where is The Life That Late Led?	Where is The Life That Late I Led?
Always True to You (In My Fashion)	Always True to You (In My Fashion)
Bianca	Brush Up Your Shakespeare
So In Love (Reprise)	From This Moment On
Brush Up Your Shakespeare	Finale Act Two: So, Kiss Me, Kate
I Am Ashamed That Women Are So Simple	
Finale Act Two: So, Kiss Me, Kate	

Figure 7.4 Song breakdown from the original Broadway musical and the 1953 film soundtrack

or of *Gentlemen Prefer Blondes* (1953), where significant proportions of the stage score were abandoned, MGM's *Kiss Me Kate* retains fifteen of nineteen songs as well as Porter's adapted lyrics to "I Am Ashamed That Women Are So Simple." By contrast, the MGM films retain just five songs from by Bernstein from *On the Town* (originally staged in 1944) and just three of Jule Styne's contributions to the original Broadway production of *Gentlemen Prefer Blondes*. As a result of the overlap between song lists, it is possible to underestimate how the musical landscape of *Kiss Me, Kate* is revised in the film. Figure 7.5 stratifies the key changes into different actions: cutting, reordering, editing, and adding songs. When laid out in this way, we see subtle but meaningful changes to the song list emerge.

From the original Broadway score, only "Another Op'nin', Another Show," "I Sing of Love," "Bianca" (and the reprise of "So in Love") are cut from the film's vocal music.[24] However, this has significant consequences for the ensemble because, with the repurposing of "Too Darn Hot" for Miller, the biggest whole or large group musical numbers are stripped from *Kiss Me,*

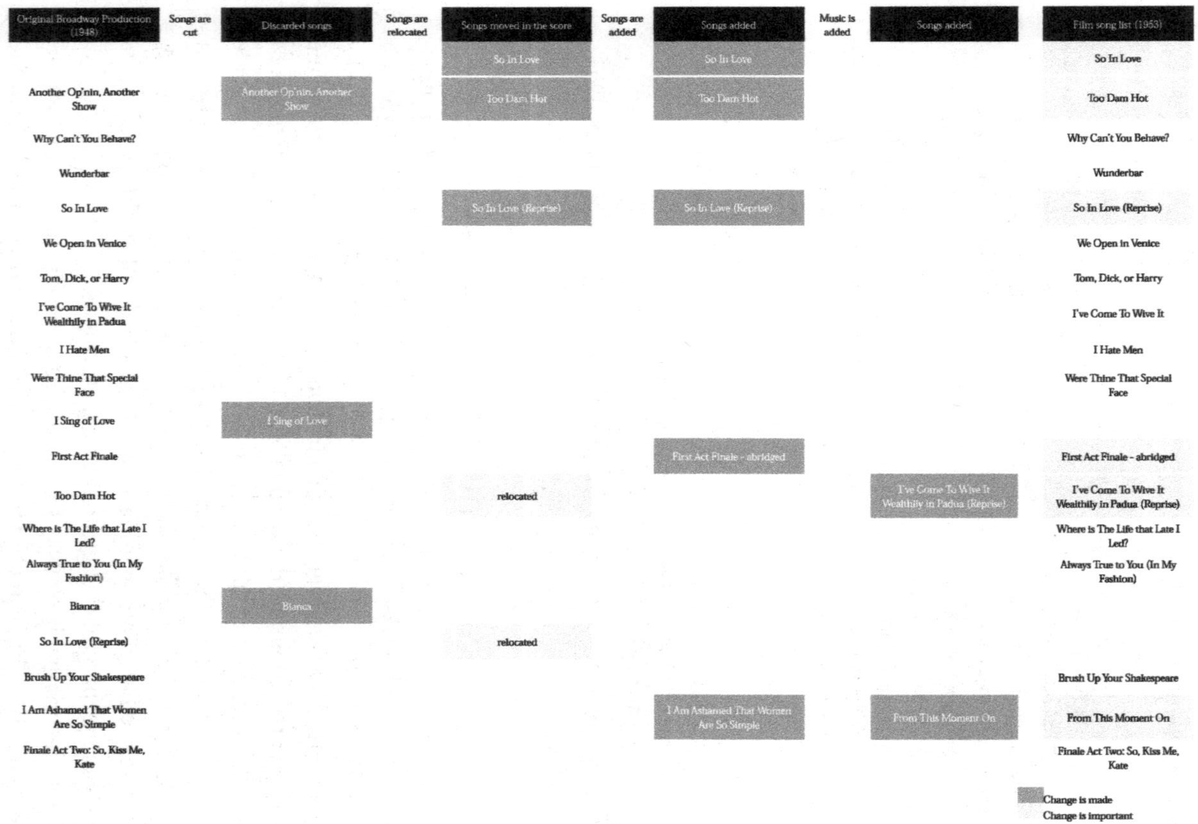

Figure 7.5 Transition from Original Broadway score to *Kiss Me Kate* (1953) soundtrack, structured by action taken

Kate. In my chapter for *The Oxford Handbook of Musical Theatre Screen Adaptations*, I outline in detail the significance of this change.[25] Most notably, the film removes the bustle of people and the business of making a musical from its songs. Instead, the ensemble provide set dressing and visual impact, while being limited to some supportive singing in numbers led by the main characters.

The changes to "Another Op'nin', Another Show" and "Too Darn Hot" also have more insidious consequences by stripping the feature roles for the Black actors playing Hattie and Bill from MGM's *Kiss Me Kate*. In fact, the three specialty performers who lead "Too Darn Hot" and Lilli's maid, Hattie, are reimagined as elderly, non-singing white servants. MGM also whitewashes the two racially integrated songs in the score while repurposing one as a solo song-and-dance routine for a star white performer. Not only does this remove diversity from the musical (written into the stage show and acknowledging the musical style of the song with idiomatic choreography developed by the dancers), but the film also reorchestrates "Too Darn Hot" to emphasize a faux-Latin sound. The revised accompaniment features an acoustic guitar instead of horns and uses bongos and countermelodic details on a solo clarinet, instead of *tutti* orchestral gestures.

"So in Love" is also resituated in MGM's *Kiss Me Kate* and is presented as a duet from *The Taming of the Shrew* that Fred uses to attract Lilli into the production. Fred starts the song in a casual manner, accompanied by "Cole Porter" (Ron Randell) at the piano, and Lilli joins in, picking up on the melodic gestures of the song and exchanging the title lyric between them in the final bars. The spell is broken when Lois arrives to audition with "Too Darn Hot," although it later transpires that it has been cut from the performance. When "So in Love" is reprised a few scenes later, Lilli is reflecting on her renewed connection to Fred. Importantly, Fred does not return to "So in Love" in the film, and we do not hear him sing when Lilli has left. MGM's *Kiss Me, Kate* gives Fred no musical outlet for any feelings he has for Lilli. Instead, she is bound up in a romance that Fred seems less invested in.

When examining Figure 7.5, it becomes clear that Lilli's reprise of "So in Love" and the other musical additions—"I've Come to Wive It Wealthily in Padua (Reprise)" and "From This Moment On"—fall in places where there were song moments already. While MGM's musical adaptation did some streamlining, including cutting verses and refrains from most songs, they were not concerned with restructuring the score or the volume of music in the film. Instead, it clarifies that Fred, Lilli, and Lois will deliver most of the singing, with some assistance from Rall, and background support from the ensemble. The vocal talents of Grayson and Keel facilitated an exciting performance of the finished song list as well as the energetic dynamic of Fred and Lilli's relationship. Grayson's classical soprano is particularly well matched to *Kiss Me, Kate*'s Lilli, echoing the initial casting intentions for the role in 1948. Yet, arrangers Previn and Chaplin expunged several semi-operatic features from her vocal part, including removing Katherine's cadenza from "Finale Act One." Kingsley also decided, in March 1953, to revert "I Am Ashamed That Women Are So Simple" from a song to a speech, noting that "Katherine recites, in ballad form, to musical accompaniment, while the men listen approvingly."[26]

As part of his involvement in *Kiss Me, Kate*, Porter was contracted to produce up to three additional songs for the film but was let out of this agreement by permitting MGM to use the song "From This Moment On" (cut from *Out of This World*), which was also added in March 1953.[27] "From This Moment On" offers a new spectacle near the close of the film, following the wedding of Bianca and Lucentio and introduces a third song-and-dance number for Miller and Rall.[28] It also pairs with "Tom, Dick, or Harry" as Bianca and her suitors, played by Rall, Bobby Van, and Bob Fosse, are reunited on stage with two additional partners (Carol Haney and Jeanne Coyne.)

"From This Moment On" is a playful song about fidelity and commitment, briefly subverted by Hermes Pan's choreography where Bianca flirts with all of the men in the opening verse. This prefaces an extended dance sequence, including whole group sections and feature spots for the pairs to perform specialized micro routines. The number includes a now iconic passage of choreography by Bob Fosse (often deemed his first significant intervention in musical theater dance), which announced his future as a changemaker in dance aesthetics to come. Fosse's choreography comes third of three feature spots, prefaced by the other pairs. Leading the feature sections, Miller and Rall dance to a lush, if traditional, arrangement of the refrain. Pan's choreography prioritizes balletic leaps, spins, and tap to showcase the traditional skill sets of the two stars. Van and Coyle's twelve-second intervention is set to a fragment of the bridge, in a speedy, bent-over tap style, recalling the mannered performances of Gower and Marge Champion.

Pan then relinquished nearly ninety seconds of the four-minute song to Fosse who, paired with Haney, commands the longest section of choreography in all of "From This Moment On." The musical arrangement underscoring their sequence embraces Fosse's distinctively modern style, including contrasts of dramatic pauses, leaps, and unpredictable changes in speed accented by the shrugs and languorous movements quite unlike the classic material before it. The orchestration delivers a disjointed blues setting of the melody, dominated by brass, and punctuated by a solo walking bass, passingly reminiscent of the opening riff to Kander and Ebb's "Roxie" in *Chicago* (1975). This allows Fosse and Haney's clicks, likely recorded with the orchestra, to be heard as part of the percussion of the sequence, a fresh interpretation of the tap tracks we hear in Miller's solo routines. The contrast in styles is made clear in similarly unusual cinematographic and lighting choices. Figure 7.6 shows this contrast between Miller and Rall's expansive postures, Van and Haney's tight mirroring of each other, and Fosse and Haney's different shapes, appearing under blue light, featuring what Kevin Winkler describes as "aggressive jazz stylings, burlesque traces, and witty comic touches."[29]

By adding "From This Moment On" to the internal *Taming of the Shrew* musical while moving "Brush Up Your Shakespeare" to the theater back alley, MGM's *Kiss Me, Kate* amplifies the differences between the backstage and onstage scenes. While the intertextual parallels of character remain, this version adds more modernity to the song-and-dance numbers of *The Taming of the Shrew*, while cutting the less sophisticated "I Sing of Love," de-musicalizing "I Am Ashamed That Women Are So Simple," and abridging "Finale Act One." This functionally reduces the Shakespeare-by-Porter elements of the show. Kathryn Grayson's vocal dexterity is also showcased backstage as Lilli, instead of as part of *The Taming of the Shrew*. Meanwhile, the songs about the conditions or nature of performance—"Another Op'nin', Another Show," "Too Darn Hot," and "Brush Up Your Shakespeare"—are reimagined or removed so that most of the theatricality is contained within the internal performance. While most of Porter's songs endure, the editorial changes to song list recast the performers, the contexts for song, and the

Figure 7.6 Stills of the three pairs in the dance break in "From This Moment On"

blurred musical language of the stage production into more linear and unimaginative versions of themselves.

Censoring *Kiss Me, Kate*

While most of the constituents of the original Broadway song roster were preserved in the film adaptation, Cole Porter's lyrics were subjected to new scrutiny, impacting the tone of the material in additional ways. At the time, all pre-existing material was vetted by the Motion Picture Production Code Office for suitability on screen.[30] The "Hays" Code or Motion Picture Production Code aimed to limit offensive and immoral content in films, restricting any sexual content, such as "lustful kissing" and suggestive gestures.[31] As a result, there were lots of filming conditions, like refraining from showing couples (married or otherwise) sharing a bed, as well as restrictions on language, meaning that expressions like "Oh, God" were prohibited.[32] Kingsley's adapted screenplay tackled the minor challenges in the book, replacing details like Lilli's explosive outbursts of "bastard" with "you louse." The *Taming of the Shrew* segments survived generally unscathed, although the text "But that our soft conditions and our hearts / Should well agree with our external parts?,"[33] extracted by Porter for "I Am Ashamed That Women Are So Simple," was provisionally flagged as objectionable. Clearly, these lines did not provoke too much concern, as Grayson speaks them in the final scene of the film.

Correspondence between Porter and musical arranger Chaplin offers some insight into the process of adapting the song lyrics. Changes were suggested from MGM, based on their understanding of the Code's boundaries, and submitted for Porter's approval.[34] Unlike the commercial sheet music versions or the lyrics for London transfer of *Kiss Me, Kate*, Porter did not draft the revised lines himself. In one example, Chaplin enclosed a verse of "I Hate Men," which they had redrafted to omit a playful reference to extramarital affairs. Chaplin writes:

> In the song I HATE MEN, the censors objected to certain lines. We are using therefor: [*sic*]
>
> "... I Hate Men.
> They should be kept like piggies in a pen.
> Don't wed a traveling salesman,

> Though a tempting Tom he may be.
> For on your wedding night he may be off to far Araby.
> While he's away in Mandalay,
> It's thee who'll have the baby.
> Oh, I Hate Men.
>
> "If Thou shouldst wed a businessman,
> Be wary, oh, be wary.
> He'll tell you he's detained in town on business necessary.
> His business is the business with his pretty secretary.
> Oh, I Hate Men . . ."
>
> The above lyrics are acceptable to the censors. We will, of course, welcome any suggestions or improvements.[35]

This edit softens Porter's previous lyric "But don't forget 'tis he who'll have the fun / And thee the baby" and makes a subtle change to the earlier lyric "His business is the business that he gives his secretary."[36] It lightly recasts infidelity and likely sexual activity as a suggestive absence.

While seemingly innocuous, this change was indicative of an overarching adjustment to the humor and themes of *Kiss Me, Kate*, dampening Porter's more impish sensibility from the musical, and especially in Katherine's positional song. As Kingsley's screenplay places Lilli and Lois in open competition and Lilli is characterized as starchy and judgmental of Lois in their first meeting, it is significant that the film also desexualizes Katherine's lyrics. The contrast of Lois singing "Too Darn Hot" in her skimpy pink leotard opposite Lilli's sober two-piece prefaces a new conservatism that makes Lilli/Katherine (the heroine) primmer and Lois (the "bit on the side") newly sexualized through her subjection to the male gaze in this performance. The sanitization of the lyrics to "Too Darn Hot," previously layered with euphemisms for failed ejaculation due to the heat, focus more explicitly on the weather but are also covered by the objectification of Miller by her onscreen audience. The spectacle of her dance, in that costume, distracts from any "maleness" that survives in the lyric.[37] Then, later, Katherine is framed as unromantic and sings about ungentlemanly conduct in a static musical number. Meanwhile, Bianca is flirtatious, playful, and desirable. Their conflict is defined and communicated through subtle changes, including these acts of censorship.

On an initial impression, "Always True to You (In My Fashion)" and "Brush Up Your Shakespeare," both about sexual conquest, seem ripe for censorship. Like many of the musical numbers, both songs are stripped of at least two refrains, and the sections are reordered. In cutting the running times of these numbers, they were also able to censor any especially problematic material. For example, Lois's refrain about a possible assault is omitted:

> There's a mad man known as "Mack"
> Who is planning to attack,
> If his mad attack means a Cadillac, okay![38]

More significantly, these songs are reframed by new performance contexts. In the film adaptation, Lois sings "Always True to You (In My Fashion)" with Bill, rather than in his absence, in the back alley next to theater. They split the opening verse so that Bill asks: "Why can't you behave?," turning Lois's earlier lament back on her. Then, he recounts some of the refrains as examples of her misdemeanors. As a result, Lois's cheeky solo number about compartmentalizing transactional relationships and her love for Bill becomes (playful but recast) scrutiny of her choices after she bumps into Lilli's fiancé, Tex. Audiences familiar with *Kiss Me, Kate* may recognize that the film ditches Harrison Howell, the elder statesman, for a new prospective fiancé Tex, whose name is taken from the discarded second refrain of Lois's song.

Almost immediately after, the gunmen discover that their employer has been assassinated and prepare to leave. As they leave, they see Lilli quit the production and sing "Brush Up Your Shakespeare" to Fred, who is left dejected. Because it is no longer delivered to a theater audience, the song does not achieve the raucous, and knowing, laughter it often elicits in live performance. Instead, the gunmen perform it to raise Fred's spirits, giving the Porter's song a narrative purpose (of a kind) for the first time. Like "Always True to You," the film version substantially abridges the song's structure from an introductory verse and five refrains to a verse and two refrains plus an instrumental version. The adaptation scraps all material from the third refrain, including the censored language "a damn or a damnlet," the undeniably provocative "your lap'll have 'honey' upon it," and "Better mention *The Merchant of Venice* / When her sweet pound o' flesh you would menace" from the fourth.[39] Instead, the arrangers reconfigure content from different

Location in original Broadway lyric	**1st Refrain**
Every refrain	Brush up your Shakespeare, Start quoting him now, Brush up your Shakespeare, And the women you will wow.
1st refrain	Just declaim a few lines from Othella And they'll think you're a helluva fella,
1st refrain	If your blonde won't respond when you flatter'er Tell her what Tony told Cleopaterer.
Original to film 4th refrain	And if, still, to be shocked, she pretends well Just remind her that *All's Well That Ends Well*
Every refrain	Brush up your Shakespeare And they'll all kowtow
	2nd Refrain - *Instrumental*
	3rd Refrain
Every refrain	Brush up your Shakespeare, Start quoting him now, Brush up your Shakespeare, And the women you will wow.
5th refrain	If your goil is a Washington Heights dream Treat the kid to A *Midsummer Night's Dream*
1st refrain	If she fights when her clothes you are mussing, What are clothes? *Much Ado About Nussing.*
2nd refrain	If she says your behaviour is heinous Kick her right in the *Coriolanus*
Every refrain	Brush up your Shakespeare And they'll all kowtow

Figure 7.7 Breakdown of lyric reorganization between the Original Broadway version and MGM film version of "Brush Up Your Shakespeare"

sections into a newly concise but no less problematic vaudeville spectacle about managing women:

The film lyric resets couplets from the first, second, fourth, and fifth refrains of "Brush Up Your Shakespeare" (see Figure 7.7) with only one editorial intervention that dilutes the implied sexual violence "If her virtue, at first, she defends well" to "And if, still, to be shocked, she pretends well."[40] Unlike the songs performed by the female singers, "Brush Up Your Shakespeare" retains most of its punch from the original Broadway lyric. The gunmen also address Fred with their crude and uncomfortable jokes as a balm for his despair.

Through "I Hate Men," "Always True to You (In My Fashion)," and "Brush Up Your Shakespeare," we see how censorship acts as an important driver in defining the film version of *Kiss Me, Kate*. As the limitations on expression remove the sharpest edges from Porter's lyrics, especially as they relate to the female characters and their reflections on sex in relationships, this *Kiss Me, Kate* takes on a new, if subtle conservatism in comparison to the stage versions. When coupled with the expanded conflict between Lilli and Lois, and the addition of "From This Moment On," which advocates for monogamous heterosexual partnerships and features the dance spectacles that show everyone happily paired off, the momentum of the musical is driven toward an automatic resolution between Fred and Lilli. The culmination of Kingsley's changes, the casting decisions, edits to the score, and the influence of censorship restrict the dramatic and emotive pauses in *Kiss Me, Kate* that enrich Fred and Lilli's relationship. Instead, the film sways toward fun and spectacle above all.

Technological Matters

The creative priorities of the film may have been partially driven by the various technical innovations and experiments that were undertaken during filming. MGM's *Kiss Me Kate* is widely reported as one of the first film musicals to be filmed in 3D, marketed as a technological landmark used to diversify film festival programming. The Blu-ray release (2015) of the 3D print has made this version, which was not broadly distributed in 1953, considerably more accessible to modern audiences than it was at first release. A postwar slump in cinema box office sales, which correlates closely to increased access to television at home, encouraged production companies to invest in developing new film technologies that might re-engage audiences through experiences that they could not replicate at home.[41] By 1953, approximately 40 percent of films were released in color, reflecting a 20 percent increase since 1952 and a tenfold increase since 1939.[42]

The impetus to innovate and draw audiences was reflected in the development of *Kiss Me Kate*, which was filmed in widescreen, Ansco Color, and stereoscopic 3D. Like other films *Brigadoon* (1954) and *Seven Brides for Seven Brothers* (1954), which used Ansco technology, *Kiss Me Kate* is particularly remarkable for its heightened bright colors. Ansco Color was developed during the Second World War as a response to emergent German technology (Agfacolor).[43] The film absorbed color more quickly than other options available at the time, meaning that the prints showed images in their richest form. MGM was the only studio really to embrace Ansco Color, having secured a contract with the company in 1948.

Kiss Me Kate was also trailed as part of MGM's move to produce most of their films in the widescreen aspect ratio.[44] Similarly, the trend for 3D filmmaking was such that sixty-nine pictures were produced using 3D technology. However, a third of these were only released in a 2D flat-screen format when CinemaScope took over in popularity. Porter seems to have been particularly struck by what he witnessed during this process, immortalizing the technological chase in the song "Stereophonic Sound," written for *Silk Stockings* (1955). In this song, an actress explains all the different sensations that studios are mounting to try and entice audiences to a movie theater.

In 1996, Howard Keel also reflected on the challenges of making *Kiss Me Kate* while the studio was experimenting with this new technology. In order to make 2D *and* 3D prints, every scene had to be recorded twice on different cameras. However, the experimental lighting environment required to penetrate the layers of the 3D camera filters caused a spike in studio temperatures. Keel recalled that no one was allowed to step off set and out of the reach of the lights for fear of catching hypothermia: "it would be a drop of like fifty degrees, and you'd chill and catch cold or just seize up."[45]

In *Kiss Me, Kate*, the internal production of *The Taming of the Shrew* allowed the set and lighting designers to explore the possibilities of color in varied ways less available in the pastoral and farm settings of *Brigadoon* and *Seven Brides for Seven Brothers*. Legendary art director Cedric Gibbons, who was nominated for thirty-nine Best Production Design Oscars and won eleven, and renowned costume designer Walter Plunket (best known for his designs used in *Gone with the Wind* [1939] and *An American in Paris* [1951]), collaborated to enhance the impact of this technology. Gibbons and Urie McCleary designed the *Taming of the Shrew* sets on perspective ratios to give extra depth and amplify the 3D print. They also expanded the topographical designs by Lemuel Ayers, printing them in oppositional colors that would pop on Ansco film.[46] Not only did the color palette enrich the spectacle of *Kiss Me Kate* but it also facilitated a wider variety of cinematographic and directorial decisions.[47] For example, Sidney incorporated several "to the camera" shots with actors performing straight down the lens, often in extreme close-up. Additionally, the film's lighting mimics the effects of live theater, using spotlights in "I Hate Men," "Where Is the Life That Late I Led," and during the final scene to focus on Grayson. Sidney was interested in theatrical camera work and in experimenting with space, color, and movement to tell his story.

In his 1952 picture *Scaramouche*, Sidney used a variety of techniques to capture the *commedia dell'arte* performances within its melodramatic revenge/romance plot. Adapted from the novel by Rafael Sabatini (1921), *Scaramouche* follows the hero Andre-Louis Moreau, who is seeking revenge on master swordsman the Marquis de la Tour d'Azyr. To defeat the Marquis, Andre goes into hiding in the theater troupe of his former lover, Lenore, taking on the masked role of Scaramouche (a clown, lazzi-like character from the *commedia dell'arte*).[48] Although different from *Kiss Me Kate* in many ways, *Scaramouche* was allegedly considered by MGM as a film musical property to star Gene Kelly, and there are some obvious parallels between it and his role in *The Pirate*.[49]

Significantly, Sidney appears to have experimented with many of the filming techniques used in *Kiss Me Kate* in the theatrical scenes of *Scaramouche*, including having the camera follow a swordfight around and through the auditorium. He reused this sense of motion to trace the rise and fall of jumps in *Kiss Me Kate*'s dance choreography, reflecting the natural movement of the eyes. The effect is most obvious in Bill's rooftop dance at the end of "Why Can't You Behave?" as Tommy Rall jumps on hidden trampolines and, later, when the male dancers leap unnaturally high, thanks to hidden wires, during the closing sequence of "From This Moment On."[50]

Sidney also incorporated "the audience" as a visible part of both films. Sections of *Kiss Me Kate* are shot from the back of the stage looking out into the audience and from the back of the auditorium, looking at the entire stage. The soundtrack is layered with canned laughter to simulate a live and reactive audience, and some *Taming of the Shrew* scenes include cuts to audience reaction and to a full auditorium watching the performance. There are other smaller nods to his previous film, including when Keel throws a ball of red paint into the camera lens so that a swirl of powder covers the cut from "We Open in Venice" to the opening sequence of *The Taming of the Shrew*. Sidney used the same device to signal the beginning of a theatrical performance in *Scaramouche*.

To a modern viewer, there is a lot of fun to be found in the 3D print. The title cards have new dimensions, and they float like banners. At the start of *The Taming of the Shrew*, we are treated to extra seconds of film including flame throwers and confetti canons. In the dance sequences, Tommy Rall's feet rush into the faces of the audience and Ann Miller tosses her gloves, scarf, and jewelry through the screen. However, the effect is sometimes

Figure 7.8 Stills from *Kiss Me Kate* (1953) showing Ann Miller throwing her glove at the cinema audience and it then reappearing "onscreen"

Figure 7.9 Stills from MGM's *Kiss Me Kate*, showing Fred and Lilli's onscreen progress in the final frames of the film

limited. For example, Ann Miller's gloves fly out at great pace. However, the items land back in scene in the next frame so the illusion of them breaking through the screen threshold is undermined (see Figure 7.8). Similarly, in the final frames of *Kiss Me Kate*, Fred/Petruchio sweeps Lilli/Katherine into his arms, carrying her up some stairs to the left of the shot, before their closeup image is superimposed, and grows in size, over the background of the theater (Figure 7.9). In the 3D version, they feel as though they are projected over the cinema audience.

MGM's *Kiss Me Kate* negotiates a range of adaptative and creative considerations. It is never entirely committed to a fantastical or to a realistic spectacle, and this is borne out in the different options that Dorothy Kingsley explored when determining how to frame the play-within-a-play, the intertextuality, and the overt theatricality of the musical. In many ways, Sidney, Kingsley, Cummings, and the wider creative team embraced the opportunity to heighten as many details as possible. Knowing that the film would be shot in Ansco Color, the set and costume design is vivid with bright accents used to against dark tones to direct the eye to the key focuses of each shot. The direction interacts the musical's comedy and light melodrama with unnatural movement direction, 3D additions, and a shifting sense of "real" and "unreal" as numerous scenes fluctuate between a theater set with live audience and film stages with no boundaries or architecture beyond the camera lens. When considering whether to embody William Shakespeare in the layers of their adaptation, Dorothy Kingsley explored a "heavenly" frame, which adds to artificial character of the film.

Ultimately, Kingsley mobilized the redefinition of Lois and Lilli as sexpot and "Shrew" to add new gendered polarity to the material. This is reinforced by the casting and song lists that place Lilli and Lois as contemporaries with equivalent star power and allocates Lois considerable flirtatious and extravagant performance opportunities with her love interest(s) while reducing Lilli's musical interactions with Fred, in role as Katherine, and as a leader of the company. This is a *Kiss Me, Kate* of contrasts and gimmicks used to highlight the staginess of the source material while toning down its more adult understanding of love, marriage, and show business. The female rivalry trivializes the power struggles between Fred and Lilli, which do not directly involve Lois on stage. Meanwhile, the song spectacles are prioritized over the more static and romantically charged backstage encounters without disrupting the *Taming of the Shrew* adaptation. Therefore, MGM's *Kiss Me Kate* presents audiences with a superficially faithful adaptation, which actually undermines and regresses the gender politics explored in the creation of the original Broadway musical.

8

Kiss Me, Kate and the Contemporary

Over the last twenty-five years, revivals of *Kiss Me, Kate* have grappled with the tension of staging any part of *The Taming of the Shrew* within the musical. For a long time, the MGM film became the most familiar version of *Kiss Me, Kate*, promoting a more limited understanding of its gender politics than had been seen on stage. Various attempts were made to revise the book for performance, but they were repeatedly rejected in the knowledge that Sam and Bella Spewack had jealously protected their work for decades after the original Broadway opening. However, at the end of the century, one hundred years after the birth of Bella Spewack and fifty years since *Kiss Me, Kate* premiered on Broadway, Michael Blakemore's 1999 Broadway revival was granted permission to make changes.

Under the headline "Another Op'nin', but Hardly Another Show," *New York Times* reporter Robin Pogrebin emphasized that "the name of the playwright John Guare is nowhere to be found in the program" despite his work on the amended book for the 1999 *Kiss Me, Kate*.[1] The article, with its subheading "Vigilant Guardians Keep *Kiss Me, Kate* True to Its Roots," outlines how Bella Spewack left her controlling rights to friends Lois and Arthur Elias, who scrupulously reviewed any proposed changes. This ultimately unraveled the plan to stage a production in 1994, starring Kevin Kline. The Eliases told Pogrebin: "their main directive was that Lilli and Fred clearly adore each other. [. . .] If you don't have that, you don't have *Kiss Me, Kate*."[2]

Blakemore's production rivaled the success of the original Broadway production, playing 881 performances and enjoying a popular West End transfer. It confirmed that there was still appetite to enjoy *Kiss Me, Kate*, but also foreshadowed twenty years of conversation about changing the musical now that there was scope to amend the script. Published almost twenty years before Paulson's thinkpiece on reviving musicals and #MeToo, Pogrebin's article couches the revisions to *Kiss Me, Kate* as gentle, unlike rewrites to *Carousel*, which Paulson also problematizes. As this book has shown, negotiated amendments to the content of musicals are a typical part of the business of new stagings and reviewers are aware of this convention.

Too Darn Hot. Hannah Robbins, Oxford University Press. © Oxford University Press 2026.
DOI: 10.1093/9780190082437.003.0008

However, the opportunity to change *Kiss Me, Kate* after all those years was big news and undeniably encouraged new scrutiny of the material and the preference to have the 1999 script as a licensable version for future productions.

When Patricia Morison starred as Lilli/Katherine, her beautiful but characterful manner was captured through lots of production stills that generally showed her frowning and pouting. By contrast, there are several delightful behind-the-scenes photos, taken by Harold Lang,[3] where she is beaming and full of fun. Her offstage demeanor was subsequently captured in the "about town" press she did with Porter once *Kiss Me, Kate* had become a success. However, the visual culture of the original Broadway production capitalized on the staging, costumes, and set design of *The Taming of the Shrew*. Therefore, Morison's Lilli/Katherine was routinely shown in opposition to Alfred Drake's Fred/Petruchio holding a whip over her or as looking jealously at Lisa Kirk's Lois/Bianca. This continued in the promotion for the MGM film, which persistently used stills of Grayson being spanked by Keel as the central marketing image. Similar presentation remained for the 1999 revisal with photographs of Brian Stokes Mitchell strongarming Marin Mazzie in much of its press coverage. In this context, the 2019 Roundabout production introduces vital changes by using images of Broadway icon Kelli O'Hara, a Broadway icon herself, standing over other members of the cast on the cover art for the 2019 revival cast album.

Introducing New Sexisms

The 1999 revisal introduced foundational revisions to *Kiss Me, Kate*, which are represented in most contemporary productions. The licenser Tams-Witmark characterizes this as "keeping in mind evolving social values," explaining that "the book was carefully refined, not changed."[4] In practice, they cut the overture and made "Another Op'nin', Another Show" the first business of the musical rather than the finale to the first scene. The script also edits or omits some of the Spewack-authored "Shakespeare" and a couple of sentences from the Baltimore scenes. However, its most substantive "refinement" is the re-characterization of Lilli's fiancé Harrison Howell, who is transformed into a domineering military general, obsessed with order and American values. The revised scenes between General Howell and Lilli, also including Fred and the gunmen, redefine the power dynamics of Act 2, but not necessarily for the better.

In the 1948 dialogue, Harrison is described as set-in-his-ways and dull. He likes a precise routine in his rural home. Although the dialogue implies that he believes Lilli will also enjoy his lifestyle, the joke is that Harrison is uninteresting and unappealing to Lilli beyond the social status he offers. He is not malicious nor is he particularly aware of Lilli as a personality. Because of this, the Broadway production allows Fred to demonstrate that it is he who really understands Lilli, knows what she likes, and how to upset her. The 1999 version does not introduce any new notions of love between Lilli and the General, but it does extend his interactions with other characters.

When the General arrives, the new script is littered with military references, and he threatens to court-martial Fred for telling Lilli off, claiming that right for himself:

GENERAL: Chastising the little woman is the sacred privilege of a husband and no one else. You were out of line there, soldier.

FRED: Yes sir, General!

GENERAL: Restoring family discipline, Graham. Cherishing our women no matter what it takes. That is my message to the American people. That is why I am letting her make her farewell appearance in this little show of yours. "The Taming of the Shrew." I like the title and I like what it has to say.[5]

The new script also gives him a superficial appreciation of *The Taming of the Shrew* and its misogynistic attitudes. While this attempts to situate *Kiss Me, Kate* in the historical 1940s using an outdated attitude to gender equality, the scene introduces new sexism. For the first time, Fred appears to sympathize with Petruchio and the General's derogatory attitudes to women. This was never part of the Spewack script, which presented Fred's poor decision-making as spur of the moment opportunism. Looking at these changes, the General could be referencing Alfred Drake's suggestion that Bella Spewack did not know how to behave and had to be told her place. It also overlaps closely with comments made by President Donald Trump, when campaigning for a second term of office, where he claimed that he would "protect the women whether they like it or not."[6]

The 1999 version further complicates the prospect of Lilli's forthcoming marriage by introducing "From This Moment On," reconfigured from the MGM film as a duet for her and the General. It falls after a celebration of his latest professional success as they look forward to their wedding, but Lilli's joy is curtailed when the General chastises her for eating a late dinner and being unpatriotic by preparing to wear a French (Dior) hat out in public. The extended scene also introduces excerpts from *The Taming of the Shrew* to the backstage dialogue for the first time, using lines that the Spewacks immediately cut from *Kiss Me, Kate.*

In effect, the 1999 script splices two "taming" passages from Shakespeare's Act 4, Scenes 1 and 3, which Fred and the gunmen use to interrupt Lilli and the General's song. As a result, Lilli's celebration of her engagement is tempered by the General's controlling demands and then by the three men responsible for trapping her in the theater, quoting dialogue from scenes played wholly at Katherine's expense. Despite its ambitions to place *Kiss Me, Kate* in a time with different gender politics, these changes to Harrison, and the new scene containing "From This Moment On," alter Lilli's agency and weaken the intertextuality of her modern emancipation.

In 2018, a revival of *Kiss Me, Kate* at the Crucible Theatre, Sheffield (UK) used the 1999 book as a backdrop for an especially harrowing depiction of the escalating violence against Lilli. Paul Foster's adaptation shows Fred chasing Lilli on and offstage before publicly beating her. Then, in the Act 1 finale, he leads her onto the stage with her wrists bound and she is unable to fight him during the closing song, traditionally blocked (and scripted by the Spewacks) as a continuation of their physical struggle. When interviewed about these production choices, actress Rebecca Lock, starring as Lilli/Katherine, reflected that their new "raw" staging showed that "it isn't at all hilarious that this man is hitting a woman."[7] The Crucible production argues that, although Lilli starts and wholeheartedly participates in the punches pulled, Fred is just like Petruchio, and she cannot overpower him.

Alternative Approaches

By contrast with the 1999 version, the 2019 Roundabout revival aimed to make *Kiss Me, Kate* a "fair fight,"[8] working with the 1999 script but making new adjustments. This included redrafting part of lyric to "I Ashamed That Women Are So Simple," retitled "I Am Ashamed That *People* Are So Simple" and controversially editing the original Shakespeare (via Cole Porter). Figure 8.1 contrasts the new lyric, which has a significant impact on the politics of *Kiss Me, Kate*'s ending.

1948	2019
I am ashamed that women are so simple	I am ashamed that people are so simple
To offer war, where they should kneel for peace	To offer war when we should kneel for peace
Or seek for rule, supremacy, and sway	Or seek for rule, supremacy, and sway
When they are bound to serve, love and obey	**When everything but love must die away**
Why are our bodies soft and weak and smooth	**Why are our bodies finite, bound for dust**
Unapt to toil and trouble in the world	**The time we share so brief and yet, so dear**
But that our soft conditions and our hearts	**If not to teach our proud and stubborn hearts**
Should well agree with our external parts?	**To love the best we can while we are here**
So, wife, hold your temper	So **mates**, hold your temper
And meekly put	and humbly put
Your hand 'neath the sole of	Your hand 'neath the sole of
Your husband's foot	your **lover's** foot
In token of which duty	In token of which duty, if he
If he please	please
My hand is ready	My hand is ready
Ready	Ready
May it do him ease	May it do him ease

Figure 8.1 The two versions of "I Am Ashamed That Women/People Are So Simple" (1948 and 2019)

Instead of addressing the "wives," Katherine calls the company "mates," diluting the gendered emphasis that she is schooling other women in how to behave. All allusions to female bodies as weaker than men's and the inference that one gender should capitulate to another are scrubbed. Instead, Lilli's choice to return to the performance is presented as an act of *love*, and not an act of *service*.

The Roundabout production also tackled the second of *Kiss Me, Kate*'s "problem three," retaining but fundamentally restaging the "slapping scene." As in previous versions of *Kiss Me, Kate*, Kelli O'Hara's Lilli/Katherine repeatedly strikes Will Chase as Fred/Petruchio. However, Amanda Green's edits makes clear that she is also stepping out of their blocking, so that Fred is forced to keep resetting the scene. Lilli refuses to let him take her hand, when prompted in the Shakespeare, and enjoys snatching it repeatedly out of reach. Eventually, Fred wraps his arms around her to ground Lilli in one place, but the new stage direction has O'Hara knee Chase in the groin and kick him repeatedly, leading him to lift her onto his shoulders to protect himself. She bites his arm holding her in place and they end up, after a very silly maneuver, with her legs split in his face and head between his knees as other characters enter. She continues to attack him through the closing dialogue until he cracks, kicking her back, so she slaps him, and they pounce on each other, breaking into a passionate fight as the curtain is dropped.

By reimagining the escalation of this scene into an all-out brawl rather than Fred overpowering Lilli, the power balance is completely reformed. The end of the scene is also deliberately refocused as three members of the ensemble are pushed in front of the curtain to cover the noisy chaos behind it. Fred is never shown with the upper physical hand, and their antics are shocking to the rest of their castmates. In the next *Taming of the Shrew* scene, after Katherine and Petruchio's wedding, O'Hara enters freely; she is not strongarmed by the gunmen or driven by the crack of Petruchio's whip. Instead, *she* (Lilli/Katherine) finds the whip, which she uses to threaten Fred and trip him up before standing over him for most of the Act 1 finale. This change of posture does not stop one of the gunmen from producing a weapon, but it revises the impact of Fred enjoying punishing her and Lilli/Katherine being coerced onto stage with the threat of violence from both sides of the script.

In 2018, Melissa Errico, another Broadway star who played Lilli, published a follow-on op-ed to Paulson's piece on revivals, explaining that she approached the politics of *Kiss Me, Kate* with trepidation until they began rehearsing and it became fun. Of the "slapping scene," she wrote:

> I will add that these roles are written as two mature performers with an excess of ego and bluster, and Lilli isn't exactly unafraid to throw things, including chairs and punches. An actress and actor keeping that in mind can play it with consensual relish.[9]

Her reflections preface the changes made for the 2019 revival, which takes the "consensual relish" without attributing a clear victor, attracting complicated reviews like:

> The *Kiss Me, Kate* of 2019 is more screwball comedy than sexist dinosaur, or an interrogation of the latter. If *Carousel*'s overt anti-female violence shocked you last season, or if the twist at the end of *My Fair Lady* was a nod to #MeToo debates, Kiss Me, Kate 2019 takes a swerve away from cultural confrontation. Instead, O'Hara's Kate literally kicks Will Chase's Fred's butt over and over again. She gets hoisted over a shoulder but doesn't get spanked, he most surely does get bruises. She is nobody's fool, nobody's victim, but the show isn't so much rewritten that she stands up to her suffocating husband-to-be, nor does it explain how and why she settles for what and who she settles for at the end.[10]

In his appraisal, Tim Teeman labels the changes as a "conservative, conventional tweaking rather than audacious re-scaffolding of a classic," highlighting more radical directorial choices like Eliza walking out on Henry Higgins at the end of Barlett Sher's 2018 revival of *My Fair Lady*. In the *Chicago Tribune*, Chris Jones suggests that director Scott Ellis deliberately limits audience exposure to *The Taming of the Shrew*:

> Sure, the song "I Hate Men" still plays, but there's really no need to try and milk awkward laughs from gender-based coercion when the list of Cole Porter musical numbers in the program includes the self-protected likes of "Wunderbar," "So in Love" and "Too Darn Hot."[11]

In the reactions to 2019 changes, reviewers and fans navigate the extent to which they continue to like *Kiss Me, Kate* as they had previously seen it (1999, film, or a using the 1948 script). In many ways, the crafting of the original Broadway production inevitably restricted opportunities for flexibility because the cuts to *The Taming of the Shrew* are reciprocal to the additions by Bella Spewack and Cole Porter. The decision to newly adapt a famous Shakespearean speech and distance *Kiss Me, Kate* from *The Taming of the Shrew* is a plausible tool that the original creative team could have explored, given Bella Spewack's attempts to create new scenes for Katherine. However, their final draft of *Kiss Me, Kate* diverted from the Shakespeare where it suited them rather than updating its message. Perhaps future versions of *Kiss Me, Kate* might consider whether to omit or redesign the final scene altogether. This would be more in tune with Porter and the Spewacks' actual philosophy for *The Taming of the Shrew*. However, the 2019 changes prove that the substance of *Kiss Me, Kate* does not require structural or extensive change. The original creative team had already gone most of the way in achieving an acceptable reckoning of *The Taming of the Shrew*.

A Classic Musical for Modern Times

This volume consciously centers on the original Broadway production of *Kiss Me, Kate* as essential to understanding more contemporary approaches to the musical. This is not to privilege the 1948 production as a fixed or "definitive" text, but to demonstrate patterns of reactivity to its first incarnation, and the way it was conceived. From 1948 onward, *Kiss Me, Kate* has often been negatively compared to more "ambitious" musicals of the period, situated with *Annie Get Your Gun*, as a best attempt to update the old-fashioned writing preferences of Porter and Berlin.

In January 1949, *New York Times* critic Brooks Atkinson led this narrative, contrasting his celebration of *Kiss Me, Kate* by calling it less significant than other more lofty works:

> Everyone agrees that "Kiss Me, Kate" is a blissfully enjoyable musical show. Cole Porter has set it singing with the finest score that has popped out of his music-box in years. And Bella and Samuel Spewack, who settled one of the great literary problems of the century with "Boy Meets Girl" in 1935, have put together a book that is genuinely humorous without the mechanical aid of gags. Of this there is no probable possible shadow of a doubt; no possible doubt whatever. The only doubt concerns the definitive quality of the best musical comedy of the season. Does it rank with the immortal "Show Boat," "Porgy and Bess" and "Oklahoma!" as some of its idolaters believe, or with "Annie Get Your Gun," which is perfection in the more modest field of book-and-song entertainment? In my opinion that is where it belongs. Although the gods are very likely enjoying it, they are not moving over to make room for it on the celestial reviewing stand.[12]

This framing of *Kiss Me, Kate* has meant that scholars and critics, including myself, telegraph Porter's reflections on Rodgers and Hammerstein as essential to *Kiss Me, Kate*'s success. Meanwhile, we sometimes underplay that Porter credited the scale of the *Kiss Me, Kate* score to the impact of seeing *Annie Get Your Gun*:

> I enjoyed writing the songs of "Kiss Me, Kate." I think the show has more music in it than any I have ever done. I liked what Irving Berlin had done with "Annie Get Your Gun." His having so much music in it made me feel like trying a similar thing.[13]

Porter was motivated by an ambitious musical comedy with recurring songs and a significant volume of music, and this shows in his approach to *Kiss Me, Kate* including imposing unsolicited songs on Bella Spewack after she had given him prompts to write from. By obfuscating that Porter and Berlin were influenced by each other as well as Rodgers and Hammerstein, we misalign the parallels in the creative impacts of these musicals, which both consciously feature melodrama, farce, slapstick, and comedy of personality to tell their stories. Simultaneously, the "composer as auteur" approach masks the extent to which other members of two creative teams made vitally sophisticated interventions that enable the success of the score.

Throughout this book, I evidence the depth of thinking and skill required to present an entertainment that reflexively comments on its own metalevels. Ayers's contrastingly graphic costumes and artificial backstage settings, Holm's innovative choreography that melds styles, Porter's modern commentary in song, and Bella Spewack's ambition to reinvent Katherine reveal a highly ambitious gamble. Through each of their contributions, *The Taming of the Shrew* is made integral to the fabric of *Kiss Me, Kate* and the backstage shenanigans redefine the Shakespeare. Neither can stand alone from the other, and recognizing the layered collaboration in developing *Kiss Me, Kate* recasts our understanding of various new and familiar approaches to this work.

Fascination with the appeal of Porter's score is matched by investment in the role of *The Taming of the Shrew*, as modern revivals highlight. We question whether this musical adds, extends, or remakes Shakespeare's play, focusing very proscriptively on the relationship of form and the representation of misogyny in each. Among many rich details of adaptation in *Kiss Me, Kate*, I reveal Bella Spewack and Cole Porter's treatment of Katherine, which addresses her lack of voice and visibility in the play without solving her unhappy ending. *Kiss Me, Kate* is censured because Lilli returns to Fred while the creative team refused to sanitize Petruchio, expanding his persona as a successful womanizer. This contrasts the approach taken in another successful reimagining of Shakespeare's play, the teen romantic comedy *10 Things I Hate about You* (1999), which reforms Petruchio into a charismatic rebel who is, deep down, a "good person."

Kiss Me, Kate is differently motivated to this later adaptation because its Petruchio is ultimately a villain. The intertextuality of this musical uses Petruchio to caution against the worst potential of Fred (and men in general). Through their adaptation choices and original contributions, Porter and the Spewacks take a stance on *The Taming of the Shrew* that validates Katherine by making Petruchio undeniably objectionable. Shakespeare's play explores how Katherine's lack of palatable civility empowers men to treat her poorly. *Kiss Me, Kate* refuses this outright. Whether you invest in the musical as comic or horrifying, the creative team offer you a version of *The Taming of the Shrew*, without most of the taming, that condemns Petruchio's actions and shows the traps faced by women encountering such men.

Like *Kiss Me, Kate*, *10 Things I Hate about You* uses external, up-to-date references to present its heroine Kat as unpopular for her feminist views until she meets a man able to argue with her. Rather than being a successful film star, Kat is recast as a pseudo-intellectual, polarized from her high school classmates while she reads Simone de Beauvoir's *The Second Sex* (1949), Betty Friedan's *The Feminine Mystique* (1963), Sylvia Plath's *The Bell Jar* (1963), and Alice Walker's *The Color Purple* (1982). She is a smart, pro-woman misfit navigating an environment with social rules that she does not value. It is intriguing to see Kat with a copy *The Second Sex*, published during *Kiss Me, Kate*'s first year on Broadway, because de Beauvoir captures part of the politic of the musical in one of the work's most famous quotes:

> No one is more arrogant toward women, more aggressive or more disdainful, than a man anxious about his virility [. . .] they know what they lose by relinquishing the woman of their dreams, but they do not know what the woman of tomorrow will bring them.[14]

Despite resistance to any positive feminist reading of *Kiss Me, Kate*, it is telling that Bella Spewack and Cole Porter offer a version of Katherine, via Lilli, so closely aligned to such a significant critical framing of gender politics and the restriction of female freedom. I am not claiming that they meant to offer an overtly feminist adaptation of *The Taming of the Shrew*. Porter's enjoyment in writing Petruchio's overbearing qualities, and in crafting "Brush Up Your Shakespeare," speaks against it. However, I suggest that they are in conversation with questions of female empowerment and the ways in which men, and the patriarchy, benefit from its limitation.

Ultimately, this musical continues to spark interest and comment because of its differently motivated approaches to entertainment and the treatment of Katherine. Porter's score is consistently excellent, and the Spewacks' book highlights the appeal of romantic comedies and the relevance of Shakespeare's play, familiar or otherwise. Porter and the Spewacks developed *Kiss Me, Kate* in a deliberate direction with considerable support from Ayers, Holm, Subber, and Wilson. However, they could not have conceptualized its reach more than seventy-five years later. The highs and lows of making *Kiss Me, Kate* are often paralleled by the characters, but the style and panache of its execution continue to supersede any struggles that they experienced along the way.

Now *Kiss Me, Kate* holds a torch for a type of musical that has not broadly survived the transition to musical plays and megamusicals. The fun sensation achieved in 1948 endures as revivals persist in countries around the world, as does our debate about the motivations of this musical toward Katherine, and to women in general. *Kiss Me, Kate* remains bold and irreverent, while its exploration of entertainment, love, and power has kept its musical comedy properties relevant. It honors its creators' "spirit to resist" the trends of their time and the pulls to sanitize, rather than explore, sensitive themes in *The Taming of the Shrew*. In revival, Bella and Sam Spewack fought to preserve this intention and the balance that they had crafted. Any comedy at the expense of Katherine is matched by their unflattering portrayal of Petruchio. New revisions to *Kiss Me, Kate* grapple with this tension, knowing that audiences find fun and romance in this work but also recognizing changes in acceptable representations of marriage. However, *Kiss Me, Kate* embodies the original creative team's view of Lilli/Katherine. It is confrontational, funny, quick-moving, and full of glamour. The creators understood the adaptation choices they made and offered their entertainment to the world with tongues in their cheeks and their lips in a smile.

Notes

Introduction

1. Louis Calta, "Premiere Tonight of 'Kiss Me, Kate,'" *New York Times*, December 30, 1948.
2. The production then transferred to Łódź in 1958. It has been revived in Poland several times, most recently in 2012.
3. Cole Porter, *Kiss Me, Kate: A Musical Play*, ed. David C. Abell and Seann Alderking (Van Nuys, CA: Alfred Publishing Co., 2014). Referred to as *Kiss Me Kate*, Critical Edition hereafter.
4. Cole Porter, Sam Spewack, and Bella Spewack, *Kiss Me, Kate* (New York: Alfred A. Knopf, 1953), 274. Referred to as *Kiss Me, Kate* (Knopf) hereafter.
5. Ibid.
6. Ibid., 278.
7. Ibid., 288.
8. Ibid., 303.
9. Ibid.
10. Ibid., 305.
11. Ibid., 306.
12. Ibid.
13. Ibid., 345.

Chapter 1

1. Eagle-eyed fans of MGM's screen adaptation will know that there is a portrait of Olivier as Hamlet hanging over the mantelpiece in the first scene of *Kiss Me Kate*, which Fred stops to admire (1953).
2. There is some confusion about why *Song of the South* received awards in 1948 when it should, in theory, have been included in the 1947 Oscars. As a result, various sources correct the date, reported by the Academy Awards as March 20, 1948, to the year previously. However, press clippings from 1948 confirm that "Zip-A-Dee-Doo-Dah" and James Baskett were honored a year late, shortly before James Baskett died in July.
3. Quoted in Edward Mapp, *African Americans and the Oscar: Decades of Struggle and Achievement* (New York: Bloomsbury, 2008), 5.
4. *Time Magazine*, December 27, 1948, no. 26, 59.
5. "Report: The 2023–24 Broadway Season Has the Most Female Directors Ever," *Playbill*, March 8, 2024, https://playbill.com/article/report-the-2023-24-broadway-season-has-the-most-female-directors-ever.
6. Ibid.
7. The 1925 play *The Cradle Snatchers* upon which *Let's Face It!* is based was also coauthored by a woman, the actress Norma Mitchell.
8. Joseph P. Swain, *The Broadway Musical: A Critical and Musical Survey* (Lanham, MD: Scarecrow Press, 2022), 139–164; Geoffrey Block, *Enchanted Evenings: The Broadway Musical from "Show Boat" to Sondheim to Lloyd Webber*, 2nd ed. (New York: Oxford University Press, 2009), 215–232; Lynn Laitman Siebert, "*Kiss Me, Kate*," in *A Cole Porter Companion*, ed. Don M. Randel, Matthew Shaftel, and Susan Weiss (Urbana: University of Illinois Press, 2016), 286–304.
9. This is the title of Swain's chapter. Block playfully offers "The Taming of Cole Porter" as a comparable acknowledgment of the pull of Shakespeare. Swain, *The Broadway Musical*, 139; Block, *Enchanted Evenings*, 215.
10. This is a lesser-known British hip-hop reworking of *The Boys from Syracuse*, which premiered at Theatre Royal, Stratford East.
11. Julie Sanders, *Adaptation and Appropriation* (Abingdon: Routledge, 2006), 28.
12. Ibid., 28–29.

13. Irene G. Dash, *Shakespeare and the American Musical* (Bloomington: Indiana University Press, 2010), 52.
14. James Shapiro, *Shakespeare in a Divided America* (New York: Faber, 2020), 186.
15. These songs are taken from three less well-remembered musicals: *Gay Divorce* (1932), *Leave It To Me!* (1938), and the revue *Seven Lively Arts* (1944) respectively.
16. Cole Porter quoted in Gilbert Millstein, "Words Anent Music by Cole Porter," *New York Times*, February 20, 1955, SM16.
17. Millstein, "Words Anent Music by Cole Porter," SM16.
18. Ibid.
19. Block, *Enchanted Evenings*, 215–232; Joseph P. Swain, "Shakespeare as Musical," in *The Broadway Musical*, 139–164.
20. Siebert, "*Kiss Me, Kate*," 286–304.
21. Raymond Knapp, *The American Musical and the Performance of Personal Identity* (Princeton, NJ: Princeton University Press, 2009), 273–284.
22. Michael Buchler, "Musical Structure, Dramatic Form, and Song Pairings in Cole Porter's *Kiss Me, Kate*," *Journal for the Society of American Music* 12, no. 1 (2018): 37–54, https://doi.org/10.1017/S1752196317000517.
23. Block, *Enchanted Evenings*, 219.
24. Maya Cantu, *American Cinderellas on the Broadway Musical Stage: Imagining the Working Girl from Irene to Gypsy* (New York: Palgrave Macmillan, 2015), 100–156.
25. Porter later revisited this trope (and *The Philadelphia Story*) during the making of the film musical *High Society* (1956).
26. Duane Byrge and Robert Milton Miller, *The Screwball Comedy Films: A History and Filmography 1934–1942* (Chicago: St. James, 1991), 3.
27. Toni Anita Hull, "Anita Loos: A Girl Like Her," in *When Women Wrote Hollywood: Essays on Female Screenwriters in the Early Film Industry*, ed. Roseanne Welch (Jefferson, NC: McFarland & Co., 2018), 44–45.
28. Ibid., 37.
29. While it can be said that Fred grossly violated the boundary of onstage stage fighting in their conflict during Act 1, Scene 5, it is important to remember that Lilli retaliates again after the curtain goes down. There is no safety in any impromptu violence from either actor. However, the assumption that Fred will always win in any exchange is a relic from the social infrastructure of *The Taming of the Shrew* and not from the construction of *Kiss Me, Kate*.
30. Michael Paulson, "The Problem with Broadway Revivals: They Revive Gender Stereotypes, Too," *New York Times*, February 22, 2018, https://www.nytimes.com/2018/02/22/theater/gender-stereotypes-carousel-my-fair-lady-pretty-woman.html.
31. Ibid.
32. Barbara Hodgdon, *The Shakespeare Trade: Performances and Appropriations* (Philadelphia: Penn University Press, 1998), 22.
33. Carol E. Silverberg, "If It's Good Enough for Shakespeare: The Bard and the American Musical" (PhD diss., State University of New York at Binghamton, 2009), 72–73.
34. Ibid., 71.
35. Howard Bloom, *Shakespeare: The Invention of the Human* (London: Fourth Estate, 1998), 29.
36. Ann Blake, "The Taming of the Shrew: Making Fun of Katherine," *Cambridge Quarterly* 31, no. 3 (2002): 237–252.
37. Ibid., 240.
38. Frances Teague, *Shakespeare and the American Popular Stage* (Cambridge: Cambridge University Press, 2006), 142.
39. Gordon Cox, "Listen: How Kelli O'Hara Brings #MeToo to 'Kiss Me, Kate,'" *Variety*, April 23, 2019, https://variety.com/2019/legit/news/kelli-ohara-kiss-me-kate-metoo-1203193515/.
40. David Cote, "Kiss #MeToo Kate: A Broadway Classic Gets Consent," *Observer*, March 14, 2019, https://observer.com/2019/03/kiss-me-kate-review-a-broadway-classic-gets-consent/.
41. Bailey Sincox, "Resistance and Reconciliation in Roundabout's 'Feminist Update' to *Kiss Me, Kate*," *Borrowers and Lenders: The Journal of Shakespeare and Appropriation* 13, no. 2 (2021), https://doi.org/10.18274/VZYJ7220.
42. Kristen N. Gragg, "'To kill a wife with kindness': Contextualizing Shakespeare's *The Taming of the Shrew*." in *Renaissance Papers 2019*, by Jim Pearce and William Given (New York: Camden House, Boydell & Brewer, 2020), 37–48.

43. Dash suggests that while *Kiss Me, Kate* is about "the woman's dilemma of marriage versus career" and that while Porter and Spewack have truly modernized *The Taming of the Shrew*, each of the layers of the text can be traced back to Shakespeare's play. Dash, *Shakespeare and the American Musical*, 49–76 (49).
44. Hodgdon, *The Shakespeare Trade*, 20.
45. Hodgdon, *The Shakespeare Trade*; Dash, *Shakespeare and the American Musical*; Teague, *Shakespeare and the American Popular Stage*; Robert Lawson-Peebles, "Brush Up Your Shakespeare: The Case of *Kiss Me, Kate*" [*sic*], in *Approaches to the American Musica* (Exeter: University of Exeter Press, 1996), 89–108.
46. Dash, *Shakespeare and the American Musical*, 76.
47. Joe Dziemianowicz, "Raunchy, Gutsy 'Kiss Me, Kate' Showcases Glorious Kelli O'Hara," *New York Post*, March 14, 2019, https://nypost.com/2019/03/14/raunchy-gutsy-kiss-me-kate-showcases-glorious-kelli-ohara/.
48. Blake, "The Taming of the Shrew," 240.
49. LC AD 2/2: Drake rehearsal script, 2-6-34.
50. John C. Wilson, *Noel, Tallulah, Cole and Me: A Memoir of Broadway's Golden Age*, ed. Thomas S. Hischak and Jack Macauley (Lanham, MD: Rowman & Littlefield, 2015), 171–181.
51. CU BSS 21/*Kiss Me, Kate* Correspondence (1948): letter from Bella Spewack to Walter Kane, April 1, 1948, 1.
52. Ibid.
53. CU BSS E/Correspondence from Cole Porter: telegram from Cole Porter to Sam Spewack, 16 June 1948.
54. CU BSS 27/*Kiss Me, Kate* Scripts: rehearsal script, cover.
55. CU BSS 26/Notes and Worksheets [1]: outline of *Backstage*, April 22, 1948; CU BSS 26/Notes and Worksheets [2]: untitled scene outline, dated April 28, 1948, 9pp; CU BSS 27/*Kiss Me, Kate* Scripts: first complete draft [listed as "Script B with notes" in the folder]; NYPL HH 21/501: undated script 1 [known as the "interim script" in this volume]; CU BSS 27/*Kiss Me, Kate* Scripts: October 11 Script [listed "Script C with notes" in the folder]; CU BSS 27/*Kiss Me, Kate* Scripts: rehearsal script [listed "Script C final" in the folder]. All of these drafts are all contained in Folder 27 of the Spewack papers at Columbia University, except the interim script, which is in the Hanya Holm papers at the New York Public Library.
56. CPT 1/1: Drake Transcript, 3–4.
57. William McBrien, *Cole Porter: The Definitive Biography* (New York: Knopf, 1998), 317; George Eells, *The Life That Late He Led* (London: W. H. Allen, 1967), 249.
58. David Grafton, *Red, Hot & Rich: An Oral History of Cole Porter* (New York: Stein & Day, 1987), 167.

Chapter 2

1. Bella Spewack and Sam Spewack, "Introduction," in *Kiss Me, Kate* (Knopf), vii–xxii.
2. CU BSS 21/*Kiss Me, Kate* Correspondence (1948): "Proposed Letter to be sent by Bella Spewack to Lem Ayers', etc.," August 10, 1948.
3. Wilson, *Noel, Tallulah, Cole, and Me*, 180.
4. This is expanded more thoroughly in the following section of this chapter.
5. Stephen Holden, "Saint Subber, Theatre Producer and a Neil Simon Partner, 76," *New York Times*, April 21, 1994, http://www.nytimes.com/1994/04/21/obituaries/saint-subber-theater-producer-and-a-neil-simon-partner76.html; Dan Dietz, *The Complete Book of Hollywood Musicals* (Lanham, MD: Rowman & Littlefield, 2012), 282, 358.
6. Orville Kurth Larson, *Scene Design in the American Theatre from 1915 to 1960* (Fayetteville: University of Arkansas Press, 1989), 131.
7. Ayers also directed a short sequence of MGM's *Ziegfeld Follies* (1946), "Love," featuring Lena Horne. Later, he co-produced Porter's *Out of This World* (1950) and designed set and costumes for Wright and Forrest's *Kismet* (1953) and Adler and Ross's *The Pajama Game* (1954) before his untimely death in August 1955. Earl J. Hess and Pratibha A. Dabholkar, *The Cinematic Voyage of THE PIRATE: Kelly, Garland, and Minnelli at Work* (Columbia: University of Missouri Press, 2014), 32; Larson, *Scene Design in the American Theatre*, 131.
8. Wilson, *Noel, Tallulah, Cole, and Me*, 169.
9. Holden, "Saint Subber, Theater Producer and a Neil Simon Partner, 76."
10. McBrien, *Cole Porter*, 303.

11. Elizabeth Schafer, Introduction to *The Taming of the Shrew*, by William Shakespeare (Cambridge: Cambridge University Press, 2003), 30.
12. Ibid.
13. Ibid.
14. McBrien, *Cole Porter*, 303.
15. Ibid.
16. Dennis Hevesi, "Bella Spewack, Author, 91, Dies; 'Kiss Me Kate' Is One of Her Hits," *New York Times* [online], April 29, 1990. http://www.nytimes.com/1990/04/29/obituaries/bella-spewack-author-91-dies-kiss-me-kate-is-one-of-her-hits.html.
17. Wilson, *Noel, Tallulah, Cole, and Me*, 173.
18. McBrien, *Cole Porter*, 303.
19. "DICK LAMARR GETS 40G IN 'KISS ME, KATE' CLAIM," *Variety*, January 24, 1949, 51; "L'Marr Wins 40G In 'Kate'% Suit," *Billboard*, January 27, 1951, 42.
20. CU BSS 37/*Kiss Me, Kate* Clippings: Spewack Memorandum, 1.
21. According to notes on a meeting in 1950, Spewack discounted the television and film composer Sol Kaplan because she knew he had other contractual obligations. YISG MCB 5/83-85: "Notes on Conference held at Edward Colton's office at 551 Fifth Avenue, New York City on March 22, 1950."
22. CU BSS 37/*Kiss Me, Kate* Clippings: Spewack Memorandum, 4; YISG MCB 5/83-85 "Notes on Conference held at Edward Colton's office at 551 Fifth Avenue, New York City on March 22, 1950," 2.
23. CU BSS 37/*Kiss Me, Kate* Clippings: Spewack Memorandum, 4.
24. Ibid., 3–4; Eells, *The Life That Late He Led*, 239.
25. Charles Schwartz, *Cole Porter: A Biography* (London: W. H. Allen, 1997), 231.
26. CU BSS 37/*Kiss Me, Kate* Clippings: Spewack Memorandum, 4.
27. Ibid., 5.
28. Porter explained: "I commenced sweating on an idea with a soap opera writer [Elaine Carrington]—a notion of how desperate I was may be given—when the famous writing team of Sam and Bella Spewack came to me with the suggestion of doing Shakespeare's *The Taming of the Shrew* as a musical." Cole Porter as quoted in Richard G. Hubler, *The Cole Porter Story* (New York: World Publishing Co., 1965), 50. There is also a brief allusion to Porter's potential collaboration with Carrington in Eells, *The Life That Late He Led*, 239.
29. Jarmila Novotná, *Jarmila Novotná: My Life in Song* (Lexington: University Press of Kentucky, 2018), 135.
30. Ibid., 136.
31. CU BSS 26/Notes and Worksheets [1]: undated script draft, c. March 1948, 1.
32. CU BSS 262/*Kiss Me, Kate* Notes and Worksheets [1].
33. YISG MCB 5/83-85: "Notes on Conference held at Edward Colton's office at 551 Fifth Avenue, New York City on March 22, 1950," 6; McBrien, *Cole Porter*, 305.
34. CU BSS 26/Notes and Worksheets [1]: undated script draft, c. March 1948, 1.
35. CU BSS 26/Notes and Worksheets [1]: undated draft of "Scene One," c. March 1948, 6–7.
36. Ibid., 7.
37. CU BSS 37/*Kiss Me, Kate* Clippings: Spewack Memorandum, 5.
38. Porter indicates that "We Shall Never Be Younger" was this first composition, which was cut from the score because it was too sad. Hubler, *The Cole Porter Story*, 50–51.
39. Sam Zolotow's reference to prolific Puerto Rican actor José Ferrer is the only traceable record of his name in association with *Kiss Me, Kate.* Ferrer had just won considerable acclaim in his interpretation of Cyrano de Bergerac on Broadway in 1947. However, he was not known for his ability to sing.
40. It continues: "Supposedly a secret, the plot is based on 'The Taming of the Shrew' and stems from an idea of Lemuel Ayers and Arnold Saint Subber, who will produce it next season under John C. Wilson's supervision. It isn't a feat of the imagination to deduce that Miss Novotna would be the Katherine and Mr Ferrer the Petruchio." Sam Zolotow, "Novotna, Ferrer May Do a Musical," *New York Times*, March 17, 1948, accessed November 21, 2014, https://www.nytimes.com/1948/03/17/archives/novotna-ferrer-may-do-a-musical-metropolitan-opera-star-and-actor.html.
41. CPT 1/1: Drake Transcript, 14; CU BSS 37/*Kiss Me, Kate* Clippings: Spewack Memorandum, 5.
42. Hannah Waddingham quoted in "Brief Encounter with . . . Kiss Me Kate's Hannah Waddingham," *WhatsOnStage*, June 25, 2012, https://www.whatsonstage.com/news/brief-encounter-with-kiss-me-kates-hannah-waddingham_3730/.

43. Schwartz, *Cole Porter*, 234; McBrien, *Cole Porter*, 305.
44. Robert Kimball and Brendan Gill, *Cole* (New York: Overlook Press, 1972), 72; Eells, *The Life That Late He Led*, 245.
45. Wilson, *Noel, Tallulah, Cole, and Me*, 171.
46. Louis Calta, "Wilson to Stage Musical," *New York Times*, March 9, 1948, 27, accessed November, 21, 2014, https://www.nytimes.com/1948/03/09/archives/wpcg-2vbzznxxx-uxi-cxcourier-10-pitchx2e-cowards-revival-leaves.html.
47. CPT 3/1: rider to contract for John C. Wilson (first signed March 29, 1948), June 17, 1948.
48. Chapter 3 outlines Sam Spewack's traceable interventions on the early drafts of *Kiss Me, Kate*, so this chapter will only name Bella Spewack and Porter for the remainder of its journey.
49. CU BSS 26/Notes and Worksheets [1]: outline of *Backstage*, April 22, 1948; CU BSS 27/*Kiss Me, Kate* Scripts: first complete draft.
50. CU BSS 26/Notes and Worksheets [2]: incomplete overview of Fred and Lilli's relationship history; CU BSS 26/Notes and Worksheets [1]: outline of *Backstage*, April 22, 1948, 1–2.
51. CU BSS 26/Notes and Worksheets [2]: incomplete overview of Fred and Lilli's relationship history.
52. The complete quotation reads: "He, on his part, during the years of their separation took a fling doing the PLAYBOY OF THE WESTERN WORLD, SYRANO in French in Paris, gotten his own Workshop on the air where he read Walt Whitman for a solid hour." Bella Spewack has written in pencil, "*The sponsor bowed out*" next to the French show. Ibid.
53. CU BSS 27/*Kiss Me, Kate* Scripts: first complete draft, 1-2-9; *Kiss Me, Kate* (Knopf), 28.
54. Ibid.
55. CU BSS 26/Notes and Worksheets [2]: incomplete overview of Fred and Lilli's relationship history; CU BSS 26/Notes and Worksheets [1]: outline of *Backstage*, April 22, 1948, 1–2.
56. CU BSS 26/Notes and Worksheets [1]: outline of *Backstage*, April 22, 1948, 10 pp.
57. Ibid., 1.
58. Ibid.
59. CU BSS 26/Notes and Worksheets [1]: outline of *Backstage*, April 22, 1948, 1–2; *Kiss Me, Kate* (Knopf), xxi–xxii.
60. CU BSS 26/Notes and Worksheets [1]: outline of *Backstage*, April 22, 1948.
61. Ibid., 2.
62. The agent character is not referenced in other *Kiss Me, Kate* documents available to the author.
63. CU BSS 26/Notes and Worksheets [1]: outline of *Backstage*, April 22, 1948, 3.
64. Ibid.
65. CU BSS 26/Notes and Worksheets [1]: outline of *Backstage*, April 22, 1948, 4.
66. *Kiss Me, Kate* (Knopf), 134.
67. In order to allay his disappointment, Lilli suggests that Harrison fulfill his dream "to take a whack at a drum with an orchestra" and he leaves. *Backstage* ends with a spotlight on Harrison in the orchestra pit. CU BSS 26/Notes and Worksheets [1]: outline of *Backstage*, April 22, 1948, 6.
68. Ibid.
69. Ibid.
70. Ibid.
71. CU BSS 26/Notes and Worksheets [1]: outline of *Backstage*, April 22, 1948, 2.
72. After Fred and Lilli perform "Wunderbar," Lilli receives a call (organized by Harrison) from her estate in Beverly Hills and proceeds to talk to Zuleika, the hound. "She only talks French." CU BSS 27/*Kiss Me, Kate* Scripts: first complete draft, 1-2-12.

Chapter 3

1. Spewack recalled telling Ayers and Subber how little she liked the play: "I said: 'It's a lousy play. I read it in high school. One of the worst Shakespeare wrote.'" Bella Spewack quoted in Eells, *The Life That Late He Led*, 238–239.
2. Bella Spewack, "My Life with Shakespeare," *Musical Show*, March 1967, 2. [CU BSS 37]
3. Spewack and Spewack, "Introduction" to *Kiss Me, Kate* (Knopf), x.
4. CU BSS 27/*Kiss Me, Kate* Scripts: first complete draft, 1-1-2.
5. It is likely that many of these parts would have been doubled in Elizabethan performances, requiring only fourteen performers. Ann Thompson, notes on William Shakespeare, *The Taming of the Shrew* (Cambridge: Cambridge University Press, 2003), 52.
6. Spewack and Spewack, "Introduction" to *Kiss Me, Kate* (Knopf), xvii.
7. Shakespeare, *The Taming of the Shrew*, 4.1.190.

8. CU BSS 26/Notes and Worksheets [2]: untitled scene outline, dated April 28, 1948, 9 pp.
9. Ibid., 1.
10. Ibid., 1–9.
11. CU BSS 27/*Kiss Me, Kate* Scripts: first complete draft, 1-7-31.
12. An abridged production of *The Taming of the Shrew* for *Shakespeare in the Park* (June 2016) also began their production at this line in the text.
13. CU BSS 26: Notes and Worksheets [2]: untitled scene outline, dated April 28, 1948, 4.
14. CU BSS 37/*Kiss Me, Kate* Clippings: Spewack Memorandum, 5.
15. Spewack and Spewack, "Introduction" to *Kiss Me, Kate* (Knopf), xvii.
16. CU BSS 26: Notes and Worksheets [2]: untitled scene outline, dated April 28, 1948, 1–2.
17. Ibid, 2.
18. Some feminist interpretations of *the Taming of the Shrew* suggest that Katherine never submits emotionally to Petruchio but makes a life-preserving decision to humor him, while retaining her own mental independence. Penny Gay proposes that this is a performance decision, noting that: "Many actresses, desperate for a romantic ending, argue that in the 'sun and moon' scene Kate learns to play Petruchio's game—even treating it as an erotic game." In this context, Katherine *pretends* to give way rather than breaks under the impact of being abused. Penny Gay, "Farce: *The Comedy of Errors, The Taming of the Shrew, The Merry Wives of Windsor*," in *The Cambridge Introduction to Shakespeare's Comedies* (Cambridge: Cambridge University Press, 2008), 27.
19. CU BSS 27/Kiss Me, Kate Scripts: first complete draft, 2-7-31.
20. CU BSS E/Curated correspondence with Cole Porter: letter from Cole Porter to Bella Spewack (copied from letter to John. C. Wilson), June 16, 1948, 1.
21. CU BSS 26/Notes and Worksheets [1]: outline of *Backstage*, April 22, 1948, 4.
22. Shakespeare, *The Taming of the Shrew*, 4.1.53–68.
23. CU BSS 26/Notes and Worksheets [1]: outline of *Backstage*, 6–7.
24. Millstein, "Words Anent Music by Cole Porter," 6 and 55.
25. Spewack and Spewack, "Introduction" to *Kiss Me, Kate* (Knopf), x.
26. Ibid.
27. CU BSS 26/Notes and Worksheets [1]: outline of *Backstage*, April 22, 1948, 2.
28. LC CP 11/3: folder of lyrics.
29. CU BSS E/Curated correspondence with Cole Porter: letter from Cole Porter to Bella Spewack (copied from letter to John C. Wilson), June 16, 1948, 1.
30. *Kiss Me, Kate* (Knopf), 38–39.
31. Shakespeare, *The Taming of the Shrew*, 1.2.193–196; *Kiss Me, Kate* (Knopf), 51.
32. Shakespeare, *The Taming of the Shrew*, 4.1.188; 4.1.197–202.
33. CU BSS 37/*Kiss Me, Kate* Clippings: Spewack Memorandum, 5.
34. Ibid., 1-7-37-8.
35. Shakespeare, *The Taming of the Shrew*, 1.1.62–102; CU BSS 27/*Kiss Me, Kate* Scripts: May Libretto—Spewack, 1-7-39.
36. CU BSS 27/Kiss Me, Kate Scripts: first complete draft, 1-7-37-41; 1-11-46-48; 1-13-56-60.
37. Porter's draft lyric for a song titled 'To Be or Not to Be' also makes pointed reference to *Hamlet*: "To be or not to be / I know I've got to be / In love with you." LC CP 11/1: "To Be or Not to Be" autograph lyric draft.
38. CU BSS 27/Kiss Me, Kate Scripts: first complete draft, 1-7-33.
39. The full chorus is outlined below. LC CP 11/2: "If Ever Married I'm" typed lyric sheet, April 8, 1948.

Chapter 4

1. Block, *Enchanted Evenings*, 217.
2. Swain, "Shakespeare as Musical," 139–164; Block, "*Kiss Me, Kate*: The Taming of Cole Porter," in *Enchanted Evenings*, 215–232; Knapp, *The American Musical and the Performance of Personal Identity*, 273–284; Siebert, "*Kiss Me, Kate*," 286–304; Buchler, "Musical Structure, Dramatic Form, and Song Pairings in Cole Porter's *Kiss Me, Kate*," 37–54.
3. Knapp, *The American Musical and the Performance of Identity*, 273.
4. Block, *Enchanted Evenings*, 218; Siebert, *The Cole Porter Companion*, 286–288.
5. Knapp, *The American Musical and the Performance of Identity*, 274.
6. This does not imply that other composers were not invested in comedy and/or entertainment. However, Porter's musicals prioritize these elements in ways that are less fundamental to the work of many of his contemporaries.

7. These are also outlined in: Porter, *Kiss Me, Kate: A Musical Play*.
8. LC CP 11/1: "If You Love Your Job" autograph lyric draft, undated, 1 p.
9. Sam Spewack's *Taming of the Shrew* draft does not extend into Act 2. However, he is consistent with the song list in the *Backstage* overview and the original Broadway production. I have discounted this absence in representing which songs were consistently included in *Kiss Me, Kate*.
10. This is likely to be one of the "Folders of Lyrics" held at the Library of Congress, which match this description very exactly. LC CP 11/1-5: various folders of lyrics. Contents are typed (sometimes with annotations, mainly by Porter) lyric sheets, autograph drafts, and excerpts written on notepaper from the Waldorf-Astoria, where he had his New York residence.
11. Howard Taubman, "Cole Porter Is Top Again," *New York Times Magazine*, January 16, 1949, 50.
12. Millstein, "Words Anent Music—Cole Porter," 6 and 55.
13. Jeffrey Magee, *Irving Berlin's American Musical Theater* (New York: Oxford University Press, 2014), 227.
14. An autograph lyric draft for "How Simple Life Could Be" shows Porter writing note values over the draft text. LC CP 11/1: "How Simple Life Could Be," undated, 1 p.
15. LC CP 11/1: "I Hate Men" autograph lyric draft [B2], undated, 1.
16. LC CP 11/1: "Too Darn Hot" autograph lyric draft [A6], undated, 1 p.
17. Ibid.
18. LC CP 8/12: "I Am Ashamed That Women Are So Simple" autograph lead sheet, undated, 2pp; LC CP 9/1: "First Act Finale" autograph lead sheet, undated, 2 pp.
19. LC CP 9/1: "First Act Finale" typed lyric sheet, June 26, 1948, 3.
20. Allen Forte, "Secrets of Melody: Line and Design in the Songs of Cole Porter," *Musical Quarterly* 77, no. 4 (1992): 610.
21. Ibid.
22. Raymond Alwyn, "Shakespeare's 'Kate' Is a Dollar Double-Cross!," *Daily Mirror*, March 7, 1951.
23. Ibid.
24. YISG CP 46/290: Big Sketchbook (extracts of musical ideas), undated, unpaginated.
25. In 2015, I delivered a paper on trends in Cole Porter's compositional materials while under supervision of Dominic Broomfield-McHugh, and he kindly acknowledges our collaboration on Porter's work with Sirmay in the relevant micro-section of his article. Dominic McHugh, "'I'll never know exactly who did what': Broadway Composers as Musical Collaborators," *Journal of the American Musicological Society* 68 (2015): 615.
26. YISG CP 39/254: "Always True to You (In My Fashion)," pencil sketch of unused melody (opening verse) transcribed by Albert Sirmay, undated, 4 pp.; LC CP 11/1: "Always True to You (In My Fashion)," autograph draft of unused verse, undated, 1 p.
27. Siebert, "*Kiss Me, Kate*," 287.
28. Ibid.
29. Swain, *The Broadway Musical*, 150.
30. Block, *Enchanted Evenings*, 220.
31. Ibid., 221.
32. Buchler, "Musical Structure, Dramatic Form, and Song Pairings in Cole Porter's *Kiss Me, Kate*," 38.
33. Knapp, *The American Musical and the Performance of Identity*, 276–282.
34. Buchler, "Musical Structure, Dramatic Form, and Song Pairings in Cole Porter's *Kiss Me, Kate*," 50.
35. Knapp, *The American Musical and the Performance of Identity*, 274.
36. LC CP 11/1: "A Woman's Career," typed lyric sheet, July 31, 1948, 1.
37. Knapp, *The American Musical and the Performance of Identity*, 274.
38. G. J. Decker and Michael Buchler, *Here for the Hearing: Analyzing the Music in Musical Theater* (Ann Arbor: University of Michigan Press, 2023).
39. Ibid., 281.
40. Cole Porter, *Kiss Me, Kate: A Musical Play*, 43–45.
41. YISG 39/255: "It Was Great Fun the First Time" fair copy, 7.
42. YISG 39/255: "It Was Great Fun The First Time" fair copy, undated, 2–4.
43. Cole Porter, *Kiss Me, Kate: A Musical Play*, 100.
44. YISG 39/255: "We Shall Never Be Younger" fair copy, 4–5.
45. Block, *Enchanted Evenings*, 228.
46. Ibid., 229.

47. CU BSS E/Curated correspondence with Cole Porter: letter from Cole Porter to Bella Spewack (copied from letter to John C. Wilson), June 16, 1948, 1.
48. CU BSS E/Curated correspondence with Cole Porter: letter from Cole Porter to Bella Spewack, June 16, 1948, 5–6.
49. *Kiss Me, Kate* (Knopf), 140.
50. LC CP 11/1: "Brush Up Your Shakespeare" typed lyric sheet, June 12, 1948, 2.
51. LC CP 11/1: "Brush Up Your Shakespeare" autograph lyric draft (undated), 1.
52. LC CP 9/1: "First Act Finale" autograph lead sheet (undated), 2.

Chapter 5

1. Eells, *The Life That Late He Led*, 245; Grafton, *Red, Hot & Rich*, 171–172; McBrien, *Cole Porter*, 305.
2. *Kiss Me, Kate* (Knopf), 89.
3. Ibid.
4. The Donizetti score does not include annotation of a cadenza of this nature. It has been fairly widely accepted that this feature, in which "Lucia" performs an extensive improvisation accompanied by a solo flautist, was introduced by Nellie Melba in the late 1880s. Numerous star sopranos including Maria Callas and Joan Sutherland have performed their own noted interpretations of the cadenza after Melba. Each version includes comparable echoing and doubling as seen in the extract from *Kiss Me, Kate* in Figure 5.1.
5. The full stage direction reads: "*(As* KATHARINE *starts coloratura, a girl enters carrying a bird. At the end of coloratura bird goes up in air.* FIRST GUNMAN *shoots at bird. Bird drops to stage, generally on* BAPTISTA's *hat.)*" *Kiss Me, Kate*, Critical Edition, 175–176; *Kiss Me, Kate* (Knopf), 89.
6. Porter, *Kiss Me, Kate*, 120–121. (See also *Kiss Me, Kate*, Critical Edition, 175–176.)
7. Ibid.
8. Susan McClary, *Feminine Endings: Music, Gender, and Sexuality*, rev. ed. (Minneapolis: University of Minnesota Press, 2002), 90–91.
9. Ibid., 86.
10. Ibid., 92.
11. CU BSS 37/*Kiss Me, Kate* Clippings: Spewack Memorandum, 5; YISG MCB 5/83-85: "Notes on Conference held at Edward Colton's office at 551 Fifth Avenue, New York City on March 22, 1950," 6.
12. Eells, *The Life That Late He Led*, 245.
13. Ibid.
14. "One day the phone rang, and it was Richard Rodgers saying that they had brought a new property, South Pacific. Would Miss Martin wait until she heard the music before making a decision? We knew the property. We had read it only the same week and had tried to buy it only to find Rodgers and Hammerstein had already made the deal." Richard Halliday (1965) as quoted in ibid., 245.
15. Schwartz, *Cole Porter*, 231.
16. McBrien, *Cole Porter*, 306; Scott Feinberg, "'Kiss Me Kate' Originator Patricia Morison Interviewed by Scott Feinberg," *YouTube*, 1:03:57, posted by Scott Feinberg, June 6, 2013, accessed December 15, 2016, https://www.youtube.com/watch?v=BQswR26fDFM, 43:26–43:45.
17. It is worth noting that later in this letter, Porter says that they have no one in mind for Fred/Petruchio so that Drake's suggestion was either conveyed anonymously or it was coincidental. CU BSS 21/*Kiss Me, Kate* correspondence (1948): letter from Cole Porter to Bella Spewack, June 16, 1948, 1–3.
18. George Eells, *The Life That Late He Led*, 246.
19. Feinberg, "'Kiss Me Kate' Originator Patricia Morison Interviewed by Scott Feinberg," 47:00–47:30.
20. CU BSS E/Curated correspondence with Cole Porter: letter from Cole Porter to Bella Spewack, June 16, 1948.
21. CU BSS E/Curated correspondence with Cole Porter: telegram from Cole Porter to Bella Spewack [undated but catalogued with a related telegram dated June 19, 1948].
22. CU BSS 21/*Kiss Me, Kate* Correspondence (1948): "Proposed Letter to be sent by Bella Spewack to Lem Ayers, etc.", August 10, 1948.
23. Ibid.

24. A version of this is preserved in Hanya Holm's papers at the NYPL alongside a clean copy of the first script draft. NYPL HH 21/501: undated script [1]; NYPL HH 21/501: undated script [2].
25. NYPL HH 21/501: undated script [1].
26. Ibid., 1-4-26.
27. Holm was also looking for an opportunity to incorporate a major set piece, which could be prepared behind the curtain if the song was performed in this way. NYPL HH 21/501: interim script, 2-6-32.
28. Tom Vallance, "Obituary: Alfred Drake," *The Independent*, August 6, 1992, accessed June 6, 2015, http://www.independent.co.uk/news/people/obituary-alfred-drake-1538814.html.
29. *The Beggar's Holiday* featured Drake with Zero Mostel and Herbert Ross (later to become a major Broadway choreographer). The musical featured an interracial love affair in the midst of a corrupt shanty town, which led to picketing outside the theater. It closed after fourteen weeks. Uwe Böker, ed., *John Gay's The Beggar's Opera, 1728–2004: Adaptations and Re-writings* (Amsterdam: Rodopi, 2006), 22.
30. CPT 1/1: Drake Transcript, 2.
31. Ibid.
32. Lewis Funke, "News and Gossip of the Rialto," *New York Times*, May 2, 1948; Lewis Funke, "News and Gossip of the Rialto: Shaw Complains about 'Superman's' Success—Other Items," *New York Times*, May 23, 1948.
33. CPT 1/1: Drake Transcript, 1.
34. Drake refers to signing "a generous" contract to play in *Kiss Me, Kate* but claimed that this was subject to an agreement that he would not take part in any of the fundraising events: "I may not have been a 'star' but I was quite well known by then." Ibid., 2–3, 10.
35. CPT 1/1: Drake Transcript, 3.
36. Ibid., 4.
37. Ibid.
38. Louis Calta, "Producers Avert Press Agents Row," *New York Times*, October 16, 1948, 9.
39. Louis Calta, "Harold Lang Gets Top Role in Show," *New York Times*, August 21, 1948.
40. See more: Carol J. Oja, *Bernstein Meets Broadway: Collaborative Art in a Time of War* (New York: Oxford University Press, 2014).
41. CPT 1/1: Drake Transcript, 6.
42. Kirk and Fuller performed with Earl Wrightson, Christina Lind, and pianist Joe Moon to help sure up *Kiss Me, Kate*'s financial backing early in the summer of 1948. Wrightson, who previously starred as Benvenuto Cellini in *The Firebrand of Florence*, was later cast as Fred for part of the touring production.
43. Louis Calta, "Lisa Kirk Is Signed for 'Kiss Me, Kate," *New York Times*, October 2, 1948. Louis Calta, "Miller Play Casts Its Leading Roles: Lee J. Cobb, Anne Revere Join 'Death of a Salesman," *New York Times*, October 28, 1948.
44. The parallels between Stanley—"a lubberly, wooden-faced lout"—and the second gunman are noticeable, as are the general similarities in style between Weill and Nash's barbershop waltz "The Trouble with Women" and Porter's "Brush Up Your Shakespeare." S. J Perelman, Ogden Nash, and Kurt Weill, *One Touch of Venus* (Radnor, PA: Chiltern Book Co., 1973), 150.
45. Feinberg, "'Kiss Me Kate' Originator Patricia Morison Interviewed by Scott Feinberg," 42:44–44:20.
46. David Ewen, *The Cole Porter Story* (New York: Holt, Rinehart & Winston, 1965), 126.
47. YISG MCB 5/83-85: "Notes on Conference held at Edward Colton's office at 551 Fifth Avenue, New York City on March 22, 1950," 6.
48. In a note written on the envelope holding this letter, de Mille explains that her son had been about to undergo a serious operation and that she had not felt able to take on a Broadway musical at that time. NYPL ADM IX-10: Letter from Agnes de Mille to John C. Wilson, September 8, 1948.
49. In June, Bella Spewack indicated that they had already amassed $100,000 in financial support, but the auditions for backers continued into October, delaying the start of rehearsals. NYPL ADM IX-10: Letter from John C. Wilson to Agnes de Mille, September 15, 1947.
50. Ibid.
51. "VERY INTERESTED IN DUSCUSSING [*SIC*] THE NEW COLE PORTER SHOW WITH YOU. REHEARSAL LATTER PART OF OCTOBER. WOULD YOU WIRE WHETHER YOU ARE INTERESTED AND AVAILABLE ALSO WHEN YOU RETURN TO CITY BECAUSE PREPARATION SHOULD START IMMEDIATELY?" NYPL

HH 20/497: telegram from Arnold Saint Subber to Hanya Holm, August 30, 1948; NYPL HH 20/498: Hanya Holm—*Kiss Me, Kate* contract [signed by Subber], September 30, 1948.

52. Virginia Lee Warren, "Dance Should Not Attempt to Tell Story, Interpret Nature, Declare Two Leading Exponents of the Art in This Country: Martha Graham and Hanya Holm Admit They Owe Much to Ballet," *Washington Post*, February 23, 1935.
53. John Martin, "New York Debut for Hanya Holm," *New York Times*, December 29, 1937, 17.
54. Claudia Gitelman, "Finding a Place for Hanya Holm," *Dance Chronicle* 23, no. 1 (2000): 49–53.
55. Andrea Kraut, *Copyrighting Choreography: Race, Gender, and Intellectual Property Rights in American Dance* (New York: Oxford University Press, 2016), 185–188.
56. NYPL HH 21/501: undated script [1]. Interim script, 2-3-9.
57. Ibid., 1-5-40.
58. Ibid., 1-9-51.
59. Ibid.
60. NYPL HH 21/502: undated script [2] [May Libretto]; NYPL HH 21/501: undated script [1] [Interim script c. September 1948]; NYPL HH 21/503: October 11 script [Act One only].
61. NYPL HH 20/499: typed memorandum with autograph annotations.
62. NYPL HH 20/500: autograph notes on loose sheet, describing Act 1 song breakdown.
63. NYPL HH 20/500: excerpt from *Kiss Me, Kate* notebook [not paginated].
64. NYPL HH 21/503: October 11 script.
65. NYPL HH 20/500: loose sheet of notes of potential dance sequences in Act 1 of the interim script.
66. NYPL HH 20/500: *Kiss Me, Kate* notebook [one of four pages on this sequence].
67. Ibid.
68. Ibid.
69. Ibid.
70. NYPL HH 20/500: Loose sheet on "Too Darn Hot."
71. "People and Ideas: 'Kiss Me, Kate'/'Lend an Ear,'" *Vogue*, February 15, 1949.
72. Kraut, *Copyrighting Choreography*, 185–188.
73. CPT 1/1: Drake Transcript, 3, 5, 9. See also Eells, *The Life That Late He Led*, 248.
74. Bella Spewack as quoted in McBrien, *Cole Porter*, 310.
75. Patricia Morrison as quoted in ibid., 311; Feinberg, "'Kiss Me Kate' Originator Patricia Morison Interviewed by Scott Feinberg," 48:00–48:35.
76. CPT 1/1: Drake Interview, 13.
77. CU BSS 21/*Kiss Me, Kate* Correspondence (1948): letter from Edward E. Colton to Arnold Saint Subber and Lemuel Ayers, November 11, 1948.
78. CU BSS 21/*Kiss Me, Kate* Correspondence (1950): letter from Edward E. Colton to Arnold Saint Subber and Lemuel Ayers, July 27, 1950.
79. McBrien, *Cole Porter*, 310.
80. Ibid.
81. The earliest dated lyric sheet is a loose leaf in NYPL HH 21/501: undated script [1].
82. McBrien, *Cole Porter*, 311.
83. Ibid.
84. Copies of photographs including some by Darby and Kubrick are available from the Museum of the City of New York's digitized photo collection [online]. NYPL HC 2/2.5 *Kiss Me Kate* scrapbook: signed photograph of Alfred Drake as Petruchio and press clippings including photographic illustrations; NYPL HH 798-800: *Kiss Me, Kate* photographs (rehearsals and performance); NYPL HL 3/3.10: press clippings and candid photographs; Museum of the City of New York, "Kiss Me, Kate (musical)" digitized image collection, accessed October 10, 2016, http://collections.mcny.org/C.aspx?VP3=SearchResult&VBID=24UAYWEGU3ZPK&SMLS=1&RW=1527&RH=822#/SearchResult&VBID=24UAYWEGU31J9&SMLS=1&RW=1527&RH=822
85. Examples of this media can be found in the papers of Harry Clark, Hanya Holm, and Harold Lang. Lang's collection also includes some uncredited photographs from backstage, and pictures by Fred Fehl who documented over 1,000 theater productions. Among Lang's scrapbook of photographs are a pair of images of Morison messing around, and pulling faces, outside her dressing room, offering a tiny glimpse of her character, which is often hidden in coverage of this musical. NYPL HL 3/3.10: photographs of Patricia Morison backstage in her first *Taming of the Shrew* costume.

86. A form of street theater, the *commedia dell'arte* originated in Venice in the 1600s and was based on improvised stories, constructed around stock characters including masters, servants, and lovers.
87. Gay, "Farce: *The Comedy of Errors, The Taming of the Shrew, The Merry Wives of Windsor*." There are also passing references to the use of the *commedia* in *The Taming of the Shrew* in several chapters in Judith Chaffee and Oliver Crick, (eds., *The Routledge Companion to Commedia Dell'Arte* (Abingdon: Routledge, 2017), particularly in Edward Grenwar's chapter "The Old Man's Spectacles: Commedia and Shakespeare," 305–306.
88. Gay suggests that Katherine's character emanates from "a long tradition in English theatre and in popular ballads" that includes "a talkative, hot-tempered and ungovernable woman." She gives examples including Noah's wife in the Mystery play as well as Judy from Punch and Judy puppet shows. Gay, "Farce: *The Comedy of Errors, The Taming of the Shrew, The Merry Wives of Windsor*," 23–24.
89. NYPL HH 20/500—*Kiss Me, Kate* notebook, 14
90. Ibid., 21.
91. RSC TS/2/2/1987/KIS1: Adrian Noble, dir., *Kiss Me, Kate* (1987) [DVD], disc 1.
92. McBrien, *Cole Porter*, 317.
93. Eells recounts that Subber stowed Hart in the balcony of the theater to observe and at the end of the performance, he turned to Subber and said, "Too bad; you haven't got it." Eells, *The Life That Late He Led*, 248.
94. Ibid., 249.
95. Ibid.
96. Grafton, *Red, Hot & Rich*, 167.
97. YISG CP 49/298: letter from John C. Wilson to Linda Porter [undated].
98. Eells, *The Life That Late He Led*, 249.
99. Ibid.
100. Waters, "Plays Out of Town: *Kiss Me, Kate*," *Variety*, December 2, 1948 [YISG Scrapbook].
101. Edwin H. Schloss: "Cole Porter's '*Kiss Me Kate*' [*sic*] Opens at Shubert," *The Philadelphia Inquirer*, December 3, 1948 [CU BSS Clippings].
102. Ibid.
103. CU BS 21/*Kiss Me, Kate* Correspondence (1948): letter from Edwin H. Schloss to Bella Spewack, December 2, 1948.
104. Jerry Gaghan, "'Kiss Me, Kate' at the Shubert; Cole Porter's New Musical," *Philadelphia Daily News*, December 3, 1984 [CU BSS Clippings].
105. Maurie Orodenker, "Kiss Me, Kate," *The Billboard*, December 11, 1948 [YISG Scrapbook].
106. Ethan Mordden, *Beautiful Mornin': The Broadway Musical in the 1940s* (New York: Oxford University Press, 1999), 257–258.

Chapter 6

1. Eldon Kelley, "Cole Porter and Shakespeare Collaborate on *Kiss Me, Kate*," *New York Herald Tribune*, December 26, 1948.
2. Mark Barron, "Cole Porter Tunes Click in *Kate*," *Syracuse New York Herald Journal*, December 31, 1948.
3. Robert Coleman, "*Kiss Me, Kate* Porter's Best, a Terrific Hit," *Daily Mirror*, December 31, 1948.
4. John Lardner, "Of Sweet Kate and Mr. Porter," *New York Star*, December 31, 1948.
5. Ibid.
6. Wolcott Gibbs, "Theatre," *New Yorker*, January 8, 1949.
7. Wilson, *Noel, Tallulah, Cole and Me*, 180.
8. CU BSS 21/*Kiss Me, Kate* Correspondence (1951): letter from Selma Tamber to Bella Spewack, August 6, 1951.
9. CU BSS 21/*Kiss Me, Kate* Correspondence (1950): memorandum for Edward E. Colton (written by Bella Spewack), 1.
10. Ibid.
11. Queen Elizabeth II (then Princess Elizabeth) and the Duke of Edinburgh also attended a performance of *Kiss Me, Kate* after it had opened in London. "*The Shrew* Musicalised," *Daily Telegraph*, March 8, 1951; "Princess at the Theatre," *Manchester Guardian*, May 8, 1951, 4.
12. Daily Mail Reporter, "Queuers Wait for 22 Hours," *Daily Mail*, March 8, 1951.

13. "Coliseum: *Kiss Me, Kate*," *The Times*, March 9, 1951; "The Arts and Entertainment: Guying the Bard," *The New Statesman and Nation*, March 17, 1951.
14. "Coliseum: *Kiss Me, Kate*."
15. Harold Hobson, "*The Theatre*: Derivations," *The Sunday Times*, March 11, 1951. See also: "A Kiss Me Cry," *Daily Mail*, March 9, 1951; Cecil Wilson, "Yes, It Glows of Certain Success," *Daily Mail*, March 9, 1951.
16. Peter Williams, "Something New in Dance Routine," *Daily Mail*, March 9, 1951.
17. "Coliseum: *Kiss Me, Kate*"; Harold Hobson, "*The Theatre*: Derivations."
18. CU BSS 21/*Kiss Me, Kate* Correspondence (1951): letter from Bella Spewack to Edward E. Colton, May 24, 1951, 1.
19. CU BSS 21/*Kiss Me, Kate* Correspondence (1951): letter from Bella Spewack to Edward E. Colton, June 14, 1951.
20. George Campey, "BBC *Kiss Me Kate* Show Off," *Evening Standard*, July 19, 1951.
21. CU BSS 21/*Kiss Me, Kate* Correspondence (1951): letter from Jack Hylton to Bella and Sam Spewack, October 4, 1951.
22. Ibid.
23. CU BSS 21/*Kiss Me, Kate* Correspondence (1951): letter from Jack Hylton to Bella and Sam Spewack, October 22, 1951.
24. Ibid.
25. CU BSS 21/*Kiss Me, Kate* Correspondence (1952): letter from Selma Tamber (The Salem Company) to Bella Spewack, January 18, 1952.
26. J. Daniel Jenkins, "The Early Years of the American Musical in Vienna," *Journal of Austrian-American History* 6, no. 1 (2022): 92.
27. Hermann Weissgärber, *You Can't Copy Tradition: A View on the Eventful History and Bilateral Work of the Austro-American Institute of Education from 1926–2016. Volume 1 (1926–1971)*, 2016, [digital edition], unpaginated; Reinhold Wagnleitner, *Coca-colonization and the Cold War: The Cultural Mission of the United States in Austria after the Second World War* (Chapel Hill: University of North Carolina Press, 1994), 200.
28. Marcel Prawy, "Marcel Prawy erzählt wie er das Musical nach Österreich holte," *YouTube*, 11:32, posted by MusicalTheaterDetect, July 1, 2012, accessed June 3, 2016, https://www.youtube.com/watch?v=tdW8A13xtqs.
29. Marcel Prawy, *Marcel Prawy Erzählt aus seinem Leben: . . . und seine Vision der Oper des 21. Jahrhunderts; 30 Tage im Leben eines Neunzigjährigen* (Vienna: Kremayr & Scheriau, 2001), 112 [translation from German by the author].
30. CU BSS 21/*Kiss Me, Kate* Correspondence (1954): letter from Edward E. Colton to Bella Spewack and Robert Montgomery, November 2, 1954.
31. J Jenkins, "The Early Years of the American Musical in Vienna," 93.
32. Ibid., 92–93.
33. Ibid., 93.
34. Lewis also led many world premieres of new work by American composers, including Jack Beeson's *Lizzie Borden* in 1965.
35. Jenkins, "The Early Years of the American Musical in Vienna," 94.
36. Julius Rudel, "And Nobody Missed the Waltz!," *Theatre Arts* (June 1956), 80.
37. Ibid.
38. Ibid., 79–80.
39. "German Version of 'Kiss Me, Kate' Gets Cheers at Its Opening Night in Vienna," *New York Times*, February 15, 1956.
40. Prawy, *Marcel Prawy Erzählt*, 113 [translation from German by the author].
41. CU BSS 21/*Kiss Me, Kate* Correspondence (1956): letter from Sam H. Linch to Julius Rudel [undated].
42. CU BSS 21/*Kiss Me, Kate* Correspondence (1957): letter from Marcel Prawy to Bella Spewack, November 14, 1957.
43. CU BSS 22/*Kiss Me, Kate* Correspondence (1961): letter from Bella Spewack to Cole Porter, May 30, 1961.
44. John Gale, "How Carmen Became Kate," *The Observer*, November 1, 1970, 9.
45. Wagnleitner, *Coca-colonization and the Cold War*, 201.
46. A similar phenomenon has been seen during recent revivals of *Sweeney Todd: The Demon Barber of Fleet Street* and *Sunset Boulevard* at the English National Opera in London, and Julie Andrews's directorial debut of *My Fair Lady* at the Sydney Opera House.

47. Fred Lounsberry, "Down with Sense," *New York Times*, June 22, 1952.
48. Ibid.
49. Richard Rodgers, "In Defence of Sense," *New York Times*, June 29, 1952.
50. CU BSS *Kiss Me, Kate* Correspondence (1970): letter from Stephen Arlen to John Wharton, September 7, 1970, 1.
51. Ibid.
52. Peter Heyworth, "Coliseum Problems," *Guardian*, December 20, 1970.
53. CU BSS 27/*Kiss Me, Kate* scripts: Script A British (Sadler's Wells revival, 1970), ii; I-3-14; I-6-50.
54. Ibid., II-1-3.
55. CU BSS *Kiss Me, Kate* Correspondence (1970): note written by Peter Coe, November 11, 1970, 1–2.
56. CU BSS 26/Notes and Worksheets [2]: undated draft telegram from Sam Spewack to Stephen Arlen.
57. CU BSS 25/*Kiss Me, Kate* Correspondence (1970) [2]: letter from Adza Vincent to Sam Spewack, November 16, 1971.
58. CU BSS *Kiss Me, Kate* Correspondence (1970): letter from Edmund Tracey to Adza Vincent, December 9, 1948, 1.
59. Ibid.
60. CU BSS 25/*Kiss Me, Kate* Correspondence (1971): letter from Sam Spewack to Stephen Arlen, January 19, 1971, 1.
61. Ibid., 2.
62. "The First Rehearsal Picture of Kiss Me, Kate," *The Sunday Times*, December 20, 1970.
63. Felix Aprahamian, "Kate and Lucy," *The Sunday Times*, January 3, 1971.
64. Philip Hope-Walla, "KISS ME KATE at the Coliseum," *The Guardian*, December 28, 1970, 6.
65. Ibid.
66. Benedict Nightingale, *New Statesman* 81 (January 1, 1971): 90.
67. Jack Tinner, "Kate's Kiss Is Not So Hot," *Daily Mail*, July 20, 1971.
68. Nicholas de Jongh, "Royal Shakespeare Company at Risk after Disastrous Barbican Season," *The Guardian*, June 15, 1987.
69. The RSC production went considerably overbudget but recuperated these costs during the run.
70. Irving Wardle, "Just in It for the Money," *The Times*, February 11, 1987.
71. Francis King, "A Bridge of Size," *The Sunday Telegraph*, February 15, 1987.
72. Rod Chaytor, "Anything You Can Do, I Can Do Better," *Daily Mirror*, 1987.
73. "Fergie in Feathers Steals the Show," *Daily Mail*, February 6, 1987.

Chapter 7

1. CU BSS 21/*Kiss Me, Kate* Correspondence (1950): letter from Ira Blue to Sam Spewack, August 4, 1950.
2. CU BSS 21/*Kiss Me, Kate* Correspondence (1951): letter from Ben Schenkman to Bella Spewack, June 22, 1951.
3. CU BSS 21/*Kiss Me, Kate* Correspondence (1951): letter from Edward E. Colton to Bella Spewack, July 19, 1951, 1–2.
4. CU BSS E/Curated correspondence from Cole Porter: letter from Cole Porter to Bella Spewack, August 1, 1951.
5. Hannah Robbins, "'Too Darn Hot': Reimagining *Kiss Me, Kate* for the Silver Screen," in *The Oxford Handbook of Musical Theatre Screen Adaptations*, ed. Dominic McHugh (New York: Oxford University Press, 2019), 275–292.
6. MHL T/MGM, f.K-466: *Kiss Me Kate* script draft, November 29, 1952.
7. Ibid.
8. Ibid.
9. USC *Kiss Me Kate* scripts, f.465: script outline by Dorothy Kingsley, January 13, 1953.
10. MHL T/MGM, f.K-466: *Kiss Me Kate* script draft, January 17, 1953.
11. Ibid.
12. After the title of Hodgdon, *The Shakespeare Trade*.
13. USC *Kiss Me Kate* scripts, f.465: script outline by Dorothy Kingsley, January 13, 1953.
14. USC *Kiss Me Kate* scripts, f.465: script outline by Dorothy Kingsley, January 13, 1953.
15. See Chapter 2 for more details.
16. CU BSS 27 *Kiss Me, Kate* scripts: first script draft, 2-7-33.

17. USC *Kiss Me Kate* scripts, f.465: temporary incomplete script, dated February 6, 1953, n.p.
18. MGM's adaptation of the Broadway musical *Roberta* (1933), *Lovely to Look At*, starred Grayson as Stephanie (previously played by Irene Dunne in an RKO film adaptation (1935)). The film also featured Red Skelton, Ann Miller, Howard Keel, and Gower Champiom.
19. Block, *Enchanted Evenings*, 319.
20. CPT 1/1: Drake Transcript, 31.
21. Ibid.
22. Ibid., 32.
23. Howard Keel [recorded interview] in Sheridan Morley, "Introduction to *Kiss Me, Kate*'" *Kiss Me Kate* [live performance] BBC Radio 2, London, October 5, 1996, 07:47–09:04.
24. I specify vocal music here because the film includes fragments of these melodies in various sections of underscore.
25. Please see Robbins, "'Too Darn Hot.'"
26. USC *Kiss Me Kate* scripts, f. 465: script outline by Dorothy Kingsley, March 19, 1943.
27. CPT 4/1: letter from John Wharton to Cole Porter, April 21, 1953.
28. This is in addition to "Why Can't You Behave?" and "Tom, Dick, or Harry."
29. Kevin Winkler, *Big Deal: Bob Fosse and Dance in the American Musical* (New York: Oxford University Press, 2018), 3.
30. In addition to limiting promiscuity and other vulgarity on screen, it also restricted scenes of graphic violence and surgery and monitored the depiction of religion in film. Peter Hay, *MGM: When the Lion Roars* (New York: Turner Publishing, 1991), 90–91; John Kobal, *Gotta Sing Gotta Dance: A Pictorial History of Film Musicals* (London: Hamlyn Publishing Group, 1970), 182, 197; "The Hays Code," *British Film Institute Screen Online*, accessed June 30, 2017, http://www.screenonline.org.uk/film/id/592022/.
31. Hay, *MGM*, 90.
32. Ibid.
33. Shakespeare, *The Taming of the Shrew*, 5.2.179–180.
34. Chaplin was subsequently jointly nominated for the Academy Award Best Music, Scoring for a Musical Picture for his work with André Previn on *Kiss Me Kate*.
35. CPT 4/1: letter from Saul Chaplin to Cole Porter, April 10, 1953.
36. *Kiss Me, Kate* (Knopf), 56.
37. I also explore changes to "Too Darn Hot" and Miller's interpretation of Lois more fully in Robbins, "'Too Darn Hot.'"
38. *Kiss Me, Kate* (Knopf), 116.
39. *Kiss Me, Kate* (Knopf), 142.
40. George Sidney, dir., *Kiss Me Kate* (Burbank, CA: Warner Home Video, 2003) [DVD], 1:38:00–1:40:12.
41. Rouben Mamoulian, dir., *Silk Stockings* (Culver City, CA: Warner Home Video, 2003) [DVD].
42. By the end of the 1960s, film production had converted almost exclusively to color film production. Sheldon Hall and Stephen Neale, *Epics, Spectacles, and Blockbusters: A Hollywood History* (Detroit: Wayne State University Press, 2010), 140.
43. Dudley Andrew, "The Postwar Struggle for Color," *Cinema Journal* 18 (1979), accessed June 28, 2016, doi:10.2307/1225441; Drew Casper, *Postwar Hollywood: 1946–1962* (Malden, MA: Blackwell, 2007), 94.
44. 'MGM to Produce Wide-Screen, but Adaptable to All Ratios," *Boxoffice*, May 9, 1953, accessed November 21, 2014; Casper, *Postwar Hollywood*, 116.
45. Howard Keel [recorded interview], in Sheridan Morley, "Introduction to *Kiss Me, Kate*," *Kiss Me Kate* [live performance], BBC Radio 2, London, October 5, 1996.
46. Andrew, "The Postwar Struggle for Color"; Casper, *Postwar Hollywood*, 94.
47. George Morris, "George Sidney: A Matter of Taste," *Film Comment* 13 (1977): 56–60, accessed December 11, 2016, http://www.jstor.org/stable/43451380; Sidney, dir., *Kiss Me Kate*, 38:43.
48. Steven P. J. Knapper, "Carnival, Comedy and the Commedia," in *The Routledge Companion to Commedia dell'Arte*, ed. Judith Chaffee and Olly Crick (New York: Routledge, 2015), 103–4.
49. Jeff Stafford, "*Scaramouche* (1952)," *Turner Classic Movies* [online], http://www.tcm.com/tcmdb/title/2053/Scaramouche/articles.htm.
50. Sidney, dir., *Kiss Me, Kate*, [*Taming of the Shrew* opening sequence] 37:06; [Miller to camera] 42:48; [Finale Act One] 01:12:50; ["I Am Ashamed"] 01:47:12.

Chapter 8

1. Robin Pogrebin, "Another Op'nin', but Hardly Another Show," *New York Times*, December 7, 1999.
2. Ibid.
3. These can be found in Lang's papers at the New York Public Library.
4. "Kiss Me, Kate (Revised 1999)," *Tams-Witmark*, n.d., http://www.tamswitmark.com/shows/kiss-me-kate-1999/.
5. Cole Porter, Sam Spewack, and Bella Spewack, *Kiss Me, Kate* prompt book (Tams-Witmark, revised June 4, 1999), 74–75.
6. Donald Trump, Make America Great Again rally, Green Bay, Wisconsin, October 30, 2024.
7. Rebecca Lock quoted in Kerrie Nicholson, "Interview: Rebecca Lock Talks KISS ME, KATE at Sheffield Crucible," *Broadway World*, November 21, 2018, accessed November 22, 2023, https://www.broadwayworld.com/westend/article/BWW-Interview-Rebecca-Lock-Talks-KISS-ME-KATE-at-Sheffield-Crucible-20181121.
8. Jesse Green, "Review: A Fair Fight Makes 'Kiss Me, Kate' Lovable Again," *New York Times*, March 14, 2019, accessed November 26, 2023, https://www.nytimes.com/2019/03/14/theater/kiss-me-kate-review.html.
9. Melissa Errico, "I Love Performing Those Songs. But What about the Gender Politics?," *New York Times*, July 13, 2018, accessed November 22, 2023, https://www.nytimes.com/2018/07/13/theater/on-a-clear-day-my-fair-lady-eliza-doolittle.html.
10. Tim Teeman "'Kiss Me, Kate'? In This Broadway Revival She'll Also Kick Your Butt," *Daily Beast*, March 15, 2019.
11. Chris Jones, "'Kiss Me Kate' on Broadway Goes for the Feelings, and Kelli O'Hara Is a Pleasure as Kate," *Chicago Tribune*, March 14, 2019.
12. Brooks Atkinson, "'From Padua to Gotham' in 'Kiss Me, Kate,'" *New York Times*, January 16, 1949.
13. Howard Taubman, "Cole Porter Is 'The Top' Again," *New York Times*, January 16, 1949.
14. Simone de Beauvoir, *The Second Sex* (Vintage Digital, 2014), 24.

Bibliography

Archival materials itemized in box/folder order unless specified differently

Lord Chamberlain's Papers, British Library [BL LCP]

Kiss Me, Kate (1951)

Reader's report reviewing Hylton's application to stage *Kiss Me, Kate*, December 1, 1950.
Letter from Jack Hylton to the Comptroller, Lord Chamberlain's Office, February 16, 1951.
Bound Script
Substitute text for Kiss Me, Kate, 5 pp. [loose inserts].
Letter of complaint from Mrs M. Hanaghan to the Lord Chamberlain, March 1951.
Letter from (Sgd.) N. W. Gwatkin to Mr. Hartley, March 22, 1951.

Cole Porter Trust [CPT]

1/1: Transcript of interview with Alfred Drake [by James Klosty].
2/1: Transcriptions of letters from D. W. Abercrombie to Kate Porter (c. 1905–1909).
3/1: Rider to John C. Wilson contract, June 17, 1948 (contract signed March 29, 1948).
4/1: Letter from Saul Chaplin to Cole Porter, April 10, 1953.
Letter from John Wharton to Cole Porter, April 21, 1953.

Bella and Sam Spewack Papers, Columbia University [CU BSS]

E/Curated Correspondence with Cole Porter

Letter from Cole Porter to Bella Spewack, June 16, 1948.
Letter from Cole Porter to Bella Spewack, June 16, 1948 (John C. Wilson).
Telegram from Cole Porter to Bella Spewack, [June 19, 1948] [undated].
Telegram from Cole Porter to Bella Spewack, June 24, 1948.
Letter from Cole Porter to Bella Spewack, August 1, 1951.

21/*Kiss Me, Kate* Correspondence (1948)

Letter from Bella Spewack to Walter Kane, April 1, 1948.
Proposed letter from Bella Spewack to Lemuel Ayers and Arnold Saint Subber, August 10, 1948.
Letter from Edward E. Colton to Arnold Saint Subber and Lemuel Ayers, November 11, 1948.
Letter from Edwin H. Schloss to Bella Spewack, December 2, 1948.

21/*Kiss Me, Kate* Correspondence (1950)

Memorandum for Edward E. Colton (written by Bella Spewack).
Letter from Edward E. Colton to Arnold Saint Subber and Lemuel Ayers, July 27, 1950.
Letter from The Salem Company [signed by Lemuel Ayers] to Sam Spewack, December 11, 1950.

CU BSS 21/*Kiss Me, Kate* correspondence (1951)

Letter from Bella Spewack to Edward E. Colton, May 24, 1951.
Letter from Bella Spewack to Edward E. Colton, June 14, 1951.

Letter from Selma Tamber to Bella Spewack, June 21, 1951.
Letter from Ben Schenkman to Bella Spewack, June 22, 1951.
Letter from Edward E. Colton to Bella Spewack, July 18, 1951.
Letter from Edward E. Colton to Bella Spewack, July 19, 1951.
Letter from Bella Spewack to "Salem" (Ayers and Saint Subber), July 19, 1951.
Letter from Selma Tamber to Bella Spewack, August 6, 1951.
Letter from Jack Hylton to Bella and Sam Spewack, October 4, 1951.
Letter from Bella Spewack to Jack Hylton, October 17, 1951.
Letter from Jack Hylton to Bella and Sam Spewack, October 22, 1951.
Letter from Bella Spewack to Cole Porter, December 18, 1951.

CU BSS 21/*Kiss Me, Kate* Correspondence (1952)

Letter from Selma Tamber (The Salem Company) to Bella Spewack, January 18, 1952.

CU BSS 21/*Kiss Me, Kate* Correspondence (1954)

Letter from Edward E. Colton to Bella Spewack and Robert Montgomery, November 2, 1954.

CU BSS 21/*Kiss Me, Kate* Correspondence (1956)

Letter from Sam H. Linch to Julius Rudel [undated].

CU BSS 21/*Kiss Me, Kate* Correspondence (1957)

Letter from Marcel Prawy to Bella Spewack, November 14, 1957.

CU BSS 22/*Kiss Me, Kate* Correspondence (1961)

Letter from Bella Spewack to Cole Porter, May 30, 1961.

25/*Kiss Me, Kate* Correspondence (1970) [1]

Letter from Louis H. Aborn to Bella Spewack, August 21, 1970 (Sadler's Wells do not want a visit).
Letter from Stephen Arlen to John F. Wharton, September 2, 1970.
Copy of letter from John F. Wharton to Stephen Arlen, September 11, 1970.
Letter from Stephen Arlen to Bella Spewack, September 16, 1970.
Letter from Bella Spewack to Stephen Arlen, September 25, 1970.
Letter from Stephen Arlen to Bella Spewack, September 30, 1970.
Telegram from Stephen Arlen to Bella Spewack, October 1, 1970 (about arrival at Sadler's Wells).
(Handwritten copy of) letter from Adza Vincent to Stephen Arlen, October 18, 1970. "Sue has been so helpful and managed to keep the Waldorf at bay but . . ."
Telegram from Edward Renton to Tams-Witmark, October 21, 1970 (Bella over Peter Coe's absence).
Telegram from Edward Renton to Tams-Witmark, October 26, 1970 (Bella Spewack has agreed Coe can make special adaptation).
Copy of telegram from Bella Spewack [signed Spewak] to Stephen Arlen, October 28, 1970 (she does not agree to Coe's rewrites).
Letter from Louis H. Aborn to Bella Spewack, November 4, 1970.
Note from Peter Coe [to Sam Spewack], November 11, 1970.
Letter from Edmund Tracey to Adza Vincent, December 9, 1948 (annotated by Sam Spewack) [duplicate in Folder 2].

25/*Kiss Me, Kate* Correspondence (1970) [2]

Letter from John F. Wharton to Bella Spewack, July 14, 1970 (asking about "What Does Your Servant Dream About?").

Letter from Bella Spewack to John F. Wharton, August 4, 1970 (does not know about "What Does Your Servant Dream About?").
Letter from John F. Wharton to Bella Spewack, September 21, 1970.
Telegram from Tams-Witmark to Edward Renton, October 28, 1970 (Sam wants to go to London to help).
Letter from Stephen Arlen (dictated) to Sam and Bella Spewack, November 10, 1970 (includes casting).
Letter from Stephen Arlen (dictated) to Sam Spewack, November 10, 1970.
Letter from Geoffroy Millais to Bella Spewack, November 12, 1970 (re: BBC broadcast).
Letter from [unsigned] (Adza Vincent) to Stephen Arlen, November 20, 1970.
Letter from Adza Vincent to Sam Spewack, November 16, 1971.

25/*Kiss Me, Kate* Correspondence (1971) [1]

(Handwritten) letter from Adza Vincent to Bella Spewack, January 4, 1971.
Letter from Sam Spewack to Stephen Arlen, January 19, 1971.
Letter from Stephen Arlen to Sam Spewack, January 21, 1971.
Letter to Louis H. Aborn from Edward Renton, February 17, 1971.
Telegram from Tams-Witmark to Stephen Arlen [unsigned], April 21, 1971.
Letter from Louis H. Aborn to Stephen Arlen, April 21, 1971 (heavily annotated by Sam and Bella Spewack).
Letter from Bella Spewack to Adza Vincent, April 22, 1971 (includes "Comedia del Arte hog wash").
Memorandum (re: Sadler's Wells revival) from Sam and Bella Spewack, May 10, 1971 [duplicate in Folder 2].
Draft letter to Stephen Arlen [from Sam Spewack (unsigned)], c. May 10, 1971.
Letter from Geoffroy Millais (BBC) to Sam and Bella Spewack, October 8, 1970 [filed incorrectly].

25/*Kiss Me, Kate* correspondence (1971) [2]

Letter from Stephen Arlen to Louis H. Aborn (Tams-Witmark), April 6, 1971.
Letter from Edmund Tracey to Louis H. Aborn, April 27, 1971.
Internal memorandum from Colin Graham to Stephen Arlen, May 24, 1971.
Letter from Stephen Arlen to Louis H. Aborn, June 1, 1971.
Letter from Marcel Prawy to Bella Spewack, November 22, 1971.
Letter from Bella Spewack to Julius Rudel, November 27, 1971.

26/Background

Shakespeare, William. *The Taming of the Shrew.* Edited by M. R. Ridley. New York: E. P. Dutton, 1950 [two copies].

26/Notes and Worksheets [1]

Outline of *Backstage*, April 22, 1948.
Typed list of numbers in *Brigadoon* and *Lady in the Dark.*
Incomplete draft pages of first script draft (annotated by Bella Spewack), 2 pp. [paginated 8–9].

26/Notes and Worksheets [2]

Overview of Fred and Lilli's relationship history, 2 pp. [incomplete].
Untitled scene outline, April 28, 1948, 9 pp. [probable author: Sam Spewack].
Undated draft telegram from Sam Spewack to Stephen Arlen.

27/*Kiss Me, Kate* Scripts

Script A [London script (1951)]
Script A with notes [1] [original Broadway script]
Script A with notes [2] (different annotations to A[1])
Script B [first complete script draft]
Script B [Sadler's Wells Script (1970)]
Script B with notes [first complete script draft with annotations]
Script C [October 30 Script (with annotation)]
Script C with notes (additional pages added) [October 11 Script]
Script C "final" [unmarked October 30/rehearsal Script]

28/*Kiss Me, Kate* Scripts

Script D for TV (incomplete)
Script D for TV (complete)
Script E for Hallmark Hall of Fame (annotated)
Script F for BBC2

37/*Kiss Me, Kate* Clippings

Typed memorandum of early genesis of *Kiss Me, Kate*, May 12, 1948, 7 pp. (known as "Spewack Memorandum," possibly incomplete)

42/*Leave It to Me* Correspondence

Letter from Richard Madden to Bella Spewack, December 12, 1939.

Alfred Drake Papers [unprocessed], Library of Congress [LC AD]

2/2: Rehearsal Script (annotations by several authors including Drake and Spewack)

Cole Porter Papers, Library of Congress [LC CP]

8/6: "Always True to You (In My Fashion)" (fair copy, corrected by ASZ, 6 pp.)
"Always True to You (In My Fashion)" (road company, fair copy, 8 pp.)
8/7: "Another Op'nin', Another Show" (fair copy with annotations, 6 pp.)
"Another Op'nin', Another Show" (revised ending, fair copy, 1 p.)
8/8: "Bianca" fair copy, 5pp. (corrected by Albert Sirmay)
8/9: "Bianca's Theme" (copyist's score in pencil, 2 pp.)
8/10: "Brush Up Your Shakespeare" (fair copy, edited by CP in pencil, 7 pp.)
"Brush Up Your Shakespeare" (fair copy, original lyrics, 7 pp.)
8/11: "Finale, Act II" (copyist's score in pencil with pen sections, 16 pp.)
8/12: "I Am Ashamed That Women Are So Simple" (fair copy, ASZ autograph edited by CP, 4 pp.
"I Am Ashamed That Women Are So Simple" (melodic sketch with lyrics in pencil, CP, 1 p.)
8/13: "I Hate Men" (fair copy, 4 pp.)
8/14: "I Sing of Love" (fair copy, annotated by CP and ASZ, 8 pp.)
8/15: "I'm Afraid, Sweetheart, I Love You" (copyist's score in pencil, 5 pp.)
8/16: "I've Come to Wive It Wealthily in Padua" (fair copy, 8 pp.)
8/17: "Kate's Theme" (fair copy in pencil, 2 pp.)

9/1: "First Act Finale" autograph lead sheet, 2 pp.
"Finale, Act One" (partial copyist score with annotations, 2 pp.)
"Finale, Act One" (fair copy, 19 pp.)
9/2: "Love Is the Only Thing" (melodic sketch in pencil, copyist and CP, 1 p.)

9/3: "Petruchio's Theme" (copyist's score in pencil, 3 pp.)
9/4: "So in Love" (fair copy, 5 pp.)
9/5: "Tom, Dick, or Harry" (fair copy, corrected by ASZ, 10 pp.)
9/6: "Too Darn Hot" (fair copy, corrected by ASZ, 10 pp.)
"Too Darn Hot" (road company fair copy, corrected by CP, 10 pp.)
9/7: "We Open in Venice" (fair copy, 5 pp.)
9/8: "Were Thine That Special Face" (fair copy, annotated by CP, 5 pp.)
9/9: "What Does Your Servant Dream About?" (fair copy in pencil, 6 pp.)
9/10: "Where Is the Life That Late I Led?" (fair copy, 10 pp.)
9/11: "Why Can't You Behave?" (fair copy, corrected by ASZ, 5 pp.)
9/12: "Wunderbar" (copyist score of verse in pencil, 2 pp.)
"Wunderbar" (fair copy, annotated by CP, 6 pp.)

10/1: Piano-vocal scores (#1–17)
10/2: Piano-vocal scores (#18–28)
10/3: Piano vocal scores (#29–47)

11/1: "Always True to You (In My Fashion)" (autograph draft of unused verse)
"Always True to You (In My Fashion)" (autograph draft of unused verse, labeled for publication)
"Always True to You (In My Fashion)" (autograph draft refrain, "Out of China") [B3]
"Always True to You (In My Fashion)" (autograph draft refrain, "Mainboucher") [B13]
"Always True to You (In My Fashion)" (autograph draft refrain [fourth refrain]) [C2]
"Always True to You (In My Fashion)" (autograph draft refrain [fourth refrain]) [C4]
"Always True to You (In My Fashion)" (autograph lyric draft, "Let's play strip") [D2]
"I Hate Men" (autograph draft, heavily annotated)
"I Hate Men" (autograph draft, "gag lyrics")
"I Hate Men" (autograph draft, "synonyms of hate")
"How Simple Life Would Be" (autograph draft)
"Finale, Act II" (autograph draft)
"Brush Up Your Shakespeare" (autograph drafts, 3 pp.)
"Brush Up Your Shakespeare" (typed lyric sheets, 4 pp.)
"Bianca" (fair copy of unused verses, 2 pp.)
"Bianca" (autograph notes for lyrics, 6 pp.)
"If You Love Your Job" (autograph draft)
"I'm Afraid, Sweetheart, I Love You" (autograph draft, 2 pp.)
"It Was Great Fun the First Time" (autograph draft)
"It Was Great Fun the First Time" (autograph draft, list of names)
"I've Come to Wive It Wealthily in Padua" (autograph lyric drafts, 2 pp.)
"Security or Love" (autograph draft, fragment)
"To Be or Not to Be" (autograph draft, fragment)
"Too Darn Hot" (autograph draft, list of verbs) [A1]
"Too Darn Hot" (autograph draft verse, Kinsey report) [A6] [transcribed]
"Too Darn Hot" (notes for lyric, 3 pp.)
"The Trouble with Me Is" (autograph draft, fragment)
"Were Thine That Special Face" (autograph notes for lyrics)
"Where Is the Life That Late I Led?" (autograph notes for lyrics, 2 pp.)
"Where Is the Life That Late I Led?" (autograph draft. includes of names) [A2]
"Why Can't You Behave?" (autograph draft)
"A Woman's Career" (autograph draft)
"Wunderbar" (typed lyric, 1 p.)

11/2: Folder of lyrics [1]
"If Ever Married I'm" (typed lyric sheet, April 8, 1948)
"Finale Act One"
11/3: Folder of Lyrics [2]
"I Sing of Love" (typed lyric sheet, April 7, 1948)
11/4: Typed lyric sheets (annotated by CP with lyric alterations for public broadcast)
11/5: Book of "extra lyrics" (typed)

Harry Clark Papers, New York Public Library [NYPL HC]

2/2.5: *Kiss Me Kate Scrapbook* (includes photographs, notes, and press clippings).

Benjamin Kranz Papers, New York Public Library [NYPL BK]

6: *Kiss Me, Kate* stage manager's script [Road Company].

Harold Lang Papers, New York Public Library [NYPL HL]

3/3.10: Assorted press clippings for original Broadway production and later revivals. Photos including candid photographs of Patricia Morison backstage.

Agnes de Mille Papers New York Public Library [NYPL ADM]

IX-10: Letter from Agnes de Mille to John C. Wilson, September 8, 1948.
Letter from John C. Wilson to Agnes de Mille, September 15, 1947.

Hanya Holm Papers, New York Public Library [NYPL HH]

20/497: Telegram from Arnold Saint Subber to Hanya Holm, August 30, 1948.
20/498: *Kiss Me, Kate* Contract, September 30, 1948.
20/499: Typed memorandum (with autograph annotations).
20/500: Loose notes on *Kiss Me, Kate* (Waldorf Astoria paper).
Kiss Me, Kate Notebook
21/501: Undated Script [1] [Annotated/Known as the "Blue Book"]
21/502: Undated Script [2] [Copy of the first complete script]
21/503: Script, October 11, 1948 [Act One only]
21/504: [Folder of dated lyric sheets]
"I Sing of Love"
"Tom, Dick, or Harry," April 7, 1948.
"If Ever Married I'm"
"Why Can't You Behave?"
"Wunderbar"
"Too Darn Hot"
"It Was Great Fun the First Time"
"But I'm Always True to You (In My Fashion)" [*sic*]
"Where Is the Life That Late I Led"
"A Woman's Career"
798–800: *Kiss Me, Kate* production photographs (mainly by Eileen Darby).

Royal Shakespeare Company Archives [RSC]

RSC/SM/2/1987/5: Programme for *Kiss Me, Kate* (RSC, 1987).
TS/2/2/1987/KIS1: Adrian Noble (dir.), *Kiss Me, Kate* (1987) [DVD], 2 discs [viewed at the Royal Shakespeare Company archive in December 2016].

William McBrien Papers, Irving S. Gilmore Library, Yale University [YISG MCB]

5/83-85: "Notes on Conference held at Edward Colton's office at 551 Fifth Avenue, New York City," March 22, 1950.

Cole Porter Papers, Irving S. Gilmore Library, Yale University [YISG CP]

36/239: Letter from Albert Sirmay to Cole Porter (April 13, 1948, 1 p.)
Letter from Albert Sirmay to Cole Porter (April 14, 1948, 2 pp.)
39/254: "Always True to You (In My Fashion)" (pencil sketch of unused melody; opening verse, transcribed by Albert Sirmay, 4 pp.)
39/255: "A Woman's Career" (fair copy, corrected by Albert Sirmay, 5pp.)
"If Ever Married I'm" (fair copy, 4 pp.)
"It Was Great Fun The First Time" (fair copy, 5 pp.)
"It Was Great Fun The First Time" (fair copy, 10 pp.)
"We Shall Never Be Younger" (fair copy, 5 pp.)
"What Does Your Servant Dream About?" (fair copy, 5 pp.)
46/290: Big Sketchbook (extracts of musical ideas) [not paginated]
49/298: Letter from Beatrice J. Whelton, Censor, City of Boston, Office of the Mayor to Michael Kavanaugh (November 29, 1950)
49/302: Note from Alfred Drake to Cole Porter (December 2, 1948)
Letter from Pembroke Davenport to Cole Porter (January 25, 1949)
Letter from Mrs William Vom Rath (December 4, 1948)
49/303: Letter from Marcel Prawy to Cole Porter (May 31, 1963)

Scripts

Perelman, S. J., Ogden Nash, and Kurt Weill. *One Touch of Venus.* In *Ten Great Musicals of the American Theatre,* edited by Stanley Richards, 115–162. Radnor: Chilton Book Co., 1973.

Porter, Cole, Sam Spewack, and Bella Spewack. *Kiss Me, Kate.* New York: Alfred A Knopf, 1953 [known as *Kiss Me, Kate* (Knopf)].

Porter, Cole, Sam Spewack, and Bella Spewack. *Kiss Me, Kate.* In *Ten Great Musicals of the American Theatre,* edited by Stanley Richards, 213–278. Radnor: Chilton Book Co., 1973.

Porter, Cole, Sam Spewack, and Bella Spewack, *Kiss Me, Kate* [prompt book] (Tams-Witmark, revised June 4, 1999) [unpublished] [CPT] [known as "*Kiss Me, Kate* prompt book" (1999)].

Shakespeare, William. *The Taming of the Shrew.* Edited by Ann Thompson. Cambridge: Cambridge University Press, 2003.

Shakespeare, William. *The Taming of the Shrew.* Edited by Elizabeth Schafer. Shakespeare in Production. Cambridge: Cambridge University Press, 2003.

Spewack, Bella, and Samuel Spewack. *Boy Meets Girl and Spring Song: Two Plays.* New York: Dramatists Play Service Inc., n.d.

Published Scores

Porter, Cole. *Kiss Me, Kate.* London: Chappell & Co., 1951.

Porter, Cole. *Kiss Me, Kate.* London: Faber Music, 2009. [All references are to this score unless noted otherwise.]

Porter, Cole. *Kiss Me, Kate: A Musical Play.* Edited by David Charles Abell and Seann Alderking. Van Nuys, CA: Alfred Publishing Co., 2014 [known as *Kiss Me, Kate Critical Edition* (piano-vocal)].

Porter, Cole. *Kiss Me, Kate: A Musical Play.* Edited by David Charles Abell and Seann Alderking. Van Nuys, CA: Alfred Publishing Co., 2015. [Full score.]

The critical report can also be accessed online:

Porter, Cole. *Kiss Me, Kate: A Musical Play.* Edited by David Charles Abell and Seann Alderking, Yale University Library [website]. Accessed July 12, 2016. http://elischolar.library.yale.edu/cgi/viewcontent.cgi?article=1000&context=cole_porter_critical_edition.

Magazines, Newspapers, and Pamphlets

Please note that where no author has been credited, the article or report has been listed alphabetically by publication (e.g., no author attribution in *Variety* will be found under "V" in this section).

Apthorp, Shirley. "*Kiss Me, Kate*, Komische Oper, Berlin." *Financial Times*, June 3, 2008. Accessed November 3, 2016. https://www.ft.com/content/28523cec-3188-11dd-b77c-0000779fd2ac.

Associated Press. "Cole Porter Is Dead; Songwriter Was 72." *New York Times*, October 19, 1964. http://www.nytimes.com/learning/general/onthisday/bday/0609.html.

Atkinson, Brooks. "The Play: Swinging Shakespeare's 'Dream' with Benny Goodman, Louis Armstrong and Maxine Sullivan." *New York Times*, November 30, 1939.

Atkinson, Brooks. "At the Theatre." *New York Times*, December 31, 1948 [YISG Scrapbook].

Atkinson, Brooks. "From Padua to Gotham in "Kiss Me, Kate.'" *New York Times*, January 16, 1949 [YISG Scrapbook].

Barnes, Howard. "Shakespeare Is Advanced to Musical Comedy Rank." *New York Herald Tribune*, January 16, 1949 [YISG Scrapbook].

Barron, Mark. "New Show Rings Bell." *Kansas City Times*, December 31, 1948 [YISG Scrapbook].

Blandford, Linda. "Knocking 'Em Out at the Old Vic." *The Guardian*, August 11, 1987.

"MGM to Produce Wide-Screen, but Adaptable to All Ratios." *Boxoffice*, May 9, 1953.

Calta, Louis. "Wilson to Stage Musical." *New York Times*, March 9, 1948, 27.

Calta, Louis. "Harold Lang Gets Top Role in Show." *New York Times*, August 21, 1948.

Calta, Louis. "Lisa Kirk Is Signed for 'Kiss Me, Kate.'" *New York Times*, October 2, 1948.

Calta, Louis. "Producers Avert Press Agents Row" *New York Times*, October 16, 1948, 9.

Calta, Louis. "Miller Play Casts Its Leading Roles: Lee J. Cobb, Anne Revere Join 'Death of a Salesman.'" *New York Times*, October 28, 1948.

Calta, Louis. "Premiere Tonight of 'Kiss Me, Kate.'" *New York Times*, December 30, 1948. [YISG Scrapbook].

Calta, Louis. "Harris to Direct New Miller Play: Confirms Report, Although No Contracts Are Signed—Julie Wilson Gets London Role." *New York Times*, September 16, 1952.

Campey, George. "BBC *Kiss Me Kate* Show Off." *Evening Standard*, July 19, 1951 [VA Collection (*Kiss Me, Kate*, 1951)].

Crowther, Bosley. "Inanity Strikes Back." *New York Times*, June 29, 1952 [YISG Scrapbook].

"Queuers Wait for 22 Hours." *Daily Mail*, March 8, 1951 [VA Collection (*Kiss Me, Kate*, 1951)].

"A Kiss Me Cry." *Daily Mail*, March 9, 1951 [VA Collection (*Kiss Me, Kate*, 1951)].

"The Shrew Musicalised." *Daily Telegraph*, March 8, 1951 [VA Collection (*Kiss Me, Kate*, 1951)].

Dziemianowicz, Joe. "Raunchy, Tutsy 'Kiss Me, Kate' Showcases Glorious Kelli O'Hara." *New York Post*, March 14, 2019. https://nypost.com/2019/03/14/raunchy-gutsy-kiss-me-kate-showcases-glorious-kelli-ohara/.

Funke, Lewis. "News and Gossip of the Rialto." *New York Times*, May 2, 1948, 81.

Funke, Lewis. "News and Gossip of the Rialto: Shaw Complains about 'Superman's' Success—Other Items." *New York Times*, May 23, 1948, X1.

Gaghan, Jerry. "'Kiss Me, Kate' at the Shubert; Cole Porter's New Musical." *Philadelphia Daily News*, December 3, 1984 [YISG Scrapbook].

Gale, John. "How Carmen Became Kate." *The Observer*, November 1, 1970.

Garland, Robert. "A Musical Comedy That Has Everything." *New York Journal-American*, December 31, 1948 [YISG Scrapbook].

Heilpurn, John. "This Kiss Me, Kate Comeback Is the Swellest Gig in Town." *Observer*, November 29, 1999.

Hevesi, Dennis. "Bella Spewack, Author, 91, Dies; 'Kiss Me Kate' Is One of Her Hits." *New York Times*, April 29, 1990.

Hobson, Harold. "The Theatre: Derivations." *The Sunday Times*, March 11, 1951 [VA Collection (*Kiss Me, Kate*, 1951)].

Hobson, Harold. "A Delight." *The Sunday Times*, February 24, 1952, 2.

Holden, Stephen. "Saint Subber, Theatre Producer and a Neil Simon Partner." *New York Times*, April 21, 1944. Accessed June 5, 2017. http://www.nytimes.com/1994/04/21/obituaries/saint-subber-theater-producer-and-a-neil-simon-partner76.html.

Kelley, Eldon. "Cole Porter and Shakespeare Collaborate on Kiss Me, Kate." *New York Herald Tribune*, December 26, 1948 [YISG Scrapbook].
Klosty, James. "Alfred Drake on the Life That Late He Led." *Show Music*, Winter 1998/99 (14), 25–27.
Lounsberry, Fred. "Down with Sense." *New York Times*, June 22, 1952 [YISG Scrapbook].
Maney, Richard. "Advice to Those Who Want Two on the Aisle." *New York Times*, June 5, 1949.
Martinez, Jose. "Cole Porter's Apartment at the Waldorf-Astoria Can Be Yours for $140K a Month." *New York Daily News*, July 20, 2010. Accessed September 7, 2016. http://www.nydailynews.com/new-york/cole-porter-apartment-waldorf-astoria-140k-month-article-1.467078.
Maxwell, Elsa. "A Party Line." *New York Post* (Home News), January 6, 1948, 12 [YISG Scrapbook].
Millstein, Gilbert. "Words Anent Music by Cole Porter." *New York Times*, February 20, 1955, SM16.
"The Arts and Entertainment: Guying the Bard." *The New Statesman and Nation*, March 17, 1951.
"German Version of 'Kiss Me, Kate' Gets Cheers at Its Opening Night in Vienna." *New York Times*, February 15, 1956.
"'Annie' a Hit in Vienna." *New York Times*, February 28, 1957.
"City Opera's Invigorator." *New York Times*, March 31, 1959.
Nichols, Lewis. "The Play: Seven Lively Arts." *New York Times*, December 8, 1944. Accessed May 29, 2016. http://www.nytimes.com/books/98/11/29/specials/porter-seven.html.
Nichols, Lewis. "'Around the World': Note on the Good and Bad in the New Musical and on Mr. Welles, Showman." *New York Times*, June 9, 1946, 45.
Orodenker, Maurie. "Kiss Me, Kate." *The Billboard*, December 11, 1948 [YISG Scrapbook].
Petsch, Barbara. "'Kiss Me Kate' [*sic*], schwungvoll, Witzig." *Die Presse*, October 28, 2012. Accessed November 30, 2017. https://diepresse.com/home/kultur/news/1306297/Kiss-me-Kate-schwungvoll-witzig?from=suche.intern.portal.
Porter, Cole. "Kate and I." *Sonny Disc Digest*, April 1949 [YISG Scrapbook].
"Kiss Me, Kate." *Queen*, April 11, 1951 [VA Collection (*Kiss Me, Kate*, 1951)].
Ratcliffe, Michael. "Whirling in the Wings." *The Observer*, February 15, 1987.
Rich, Frank. "Theater: Three Musicals Liven Stages in London." *New York Times*, June 18, 1987.
Rodgers, Richard. "In Defence of Sense." *New York Times*, June 29, 1952 [YISG Scrapbook].
Rouse, James. *Alfred Drake and Patricia Morison in "Kiss Me, Kate"* [illustration] from R. E. P. Sensenderfer, "Living Theater—New Cole Porter–Bella Spewack Musical Comedy Has Premiere Here at the Shubert Theater." *Evening Bulletin* (Philadelphia), December 3, 1948 [YISG Scrapbook].
Rudel, Julius. "And Nobody Missed the Waltz!." *Theatre Arts*, June 1956, 80 [LC CP 11/8].
Ryzik, Melena. "Meryl Streep Does a Number on Donald Trump at Public Theater's Gala." *New York Times*, June 7, 2015. Accessed June 10, 2017. https://www.nytimes.com/2016/06/08/theater/meryl-streep-donald-trump-public-theater.html.
Schloss, Edwin H. "Cole Porter's 'Kiss Me Kate' [*sic*] Opens at Shubert." *Philadelphia Inquirer*, December 3, 1948 [CU BSS 37].
Snow, Georgia. "*Kiss Me, Kate* to Open at London Coliseum." *The Stage*, April 6, 2017. Accessed May 10, 2017. https://www.thestage.co.uk/news/2017/opera-norths-kiss-me-kate-to-open-at-london-coliseum/.
Spewack, Bella. "My Life with Shakespeare." *Musical Show*, March 1967 [CU BSS 37].
Taubman, Howard. "Cole Porter Is Top Again." *New York Times Magazine*, January 16, 1949 [YISG Scrapbook].
"Coliseum: Kiss Me, Kate." *The Times*, March 9, 1951 [VA Collection (*Kiss Me, Kate*, 1951)].
Valance, Tom. "Obituary: Alfred Drake." *The Independent*, August 6, 1992. Accessed June 6, 2015. http://www.independent.co.uk/news/people/obituary-alfred-drake-1538814.html.
"Plays on Broadway—Boys from Syracuse." *Variety*, November 30, 1938.

"Dick Lamarr Gets 40G in 'Kiss Me, Kate' Claim." *Variety*, January 24, 1949, 51.

"Plays on Broadway: *Kiss Me, Kate*." *Variety*, January 5, 1949 [YISG Scrapbook].

Waters. "Plays Out of Town: Kiss Me, Kate." *Variety*, December 2, 1948 [YISG Scrapbook].

Watts, Richard, Jr. "New Musical Comedy Lives Up to Promise." *New York Post* (Home News), December 31, 1948, 8 [YISG Scrapbook].

"People and Ideas: 'Kiss Me, Kate'/'Lend an Ear.'" *Vogue*, February 15, 1949.

Weiler, A. H. "By Way of Report." *New York Times*, December 9, 1951.

Williams, Peter. "Something New in Dance Routine." *Daily Mail*, March 9, 1951 [VA Collection (*Kiss Me, Kate*, 1951)].

Wilson, Cecil. "Yes, It Glows of Certain Success." *Daily Mail*, March 9, 1951 [VA Collection (*Kiss Me, Kate*, 1951)].

Zolotow, Sam. "Novotna, Ferrer May Do a Musical." *New York Times*, March 17, 1948, 31.

Books, Articles, and Webpages

Abel, Lionel. *Metatheatre: A New View of a Dramatic Form*. New York: Hill & Wang, 1963.

Alonso, Harriet Hyman. *Robert E. Sherwood: The Playwright in Peace and War*. Boston: University of Massachusetts Press, 2007.

Baumann, Shymon. *Hollywood Highbrow: From Entertainment to Art*. Princeton, NJ: Princeton University Press, 2007.

Bigsby, C. W. E. "The Politics of Popular Culture." In *Approaches to Popular Culture*, 3–26. London: Edward Arnold, 1976.

Blake, Ann. "The Taming of the Shrew: Making Fun of Katherine." *Cambridge Quarterly* 31, no. 3 (2002): 237–252.

Block, Geoffrey. "The Broadway Canon from Show Boat to West Side Story and the European Operatic Ideal." *Journal of Musicology* 11 (1993). Accessed February 20, 2017. doi: 10.2307/764025.

Block, Geoffrey. *Enchanted Evenings: The Broadway Musical from "Show Boat" to Sondheim to Lloyd Webber*. 2nd ed. New York: Oxford University Press. 2009.

Bloom, Howard. *Shakespeare: The Invention of the Human*. London: Fourth Estate, 1998.

Böker, Uwe, ed. *John Gay's The Beggar's Opera, 1728–2004: Adaptations and Re-writings*. Amsterdam: Rodopi, 2006.

Boose, Lynda E., and Richard Burt. *Shakespeare, the Movie: Popularising the Plays on Film, TV, and Video*. London: Routledge, 1997.

Bordman, Gerald. *American Musical Comedy: From Adonis to Dreamgirls*. New York: Oxford University Press, 1982.

Bordman, Gerald, and Thomas S. Hischak. "Ayers, Lemuel." In *The Oxford Companion to American Theatre*. Oxford University Press, 2004 [online]. Accessed June 20, 2017. http://www.oxfordreference.com/view/10.1093/acref/9780195169867.001.0001/acref-9780195169867-e-0186.

British Film Institute Screen Online. "The Hays Code." Accessed June 30, 2017. http://www.screenonline.org.uk/film/id/592022/.

Buchler, Michael. "Musical Structure, Dramatic Form, and Song Pairings in Cole Porter's Kiss Me, Kate." *Journal for the Society of American Music* 12, no. 1 (2018): 37–54. https://doi.org/10.1017/S1752196317000517.

Buhler, Stephen M. "Musical Shakespeares: Attending to Ophelia, Juliet and Desdemona." In *The Cambridge Companion to Shakespeare and Popular Culture*, edited by Robert Shaughnessy, 150–174. Cambridge: Cambridge University Press, 2007.

Burrows, George. "Anything Goes on an Ocean Liner: Musical Comedy as a Carnivalistic Heterotopia." *Studies in Musical Theatre* 7 (2013). Accessed June 14, 2016. doi: 10.1386/smt.7.3.327_1.

Burt, Richard, and Lynda E. Boose, eds. *Shakespeare the Movie, II: Popularising the Plays on Film, TV, Video and DVD*. New York: Routledge, 2003.

Byrge, Duane, and Robert Milton Miller. *The Screwball Comedy Films: A History and Filmography 1934–1942*. Chicago: St. James, 1991.

Cantu, Maya. *American Cinderellas on the Broadway Musical Stage: Imagining the Working Girl from Irene to Gypsy*. New York: Palgrave Macmillan, 2015.
Carlson, Marvin. *Performance: A Critical Introduction*. 2nd ed. New York: Routledge, 2004.
Carter, Tim. *Oklahoma!: The Making of an American Musical*. New Haven, CT: Yale University Press, 2007.
Casper, Drew. *Postwar Hollywood: 1946–1962*. Malden, MA: Blackwell Publishing: 2007.
Cavell, Stanley. *Pursuits of Happiness: The Hollywood Comedy of Remarriage*. Cambridge, MA: Harvard University Press, 1981.
Chaffee, Judith, and Oliver Crick, eds. *The Routledge Companion to Commedia dell'Arte*. Abingdon: Routledge, 2017.
Citron, Stephen. *Noel and Cole: The Sophisticates*. London: Sinclair-Stevenson, 1992.
Clum, John M. *Something for the Boys: Musical Theater and Gay Culture*. New York: Palgrave, 1999.
Dash, Irene G. *Shakespeare and the American Musical*. Bloomington: Indiana University Press, 2010.
Dietz, Dan. *The Complete Book of Hollywood Musicals*. Lanham, MD: Rowman & Littlefield, 2012.
Donovan, Timothy, P. "*Annie Get Your Gun*: A Last Celebration of Nationalism." *Journal of Popular Culture* 12 (1978). Accessed April 4, 2017. doi: 10.1111/j.0022-3840.1978.1203_531.x.
Dudley, Andrew. "The Postwar Struggle for Color." *Cinema Journal* 18 (1979). doi: 10.2307/1225441.
Dyer, Richard. *Light Entertainment*. London: British Film Institute, 1973.
Dyer, Richard. *Only Entertainment*. 2nd ed. Abingdon: Routledge, 2002.
Eells, George. *The Life That Late He Led*. London: W. H. Allen, 1967.
Everett, William A., and Paul R. Laird. *The Cambridge Companion to the Musical*. 2nd ed. New York: Cambridge University Press, 2008.
Ewen, David. *The Cole Porter Story*. New York: Holt, Rinehart & Winston, 1965.
Faint, Pete. *Jack Hylton*. S.l: Lulu.com, 2014 [Kindle edition].
Fearnow, Mark. "Let's Do It: The Layered Life of Cole Porter." In *Staging Desire: Queer Readings of American Theater History*, edited by Kim Marra and Robert A. Schanke, 145–166. Ann Arbor: University of Michigan Press, 2005.
Feuer, Jane. "The Theme of Popular vs. Elite Art in the Hollywood Musical." *Journal of Popular Culture* 12 (1978). Accessed February 8, 2016.
Forte, Allen. "Secrets of Melody: Line and Design in the Songs of Cole Porter." *Musical Quarterly* 77 (1993). Accessed April 18, 2014. doi: 10.1093/mq/77.4.607.
Gay, Penny. *As She Likes It: Shakespeare's Unruly Women*. London: Routledge, 1994.
Gay, Penny. "Farce: *The Comedy of Errors, The Taming of the Shrew, The Merry Wives of Windsor*." In *The Cambridge Introduction to Shakespeare's Comedies*, 16–34. Cambridge: Cambridge University Press, 2008.
Gitelman, Claudia. "Finding a Place for Hanya Holm." *Dance Chronicle* 23, no. 1 (2000): 49–71. Accessed January 8, 2015. http://www.jstor.org/stable/1568013.
Grafton, David. *Red, Hot & Rich: An Oral History of Cole Porter*. New York: Stein & Day, 1987.
Gragg, Kristen N. "'To kill a wife with kindness': Contextualizing Shakespeare's The *Taming of the Shrew*." In *Renaissance Papers 2019*, edited by Jim Pearce and William Given, 37–48. New York: Camden House, Boydell & Brewer, 2020.
Grant, Mark N. *The Rise and Fall of the Broadway Musical*. Boston: Northeastern University Press, 2004.
Hall, Sheldon, and Stephen Neale. *Epics, Spectacles, and Blockbusters: A Hollywood History*. Detroit: Wayne State University Press, 2010.
Hay, Peter. *MGM: When the Lion Roars*. New York: Turner Publishing, 1991.
Henry, Matthew. "The Triumph of Popular Culture: Situation Comedy, Postmodernism and 'The Simpsons.'" *Studies in Popular Culture* 17 (1994). Accessed April 2017. http://www.jstor.org/stable/23413793.

Hess, Earl J., and Pratibha A. Dabholkar. *The Cinematic Voyage of THE PIRATE: Kelly, Garland, and Minnelli at Work.* Columbia: University of Missouri Press, 2014.

Hodgdon, Barbara. *The Shakespeare Trade: Performances and Appropriations.* Philadelphia: University of Pennsylvania Press, 1998.

Horowitz, Mark Eden. "The Craft of Making Art: The Creative Processes of Eight Musical Theatre Songwriters." *Studies in Musical Theatre* 7 (2013): 261–283. Accessed May, 2014. http://dx.doi.org/10.1386/smt.7.2.261_1.

Houchin, John H. *Censorship of the American Theatre in the Twentieth Century.* Cambridge: Cambridge University Press, 2003.

Howard, Jean. *Travels with Cole Porter.* New York: Abrams, 1991.

Hubert, Judd D. *Metatheater: An Example of Shakespeare.* Lincoln: University of Nebraska Press, 1991.

Hubler, Richard G. *The Cole Porter Story.* New York: World Publishing Co., 1965.

Hutcheon, Linda. *A Poetics of Postmodernism.* London: Routledge, 1988.

Hutcheon, Linda, with Siobhan O'Flynn. *A Theory of Adaptation.* 2nd ed. [S.l.]: Routledge, 2012.

Jablonski, Edward. *Harold Arlen: Rhythm, Rainbows, and Blues.* Boston: Northeastern University Press, 1998.

Kimball, Robert. *The Complete Lyrics of Cole Porter.* New York: Vintage, 1984.

Kimball, Robert, and Brendan Gill. *Cole.* New York: Overlook Press, 1972.

Kiski, Tetsuo. "Shakespeare and the Musical." In *Shakespeare and the Twentieth Century: The Selected Proceedings of the International Shakespeare Association World Congress, Los Angeles, 1996*, edited by Jonathan Bate, Jill L. Levenson, and Dieter Mehl, 49–64. Newark: University of Delaware Press, 1998.

Kobal, John. *Gotta Sing Gotta Dance: A Pictorial History of Film Musicals.* London: Hamlyn Publishing Group, 1970.

Knapp, Raymond. *The American Musical and the Formation of National Identity.* Princeton, NJ: Princeton University Press, 2006.

Knapp, Raymond. *The American Musical and the Performance of Personal Identity.* Princeton, NJ: Princeton University Press, 2009.

Knapp, Raymond, Mitchell Morris, and Stacy Wolf, eds. *The Oxford Handbook of the American Musical.* New York: Oxford University Press, 2011.

Kraut, Andrea. *Copyrighting Choreography: Race, Gender, and Intellectual Property Rights in American Dance.* New York: Oxford University Press. 2016.

Lamb, Andrew. *150 Years of Popular Musical Theatre.* New Haven, CT: Yale University Press, 2002.

Lancaster University. "Report on the Current State of the Jack Hylton Archive." Accessed February 22, 2026. https://www.lancaster.ac.uk/fass/doc_library/lica/mawer_jackhyltonreportfinal210407.pdf.

Larson, Orville Kurth. *Scene Design in the American Theatre from 1915 to 1960.* Fayetteville: University of Arkansas Press, 1989.

Lawson-Peebles, Robert. *Approaches to the American Musical.* Exeter: University of Exeter Press, 1996.

Leitch, Thomas. "Adaptation, the Genre." *Adaptation* 1, no. 2 (2008): 106–120. doi: 10.1093/adaptation/apn018.

Lenz, Carolyn Ruth Swift, Gayle Green, and Carol Thomas Neely, eds. *The Woman's Part: Feminist Criticism of Shakespeare.* Chicago: University of Illinois Press, 1983.

Library of Congress. "Cole Porter Collection, 1912–1957." Accessed June 1, 2017. http://findingaids.loc.gov/db/search/xq/searchMfer02.xq?_id=loc.music.eadmus.mu009008&_faSection=overview&_faSubsection=did&_dmdid.

Loos, Anita. *Gentlemen Prefer Blondes: The Illuminating Diary of a Professional Lady and But Gentlemen Marry Brunettes.* London: Penguin, 1998.

Magee, Jeffrey: *Irving Berlin's American Musical Theatre.* New York: Oxford University Press, 2012.

Mapp, Edward. *African Americans and the Oscar: Decades of Struggle and Achievement.* New York: Bloomsbury, 2008.
Markel, Howard. "Cole Porter's Eventful Nights and Days." *Journal of American Medical Association* 305 (2011): 310–311. Accessed May 8, 2017. doi: 10.1001/jama.2010.2007.
Markel, Howard. 'The painful life of Cole Porter'. *Medscape General Medicine.* 6 (2004) 47.
McBrien, William. *Cole Porter: The Definitive Biography.* New York: Knopf. 1998.
McClary, Susan. *Feminine Endings: Music, Gender, and Sexuality.* Rev. ed. Minneapolis: University of Minnesota Press, 2002.
mcclung, b. d. *Lady in the Dark: Biography of a Musical.* New York: Oxford University Press, 2007.
McHugh, Dominic. "'I'll never know exactly who did what': Broadway Composers as Musical Collaborators.' *Journal of the American Musicological Society* 68 (2015): 605–652.
McHugh, Dominic. *Loverly: The Life and Times of My Fair Lady.* New York: Oxford University Press, 2014.
McMillin, S. *The Musical as Drama: A Study of the Principles and Conventions behind Musical Shows from Kern to Sondheim.* Princeton, NJ: Princeton University Press, 2006.
Mordden, Ethan. *Anything Goes: A History of American Musical Theatre.* New York: Oxford University Press, 2013.
Mordden, Ethan. *Beautiful Mornin': The Broadway Musical in the 1940s.* New York: Oxford University Press, 1999.
Morrison, William. *Waldorf Astoria.* Charleston, SC: Arcadia Publishing, 2014.
Morella, Joseph, and George Mazzei. *Genius and Lust—The Creativity and Sexuality of Cole Porter and Noel Coward.* Brigend: Robson Books, 1995.
Morris, George. "George Sidney: A Matter of Taste." *Film Comment* 13 (1977). Accessed December 11, 2016. http://www.jstor.org/stable/43451380.
Museum of the City of New York. "*Kiss Me, Kate* (musical)" [digitized image collection]. Accessed October 10, 2016. http://collections.mcny.org/C.aspx?VP3=SearchResult&VBID=24UAYWEGU3ZPK&SMLS=1&RW=1527&RH=822#/SearchResult&VBID=24UAYWEGU31J9&SMLS=1&RW=1527&RH=822.
Novotná, Jarmila. *Jarmila Novotná: My Life in Song.* Lexington: University Press of Kentucky, 2018.
Oja, Carol J. *Bernstein Meets Broadway: Collaborative Art in a Time of War.* New York: Oxford University Press, 2014.
Parsons, Elinor. "The Framing of the Shrew: Screen Versions of the Taming of the Shrew." PhD diss., University of London, 2008.
Prawy, Marcel. *Marcel Prawy erzählt aus seinem Leben: . . . und seine Vision der Oper des 21. Jahrhunderts; 30 Tage im Leben eines Neunzigjährigen.* Vienna: Kremayr & Scheriau, 2001. [Any translations made by the author]
Randel, Don M., Matthew Shaftel, and Susan Weiss. *A Cole Porter Companion.* Urbana: University of Illinois Press, 2016.
Rebellato, D. "'No Theatre Guild Attraction Are We': Kiss Me, Kate and the Politics of the Integrated Musical." *Contemporary Theatre Review* 19 (2009): 61–73. Accessed November 27, 2016. http://dx.doi.org/10.1080/10486800802583091.
Robbins, Hannah. "'Too Darn Hot': Reimagining *Kiss Me, Kate* for the Silver Screen." In *The Oxford Handbook of Musical Theatre Screen Adaptations*, edited by Dominic McHugh, 274–292. New York: Oxford University Press, 2019.
Rodgers, Richard. *Musical Stages: An Autobiography.* Cambridge, MA: Da Capo, 2002.
Rothwell, Kenneth S. *A History of Shakespeare on Screen: A Century of Film and Television.* Cambridge: Cambridge University Press, 2004.
Sanders, Julie. *Adaptation and Appropriation.* Abingdon: Routledge, 2006.
Severn, John R. "A (White) Woman's (Ironic) Places in *Kiss Me, Kate* and Post-war America." *Studies in Musical Theatre* 6 (2012). Accessed May 20, 2017. doi: 10.1386/smt.6.2.173_1.
Schwartz, Charles. *Cole Porter: A Biography.* London: W. H. Allen, 1997.

Shaftel, Matthew. "From Inspiration to Archive: Cole Porter's 'Night and Day.'" *Journal of Music Theory* 43 (1999). Accessed April 14, 2014. http://www.jstor.org/stable/3090664.

Shapiro, James. *Shakespeare in a Divided America.* New York: Faber & Faber, 2020.

Shapiro, Michael. "Framing the Taming: Metatheatrical Awareness of Female Impersonation in *The Taming of the Shrew.*" *Yearbook of English Studies* 23, Early Shakespeare Special Number (1993). Accessed May 16, 2015. doi: 10.2307/3507978.

Shellard, Dominic, Steve Nicholson, and Miriam Handley. *The Lord Chamberlain Regrets: British Stage Censorship and Readers' Reports from 1824 to 1968.* London: British Library, 2004.

Siebert, Lynn Laitman. "Cole Porter: An Analysis of Five Musical Comedies and a Thematic Catalogue of the Complete Works." PhD diss., City University of New York, 1975.

Silverberg, Carol E. "If It's Good Enough for Shakespeare; the Bard and the American Musical." PhD diss., State University of New York at Binghamton, 2009.

Stafford, Jeff. "Scaramouche (1952)." *Turner Classic Movies* [online]. Accessed June 10, 2017. http://www.tcm.com/tcmdb/title/2053/Scaramouche/articles.html.

Swain, Joseph P. *The Broadway Musical: A Critical and Musical Survey.* Lanham, MD: Scarecrow Press, 2002.

Tams-Witmark. "*Kiss Me, Kate* (Revised 1999)." Accessed July 4, 2016. http://www.tamswitmark.com/shows/kiss-me-kate-1999/.

Taylor, Millie. *Musical Theatre, Realism and Entertainment.* Basingstoke: Ashgate, 2012.

Teague, Frances. *Shakespeare and the American Popular Stage.* Cambridge: Cambridge University Press, 2006.

Tony Awards. "Quick Facts and Tony Trivia." Accessed August 24, 2016. http://www.tonyawards.com/en_US/history/facts/.

Traubner, Richard. "From Vienna, with That Special Operetta Feeling." *New York Times,* April 8, 1984.

van der Merwe, Ann. "Music, the Musical, and Postmodernism in Baz Luhrmann's Moulin Rouge." *Music and the Moving Image* 3 (2010). Accessed April 6, 2017. doi:10.5406/musimoviimag.3.3.0031.

Wagnleitner, Reinhold. *Coca-colonization and the Cold War: The Cultural Mission of the United States in Austria after the Second World War.* Chapel Hill: University of North Carolina Press, 1994.

Weissgärber, Hermann. *You Can't Copy Tradition: A View on the Eventful History and Bilateral Work of the Austro-American Institute of Education from 1926–2016.* Volume 1, *(1926–1971).* 2016. [digital edition]

Wilson, John C. *Noel, Tallulah, Cole and Me: A Memoir of Broadway's Golden Age.* Edited by Thomas S. Hischak and Jack Macauley. Lanham, MD: Rowman & Littlefield, 2015.

Wyver, John. "'All the Trimmings?': The Transfer of Theatre to Television in Adaptations of Shakespeare Stagings." *Adaptation* 7, no. 2 (2014): 104–120. Accessed March 2017. doi: 10.1093/adaptation/apu020.

Zolotow, Maurice. *Stagestruck: The Romance of Alfred Lunt and Lynn Fontanne.* New York: Harcourt, Brace & World, 1964.

Theater Programs

Kiss Me, Kate by Cole Porter, Sam & Bella Spewack [program]. Directed by John C. Wilson. December 1948–July 1950. New Century Theatre. New York.

Kiss Me, Kate by Cole Porter, Sam & Bella Spewack [program]. Directed by Adrian Noble. May 1987. The Old Vic. London [RSC Archives, VA Archives].

Kiss Me, Kate by Cole Porter, Sam & Bella Spewack [program]. Directed by Michael Blakemore. November 1999–August 2002. Martin Beck Theatre, New York.

Kiss Me, Kate by Cole Porter, Sam & Bella Spewack [program]. [Stage] Directed by Shaun Kerrison. August 2, 2014. BBC Proms, Royal Albert Hall, London.

Kiss Me, Kate by Cole Porter, Sam & Bella Spewack [program]. Directed by Jo Davies. September–November 2015. Opera North, Grand Theatre, Leeds.

Cast Albums and Recordings (*All in format: CD*)

Drake, Alfred, and Patricia Morison. *Kiss Me, Kate*, by Cole Porter. Original Broadway Cast Recording. Sony, 2009.

Edwards, John Owen. *Kiss Me, Kate*, by Cole Porter. National Symphony Orchestra with Thomas Allen and Diana Montague. Jay Records, 1996.

Grayson, Kathryn, and Howard Keel. *Kiss Me, Kate*, by Cole Porter. Original film soundtrack. Premier, 1997.

Hockridge, Edmund, and Jackie Jefferson. *Kiss Me, Kate*, by Cole Porter. Sanctuary Records, 2002.

McGlinn, John. *Kiss Me, Kate*, by Cole Porter. Ambrosian Chorus and London Sinfonietta with Josephine Barstow and Thomas Hampson. EMI, 1990.

Royal Shakespeare Company. *Kiss Me, Kate*, by Cole Porter. First Night Records, [1987].

Segal, Vivienne, and Dick Foran. *A Connecticut Yankee*, by Richard Rodgers and Lorenz Hart. 1944 Broadway Cast Recording. Universal, 2001 [digital]. *Accessed via Spotify*.

Sinatra, Frank, and Dean Martin. *Kiss Me Kate*, by Cole Porter. Reprise Musical Repertory Theatre. Reprise Records, 2000.

Stokes Mitchell, Brian, and Marin Mazzie. *Kiss Me, Kate*, by Cole Porter. DRG Records, 2000.

DVDs and Audiovisual Materials

The Awful Truth. Directed by Leo McCarey. [S.l.]: Columbia Tristar Home Entertainment, 2003.

The Dean Martin Show. Episode No. 20. First broadcast February 3, 1966, on NBC. Directed by Greg Garrison and written by Harry Crane.

De-Lovely. Directed by Irwin Winkler. Santa Monica, CA: MGM Home Entertainment, 2005.

Feinberg, Scott. "'Kiss Me Kate' Originator Patricia Morison Interviewed by Scott Feinberg." *YouTube*, 1:03:57. Posted by Scott Feinberg, June 6, 2013. Accessed December 15, 2016. https://www.youtube.com/watch?v=BQswR26fDFM.

His Girl Friday. Directed by Howard Hawkes. Los Angeles: Delta Entertainment Corp., 2001.

Into the Woods. Directed by Rob Marshall. [Burbank, CA]: Walt Disney Studios Home Entertainment, 2015.

Kiss Me Kate. Directed by George Sidney. Burbank, CA: Warner Home Video, 2003.

Kiss Me, Kate. Directed by George Schaefer. Pleasantville, NY: Video Artists International, 2010.

Kiss Me, Kate. Directed by Chris Hunt. [S.l.]: Arthaus Musik, 2010.

"Kiss Me, Kate | Meet Tiffany Graves (Lois) & Ashley Day (Bill)." *YouTube*, 2:52. Posted by Opera North, October 20, 2015. Accessed January 15, 2016. https://www.youtube.com/watch?v=MZfaJgEomp4.

"Kiss Me, Kate | Opera North | Interview with conductor David Charles Abell." *YouTube*, 7:01. Posted by Opera North, November 5, 2015. Accessed January 15, 2016. https://www.youtube.com/watch?v=QZ-aGVZQjAE.

Komische Oper. "Kiss Me Kate (Komische Oper)." *YouTube*, 10:02. Posted by macfonts, June 8, 2008. Accessed March 10, 2015. https://www.youtube.com/watch?v=QQNl0cOUDIE.

Morley, Sheridan. "Introduction to *Kiss Me, Kate*." *Kiss Me Kate* [live broadcast] BBC Radio 2, London, October 5, 1996.

My Favorite Wife. Directed by Garson Kanin. [S.l.]: Universal Pictures UK, 2007.

Night and Day. Directed by Michael Curtiz. [Burbank, CA]: Warner Home Video, 1946.

Prawy, Marcel. "Marcel Prawy erzählt wie er das Musical nach Österreich holte." *YouTube*, 11:32. Posted by MusicalTheaterDetect, July 1, 2012. Accessed June 3, 2016. https://www.youtube.com/watch?v=tdW8A13xtqs.

Shakespeare Live!: From the RSC. Directed by Gregory Doran. [London]: BBC Worldwide, 2016.

Shrek. Directed by Andrew Adamson and Vicky Jenson. Universal City, CA: Dreamworks Home Entertainment, 2004.

Silk Stockings. Directed by Rouben Mamoulian. Culver City, CA: Warner Home Video, 2003.

The Taming of the Shrew. Directed by Franco Zeffirelli. [S.l.]: Columbia Tristar Home Entertainment, 2001.

Weekend at the Waldorf (Fin de Semana). Directed by Robert Z. Leonard. Burbank, CA: Warner Home Video, [2010].

Index

For the benefit of digital users, indexed terms that span two pages (e.g., 52–53) may, on occasion, appear on only one of those pages.